# Elizabeth Anscombe's INTENTION

Copyright © 2010 by Steven R. Bayne
All rights reserved.

ISBN: 1439266352
EAN-13: 9781439266359
LCCN: 2010903603

# Elizabeth Anscombe's INTENTION

Steven R. Bayne

*Dedicated To Gustav Bergmann*
*For his spirited defiance of philosophical orthodoxy*

*Now there can be no doubt that those which act by intellect act for some end, since they act with an intellectual preconception of what they attain by their action, and they act through such a preconception; for this is to act by intellect.*

— Aquinas (Introduction to St. Thomas Aquinas as Modern Library). p. 432.


*... freedom at least involves the power of acting according to an idea...*

— G. E. M. Anscombe (Causality and Determination)

# Table Of Contents

| | |
|---|---|
| **PREFACE** | xiii |
| **ACKNOWLEDGMENTS** | xv |
| **INTRODUCTION** | xvii |
| a. Logical Positivism and the Humanist Response | xviii |
| b. Private Languages before Wittgenstein (circa 1940) | xxii |
| c. Acts of Will and Willful Acts | xxiv |
| **PART 1: INTENTION AND KNOWLEDGE** | **1** |
| 1: 'Prediction', 'Intention', and 'Intentional' | 1 |
| 2: Prediction, Commands and the "Falsity" of Expressions of Intention | 4 |
| 3: Expressions of Intention, Prediction and Talking Leaves | 8 |
| 4: The Agent as Sole Authority in Knowledge of Intentions | 12 |
| **PART 2: REASONS, INTENTIONS, AND KNOWLEDGE** | **15** |
| 5: "...A Certain Sense of the Question 'Why?'" | 15 |
| a. Some Gricean Points | 19 |
| 6: Intentional 'Under a Description' | 20 |
| a. Anscombe's Later Discussion of 'Under a Description' | 21 |
| b. Davidson's Use of 'Under a Description' | 25 |

|   |   |
|---|---|
| c. The Intentionality of Sensation | 26 |
| d. Anscombe's Criticism of Davidson on Agency | 30 |
| e. Davidson on Tying One's Shoes 'Under a Description' | 35 |
| 7: The Involuntary | 42 |
| 8: Non-Observational Knowledge | 43 |
| a. Donnellan on 'Knowing What I Am Doing' | 46 |
| 9: A Difficult Distinction Based on Causation | 50 |
| 10: Introducing Mental Causes | 51 |
| 11: Mental Causes are neither Intentions nor Desires | 52 |
| 12: Motives vs. Intentions | 54 |
| 13: Backward Looking Motives and Motives-In-General | 55 |
| 14: Mental Causes and Backward-Looking Motives | 56 |
| 15: Mental Causes or Reasons? | 57 |

## PART 3: ACTING WITHOUT REASON — 61

|   |   |
|---|---|
| 16: "I Don't Know Why I Did It" | 61 |
| 17: "I Don't Know Why I Did It" (Continued) | 61 |
| 18: When the Answer to the Question 'Why?' Makes No Sense | 62 |
| 19: What Makes an Action Intentional? | 64 |
| 20: Non-Forward Looking Intentional Actions | 67 |
| 21: Chains Consisting of Actions | 71 |

## PART 4: SERIES OF INTENTIONAL ACTIONS — 73

|   |   |
|---|---|
| 22: Acting "with the Intention That" | 73 |
| 23: Whether an Intentional Action has a Unique Description as Such | 75 |
| 24: Individuating Actions | 78 |
| 25: Identifying Intentional Actions | 79 |
| 26: How Many Actions are There? | 81 |
| 27: Acts of Intending and Efficacy | 83 |
| a. Intentional Acts of Creation | 84 |
| 28: Observational Knowledge of Intentions, Again | 86 |
| 29: I Do What Happens | 87 |
| 30: Against the Idea of Intentions as Initiating Causes of Action | 92 |
| 31: Knowledge of Intention is not Like Our Knowledge of Commands | 95 |
| 32: Lists and Two Kinds of Error: Introducing Practical Wisdom | 96 |

## PART 5: PRACTICAL WISDOM — 101

33: Aristotle's Practical Syllogism — 102
    a. R. M. Hare and "Insane Premises" — 108
    b. Davidson and "Insane Premises" — 111
34: Wants and Practical Reasoning — 113
35: Wanting as the Starting Point of a Practical Syllogism — 115
    a. Actions as processes — 117
    b. Wants not Included in a Practical Syllogism — 118
    c. Incontinence and the Division of Responsibility — 121
    d. The Difference between Theoretical and Practical Syllogisms — 123
36: Wanting and Its Place in Reasoning — 124
37: Desirability Characterizations — 128
38: How We Arrive at Desirability Characterizations — 130
39: The Non-necessity of any Particular Desirability Characterization in Relation to Wanting — 132
40: The Similarity of the Relations of Wanting to Good and Judgment to Truth. — 133
    a. Ryle on Pleasure — 136
    b. Choice, Volition, and Intention — 139
    c. Speculative Remarks on Volition and Intention — 142
41: Ethics and Philosophical Psychology — 144
    a. 'Ought' and the Divine Law — 145
42: Practical Reasoning and Mental Processes — 147
43: The Complexity of 'Doing' — 148
44: Acting with an Idea of an End — 149
45: The Problem of Practical Knowledge — 151
46: Interest and the Why-Question — 153
47: 'Intentional' and the Form of Description — 155
    a. Animal Intentions — 157
48: Practical Knowledge and 'Knowledges' — 158
49: The Meaning of 'Voluntary' — 160
    a. Davidson on Voluntary Action without Intention — 161
    b. Observation and Voluntary Movement — 163
50. Intentions and Predictions — 165
51. Wanting and the Future — 165
52: 'I am Going to but I Won't' — 167

## PART 6: SINGULAR CAUSATION — 171

- a. Hume, Popper, and Regularity — 173
- b. Russell and the Idea of Lawlikeness — 174
- c. Singularity *vs.* Regularity — 178
- d. Anscombe on Hume — 181
- e. Russell's Anticipation of Davidson/Ducasse — 187
- f. Anscombe on the Singularity of Causation — 190
- g. Applying Kripke to Singular Causation — 193
- h. Calling into Question the Necessary *A Posteriori* — 201
- i. The Singularist View and Knowledge of Actions — 207
- j. Feynman, Bohm, and the "Magic" Box — 211
- k. Anscombe, Bohm and Mechanistic Determinism — 221
- l. Reconciling Singularity and Regularity Theories — 227

## PART 7: CAUSATION AND AGENCY — 233

- a. The Causes of Action — 234
- b. Anscombe and Chisholm — 242
- c. Chisholm's 1966 Position on Agent Causation — 242
- d. Melden's Problem(s) with Volition — 244
- e. Anscombe Critique of Chisholm — 247
- f. Davidson and Anscombe on Agent Causation — 249
- g. James, Volition, and Anomalous Monism — 251

## BIBLIOGRAPHY — 255

## INDEX — 265

# Preface

The relationship between having an idea and performing an action has a history that runs deep in philosophy. How one approaches the details of this history is determined in part by one's role as a participant, should one in fact *be* a participant. What follows is not, therefore, easily described as a work of History. So describing it would be complicated by the fact that the author has something to say about the content of the ideas under investigation. Understanding the nature of this complexity begins with comprehending the difference between two ways of writing about the history of ideas, each way corresponding to a different conception of the study of history.

One approach to the history of ideas is to accept their *logical* interdependency as determining the content of the historian's inquiry. The other approach is to be guided by *causal* relations between historical events, relations that establish a chronology constituting the unfolding process of the evolution of an idea or ideas. The former, following Gustav Bergmann, we shall call "structural history"; the latter we refer to as "factual history." (Bergmann [1957] pp. 9-11). What follows is work in "structural history."

Those who ignore it tend to regard intellectual history as a graveyard of forgotten ideas. Other, more attentive souls, believe that some proper arrangement of relics may lay bare history as an evolving process. The evolution of a species, typically, takes place at the edge of time; here there are no discontinuous boundaries within the process; this is factual history in the making. But the evolution of an idea is, somewhat, different. An idea may disappear and return long after having been discarded. During the interim there may be little or no trace of its former presence. Intellectual history is not, merely, the narrative biography of ideas, rather, it is essentially structural, and we shall regard it as such. The historian of ideas as a chronicler of "factual history" is in one sense an aesthete and little else. What we seek is, at least, an improved understanding of what might be called "the idea idea" in the theory of human action, i.e., the idea that ideas determine actions. Elizabeth Anscombe's contribution to understanding the connection of ideas and actions is what we undertake to examine. We attempt this within the historical context in which she wrote and its aftermath. In this book, our objective is not to explore abandoned philosophical castles in search of attractive museum pieces; rather we regard ourselves as interlopers in search of hidden treasure, a form of capital that may enable us, eventually, to become revolutionaries, rather than revisionists, within the caretaker government of the shrinking republic of our academic institutions.

    Steven R. Bayne
    Elmhurst, Illinois

# Acknowledgements

This book would not have been written had it not been for the persistent encouragement of Mark Pavlick. My interest in action theory originated from a lecture delivered by Myles Brand back in the late sixties. I owe a great deal, also, to Dr. David Krasner for his loyalty when the chips were down. Mrs. Rita Martin, and her husband Edward, all along, took an interest in the work and provided a great deal of encouragement. My wife, Mary, contributed substantially to my views through discussion that, frequently, turned philosophical. Her material and emotional support were invaluable as well as her assistance on a number of technical matters.

Mention must, also, be made of Roger Bishop Jones, a technology savvy researcher, who directed my course in making suitable arrangements for publishing the manuscript. Thanks go, also, to Sarah Zola of the Amazon Corporation. I would, also, like to thank Richard Lorenc of the Illinois Policy Institute for stimulating discussion as well as directing me to certain works by Ludwig Von Mises of which I had been, previously, unaware. Prof. Ron Barnette, a philosopher and one of A. I. Melden's dissertation students, provided a number of relevant details both philosophical and historical, as did Prof. John Shand of the Open University, UK. My brief discussion of Grice, which should have been longer, benefited substantially from discussion with J. L. Speranza. In addition, I have gained by the observations and comments made by Prof. Aaron Sloman (University of Leeds). I should, also mention the late Prof. Warner Morse of the University of Kansas from whom I acquired a love of Aristotle's ethical works. I owe Prof. Anne J. Jacobson (University of Houston) thanks for insights into the intellectual climate and events of the period. Shelly Thorpe has been a great friend over the duration of producing this manuscript and has, contributed to the, actual, production effort. Thanks go, also, to Lee Groban who has had to endure my philosophical rants for over 40 years and who contributed ideas pertinent to the physical layout of the manuscript. Last, but not least, I must mention discussion with Bruce Aune. Prof. Aune (University of Massachusetts, Amherst) disagrees with me on Kripke, but has been an influence on my views since around 1967. Mention must, also, be made of the work of Peter Vranas, who anticipated (and bested) me on a number of points in my discussion of work related to R. M. Hare, points not included in this manuscript. Time considerations prevented taking up aspects of Prof. Vranas's work.

The greatest influences on my philosophical thinking have come from Bertrand Russell, Wittgenstein, C. D. Broad, Gustav Bergmann, Rudolf Carnap, and Noam Chomsky. Chomsky's work showed that the study of language is a science, particularly in matters of syntax. More recently the works of Wm James and Hans Reichenbach have become the source of my renewed enthusiasm for the history of analytical philosophy and what it has to offer future generations. Finally, I would like to thank those who have supported Hist-Analytic (www.hist-analytic.org) achieve its objective of open access to numerous documents pertaining to the history of analytical philosophy.

# Introduction

Anscombe's debt to Wittgenstein is well known. The precise nature of this debt, however, is unclear, and some readers may be surprised at how often she takes exception to his views. Perhaps equally relevant is her respectful and, almost, deferential attitude towards Bertrand Russell, whose ideas differed, considerably, from her own. Notwithstanding this fact, many of her own views on causation, for example, appear to have been formulated in reaction to Russell's, just as many of Wittgenstein's positions were commentaries on Russell's early work. Neither Wittgenstein nor Russell, however, had a great deal to say about intentions, as such. In some respects, Anscombe was a pioneer, but there is a larger history that is, often, forgotten.

Before Anscombe, Wm. James had written extensively on the subject of volition and the Will. His work was addressed by F. H. Bradley in a series of remarkable papers that today would be considered by many as excessively metaphysical, or the mere musings of a now discredited philosophical psychologist. Following Bradley, others entered into the discussion, people such as G. F. Stout, A. Shand, Samuel Alexander and many others. The move towards logical positivism would contribute to putting an end to this continuing debate, and the thread which had begun with James came to an end. About this time the behaviorism of James Watson began to exert considerable influence and his impact on philosophy would become evident in the works of a number of philosophers including Russell, works such as *The Analysis of Mind* to take one example. James's philosophy, more generally, was welcomed by Russell, particularly on matters related to mind/body dualism, but this supportive attitude began to fade as Russell moved towards materialism. Although it is difficult to establish beyond a reasonable doubt, it was the later Wittgenstein who began to take James's philosophy of mind seriously, after a long period of neglect by others in the field. Anscombe it may be suggested was, indirectly, influenced by James through Wittgenstein in ways she would, almost, certainly deny. Still the case can be made, although we shall not attempt to make it here.

## *a) Logical Positivism and the Humanist Response*

Elizabeth Anscombe transformed the theory of human action. At the time she wrote *Intention* philosophy was in a state of transition. Hegel had become, pretty much, a relic of the past and philosophy continued to be influenced, heavily, by developments in science and logic, although the trend had subsided owing, largely, to the work of Wittgenstein, Austin and Ryle. Hegel been contemptuously set aside, but so had metaphysics in general, at least in the sense that it had been pursued by thinkers such as Wm. James, F. H. Bradley, Samuel Alexander, J. E. McTaggart, and others. It is not uncommon to identify the emergence of analytical philosophy with a new found respect for language and the concomitant dismissal of previous trends in metaphysics, but to leave matters at this would be to accept an oversimplification, for such a view does not take into account one other influence of profound significance to the field: the impact of the Special Theory of Relativity.

The idea of philosophy as an attempt at understanding the logic of the language of science, which we owe mainly to Rudolf Carnap, was in large measure a merging of two influences, both begun in 1905. One was Einstein's paper introducing the Special Theory and the other was Bertrand Russell's paper "On Denoting." The former introduced new content into philosophy while the latter presented a new methodology: the logistical analysis of language. The combined influence of these two movements of thought had an effect that was both subtle and yet profound.

These two developments coalesced in "logical positivism." It is well known that Einstein's thinking had been influenced by Ernst Mach's views on relativity when he came up with his own Special Theory of Relativity. (Holton [1973] pp. 219-259) The two exchanged letters and on one occasion met. It was mainly Mach's epistemology, his radical empiricism, that appealed to Einstein and it was this very empiricism that became wed with Russell's introduction of the methods of logic to general philosophy that resulted in what came to be known as "logical positivism." There would be little place for the Will in logical positivism. It would show itself, primarily, insofar as choice entered into the setting of conventions, such as those associated with measurement.

Earlier philosophers, such as Wm. James, F. H. Bradley and G. F. Stout, had taken great pains in attempting to understanding the nature of the Will. Interest in the Will waned as psychology came, increasingly, under the spell of learning theory, an approach to psychology that goes back to people such as Thorndike, Guthrie, and Watson. There can be little doubt that the earlier preoccupation with the Will was rooted in Descartes, a philosopher whose absence was to become as conspicuous as the presence of Hume, particularly among the logical empiricists. By the 1930s what Russell had described as "general philosophy" was encompassed within an ellipse of two foci: the philosophy of science and the philosophy of language. This provoked discontent among a number of philosophers.

Although there we some, such as C. D. Broad, who could step gingerly between philosophy of science and an earlier metaphysics, it was clear that there would, at some point, be a "humanistic" rebellion against a philosophy that was becoming increasingly logical and scientific. Among the first to rebel was Gilbert Ryle. In 1949, Ryle published *The Concept of Mind*, a book which was, and is, regarded as one of the most aggressive attacks on Cartesian thinking ever. However, Ryle's book did not address the nature of mind along lines that had been made fashionable by logical empiricists. There was overlap, such as a preoccupation with behaviorism and the dispositional analysis of psychological concepts, but the focus was less on formalizing these concepts and more on how they are related to ordinary discourse in a common sense world. This is not to say that Ryle was untouched by Russell's reverence for the logical approach.

Indeed, his most influential early work was, obviously, inspired by Russell's 1905 paper. (e.g. Ryle [1932]) In fact, Ryle's historical significance was augmented by the influence he succeeded in having on philosophers who, while they had not dismissed metaphysics out of hand, had been mesmerized by philosophers like Carnap. Here the work of Wilfred Sellars comes immediately to mind. Ryle's work can be regarded as something of a return to an earlier "humanism" insofar as it was not so much an analysis of the logic of the language of science as an analysis of philosophical problems from the standpoint of natural language and its conventions. Ryle promoted what would become a new found respect for "ordinary language," a respect that was not, merely, a reaction against the logistical approach to philosophy but, rather, "a defense of common sense" in a form that had, more or less, been championed by G. E. Moore in a paper of that title published in 1925. (Moore [1925]) Indeed, it was Moore who, among philosophers of his stature, stands, virtually, alone in resisting the move towards philosophy of science. Moore never received the credit due him for the role he played in Wittgenstein's change in approach to the problems of philosophy.

The true story of the evolution of Wittgenstein's ideas has yet to be, properly, examined. Although he seldom cites other philosophers, there are a few important exceptions. Carnap, however, is not on this list, although there can be little doubt that he was apprised of Carnap's work and that of others from whom his own work would soon depart even more radically than in the past. Carnap had been very much taken by Wittgenstein's early work, unlike, say, Godel who paid it little mind. Carnap had moved away from the ideas of the early Wittgenstein, owing mainly to publication of Tarski's semantical conception of truth, just as he moved away from the Russell he so admired in his *Aufbau*. Although it would appear on the basis of his published work that Wittgenstein changed directions following his repudiation of his earlier "picture theory of meaning" (Wittgenstein [1921), a good case can be made for the idea that his change of course was a reaction against philosophy conceived as a logical analysis of the language of science.

Although Wittgenstein in the *Philosophical Investigations* distances himself from his earlier "picture theory of meaning," his more extended remarks are directed against the possibility of a private language, a language understandable in principle only by the person who makes up the "rules" for that language. Many followers of Wittgenstein, such as Anscombe and Anthony Kenny (just to mention two), make considerable use of his argument against private languages in their attacks on a more traditional Cartesianism. But herein reside the makings of a profound historical misunderstanding. If we are right, the later Wittgenstein is addressing the logical positivists, not Descartes. This is not to deny the possibility of so construing many of his later views, but in all likelihood Descartes was among the things furthest from his mind when he attacked the very idea of a private language. Wittgenstein, himself, had earlier expressed belief in such private languages, such as when he asserted that "…the limits of my *language* (the language that only I can understand) mean the limits of *my* world." (Wittgenstein [1921] 5.62) His later attack on private language can be viewed as a reaction to what came to be known as the "egocentric predicament." We will examine this more closely because it has implications for the theory of action, implications that Anscombe was the first to recognize and address, albeit, in a fragmented way.

At one point, Russell had maintained that a logically perspicuous language would contain only logical terms and terms that depend on acquaintance with sense data in order to be meaningful. All other terms were definable in terms of these. This "principle of acquaintance," however, led to a predicament; for, if experience is private to the individual, meanings could not be shared. If someone pointed towards an object, referring to it with the term 'this', then, since his experience and mine are different, the term "has not the same meaning to him as to me." (Russell [1913] p. 29) Russell, at this time, believed that a solution could be found by adopting the "neutral monist" position (Russell (1913) p. 34), the view that the world's ultimate constituents are neither mental nor physical but are, rather, something "neutral." His views on neutral monism, however, were later judiciously criticized by Broad and, following publication of his *Analysis of Matter*, Russell appears to have loosened his commitment to the doctrine. There is an interesting history relating the "principle of acquaintance" and, so called, verificationism in philosophy, but it is serpentine and difficult to follow. Wittgenstein, it should be recalled, was not the first to inveigh against private languages. In fact the private language issue goes back considerably further than Wittgenstein's *Philosophical Investigations*.

## b) Private Languages before Wittgenstein (circa 1940)

Wittgenstein's discussion made the issue of private languages central to philosophy. It has, since, been applied, and misapplied, by numerous discussants in an attempt to resolve the relation between the subjective individual and the "external world"; between the "private world" of the self and the objectively given reality of science. The problem became a matter for semantics, however, long before Wittgenstein agued against the possibility of private senses for words. Carnap had raised the issue in connection with epistemological issues in science and Ayer devoted a chapter to the subject in one of the most lucid discussions of the topic ever. (Ayer [1940]) One epistemological problem faced by the early logical positivists was how to bridge the gap between the privacy of sense-data associated with the results of experiments and the "public" world which is the subject matter of science. This problem belongs with the "egocentric predicament." The logical positivists, Carnap in particular, sought to reformulate this conundrum in terms of the relation of two languages: the "protocol language," which had as its subject matter the "private" world of sense experience, and the "physical language," the language which has the public, physical, world as its subject matter.

The protocol language was originally viewed as referring to sense-data. Sense data were taken to be private, which was part of the problem. Even though Canap's approach led to a novel formulation of the difficulty, it had antecedents. Earlier, Russell had attempted to give an account of how public space could be understood as a logical construction from "private worlds," (Russell [1914] pp. 90-113) and, later, C. D. Broad would make a considerably more sophisticated effort, inspired of course by Russell's own. (Broad [1923]) What is important is that science was understood to depend on verification; verification requires sense-data; and sense-data are mental. How might we avoid basing science on private experiences taking the form of sense-data? This is how the egocentric predicament manifested itself before Carnap's introduction of two languages: the protocol language and the physical language.

Instead of talking about the relation of sense-data to public knowledge, Carnap spoke of the translatability of protocol languages into physical language. 'Translation' was moving from expressions of one language to those of another while preserving meaning. Earlier, in work that went unpublished during his lifetime, Russell had spoken of meaning as what a sentence has in common with its translation. More specifically, Russell noted that meaning is to be understood as that which we seek to preserve in translation. (Russell [1903-1905] p. 316) Anssi Korhonen has pointed out that it is likely that Russell received the idea from Frege who, circa 1897, wrote that when we speak of translation "the thought must be preserved," the relation of meaning and "thought" in Frege being well known. (cf. Beaney [1997] p. 231) This, seemingly, small move would have profound implications for the development of analytical philosophy. It could be argued that Carnap assumes this notion of meaning in much of his work, while Quine would, explicitly, adopt it. (Quine [1960] p. 32) One important feature of this approach to meaning is that 'same meaning' becomes more important than 'meaning' insofar as the latter is defined in terms of the former. This maneuver initiated by Russell and Frege may have been inspired, somewhat, by the great Italian mathematician, Peano, who had entertained the idea of defining the number of members of a set in terms of classes of classes *similar* to a given class. (Russell [1903] p. 115) Understanding Carnap's situation in light of this, somewhat, different approach to meaning led Reichenbach to remark that the issue of verifiability had been replaced by that of translation. (Reichenbach [1936] p. 148). Some had maintained that a sentence is cognitively meaningful if and only if it is verifiable. But now it could be said that a sentence is meaningful if it can be translated into another language. There are problems, of course, but the approach was "friendly" to the semantic conception of truth advanced by Tarski, an approach that emphasized the linguistic relativity of 'true'. But there remained one problem, pointed out by Neurath, that Carnap had to address.

Even though translation had displaced verifiability, there remained the fact that protocol languages, nevertheless, made reference to private experience. In giving a pointer reading as the result of an experiment, one might say "I see a black line with an arrow pointing towards it." Not only was there reference to subjective experience but the predicates were descriptive of phenomenal properties. The solution was to render the protocol language a physical language, describing sense-data in terms of brain states. Thus "logical positivism" became "logical materialism," neatly, stated by Reichenbach. (Reichenbach [1936] p. 151) How this impacted the private language issue reveals, perhaps, a significant difference between Anscombe and Wittgenstein. What *may* have influenced Wittgenstein's thinking is that if meaning is what is preserved under translation, and private languages are not translatable in principle, then there can be no such thing as a private "meaning."

Wittgenstein's in his criticism of private languages (Wittgenstein [1953] pp. 269-275, *passim*) can be view as criticizing the common logical positivist position prior to Carnap's "reduction" of protocol language to physical language. The protocol language, once disposed of, allowed Wittgenstein and his followers to disregard the idea of philosophical analysis as the construction of artificial languages. The issue of verification could no longer be formulated in terms of the relation between two languages. Attention to how natural language functions became paramount, largely *because* the idea of the usefulness of artificial languages was thought to have been debunked. This was the main conclusion Wittgenstein derived from his argument, and this is why Wittgenstein placed his argument in such a prominent position in his later work. Wherever Anscombe relies on the conclusion of Wittgenstein's private language argument, there is a conspicuous absence, however, of any discussion of the relation of languages, such as the relation of protocol languages and physical languages or the regimentation of natural languages within canonical languages. The lesson she took from Wittgenstein was not so much the idea that the positivists had been wrong but, rather, that Cartesianism had been refuted. Herein lies a fundamental difference between Wittgenstein and Anscombe. As for Carnap's relation to Descartes, it was not Descartes's appeal to private "ideas" that were of so much concern as the effort to make science "rational." (Reichenbach [1936] p. 149)

### c) Acts of Will and Willful Acts

One distinction we shall assume, one anticipated by Wm. James, is the distinction between what we shall call an "act of will" and a "willful act." The difference is important and frequently overlooked. Suppose it is a cold morning and I am lying in bed contemplating the displeasure of abandoning my warm blanket. For a time, I think about other things, but there arrives that moment when I push these thoughts aside and resolve to perform the unpleasant act; that is, I have formed an intention, and my resolve is to act on that intention. Finally, I act. In this case, what we have is an act of will. Examples abound. Another would be where I must enter cold water in order to take a swim. I know that I will be able to adjust to the temperature, once I'm in, but there is a resistance to be overcome. Again, finally, I act; and such an act is, also, an act of will. But there are other actions that we perform, actions which are not acts of will, acts we shall call "willful acts."

Willful acts are difficult to define but are easy to distinguish from acts of will. Suppose I am summoned to a meeting in another room. Quickly, I walk to the door, open it, leave the room, entering the other room. When I opened the door, I did it as part of another action. However, unlike the action of entering the other room for the purpose of attending the meeting, I have formed no intention, as such, to open the door. I simply do it as part of exercising the intention of attending the meeting next door. Such an act is what we shall call a "willful action." Consider another example. Suppose I am determined to reach high up in order to retrieve a container on the top shelf of my pantry. While reaching, the backs of my feet are raised from the floor. This is an action, but it is not an act of will. However, it is a willful action. As we shall soon discover, the distinction raises certain questions, such as whether, merely, willful actions are actions at all, and whether wrinkling a rug while deliberately walking across the room counts as a willful action. Its value as an expository device, alone, makes this a distinction worth making. We now proceed to discuss some of the details of Anscombe's *Intention*.

# PART 1:
## Intention and Knowledge

Parts 1 through 4 consist of sections numbered in correspondence with those of Anscombe's *Intention*, second edition, Harvard University Press, 1963.

### SECTION 1: *PREDICTION, 'INTENTIONAL', 'INTENTION'*

Anscombe identifies three sorts of sentences expressive of intention, but gives an example of the first, only: 'I am going to do such and such'. Besides the one for which we have been given an example, the other two sorts are exemplified by such sentences as 'I am intentionally pumping this water', and 'I am pumping this water in order to poison those people', respectively. As in the case of Kant, the points she raises might have been clearer had she ventured to provide a more extensive list of examples.

Most people think they understand the word 'intention'. However, few have attempted to explain its meaning or what it *is* to intend to do something. Anscombe begins by introducing three sorts of sentences expressive of intention. First, there are sentences expressing one's intention to perform a future action such as 'I am going to do such-and-such'. But not all expressions of intention can be of this form, since intentions may not be future directed. For example, a child walking home from school may make a game of kicking snow. What he does he does intentionally without concern for the future. Although Anscombe does not consider the possibility, it is not unreasonable to consider regarding a report such as 'I intend to do such and such' as a form of intentional behavior much as one might regard saying 'I am in pain' as a form of pain behavior. (Wittgenstein [1953] 244). The pain case is more interesting, perhaps, owing to the fact that, whereas pain is often considered a non-intentional notion, a pain report can be uttered *with an intention*, e.g. in order to explain erratic behavior. The notion of acting *with an intention*, as we shall soon discover, is of fundamental importance in arriving at some understanding of intention beyond one's intention to move one's limbs in some way or another.

Although Anscombe sees a connection between intentionality and sensation, at this point, her interest is in clarifying the term 'intention' without drawing on complex examples or remote analogies. The second sort of statement she identifies as expressive of intention is one in which we describe an action as intentional. Anscombe points out, however, that such a statement cannot capture all that we mean by 'intention' inasmuch as many intentional actions are not backed by an intention. Suppose I am concentrating on some difficult problem. I place my index finger on my upper lip. I do so intentionally, but I have no intention in doing so. Such an action is not the satisfaction of an intention, even though it is intentional.

This notion of being intentional in the absence of an intention is related to the distinction we have drawn, already, between acts of will and willful acts. Willful acts are not acts of will, but all acts of will insofar as they include an intention are willful acts. Acts of will can be thought of as intentional acts which are "backed" by an intention the agent has formed, perhaps following careful deliberation.

There is, however, a third sort of sentence which is prominent in categorizing the various ways in which intentions are expressed. One example would be 'I am pumping this water in order to poison those people'. Sentences of this sort pertain to occasions where what we do intentionally is done *with the intention* of accomplishing something with the help of nature, and by "nature" we mean in this case the forces of gravity, inertia etc. These are actions we perform with the intention of accomplishing something that goes beyond bodily movements alone; again, cases such as where I move the handle of a pump up and down with the intention that water be moved from a reservoir to some other location; or, perhaps more commonly, when I take a bus with the intention of avoiding having to drive. The idea of doing something "with the intention that" will remain prominent throughout much of *Intention*, but another distinction is touched upon which is, also, of considerable importance.

I may describe an intention as if were my immediate objective, such as when asked why I am performing some action I say "What I intend to do is pump water into the reservoir." But I may say "My intention *in* pumping water into the reservoir is to poison the people who draw their water from it." In the first instance, the intention is described independently of consequences; in the second, a consequence is described which may inform any complete statement of why I am doing what I am doing. Suppose that, instead of speaking of bodily behavior, we are talking about speech behavior, a speech act. We sometimes say "In saying that, I was drawing attention to…" Perhaps we might as well have said: 'My intention *in* saying that was to draw attention to…' It has been questioned whether the connection between the saying, and the drawing of attention to, is one requiring intention. J. L. Austin suggested that intention is not at issue but convention is. (Austin [1962] p. 128). Austin expressed these views in his Wm. James Lectures at Harvard in 1955 and it is, entirely, possible—indeed likely—that, given the extent of their philosophical exchange, Anscombe was acquainted with Austin's position, although *Intention* was published before Austin's now classic work in speech act theory.

There are, then, three sorts of cases where sentences expressing intention are applicable to the circumstances of action. Nevertheless, Anscombe resists the temptation to treat the term, 'intention' as equivocal; she does so because this requires assuming that we understand the concept of intention well enough to draw this conclusion. Of these three statement forms related to intention, it is the first that she dubs an "expression of intention," and it is this form of statement to which she first directs our attention in the next Section. Later we will be told that these three expressions do not delineate three divisions within the meaning of 'intention' (Anscombe [1963] p. 40).

Although Anscombe seldom refers to Wm. James, there are occasions where their views are related. When Anscombe speaks of an action being intentional, although there is no intention "in" it, she is alluding to an idea closely related to a distinction James drew between "ideo-motor" actions and actions that require deliberation, (James [1890] p. 522) another distinction that figures in our earlier one between willful acts and acts of will. Actions of the first sort include actions such as when, without thinking, I bend over to pick up a scrap of paper. The situation with respect to actions is not unlike that with respect to awareness: we may walk around a puddle of water in our path "without thinking," whereas if we are examining a work of art we may focus our attention on certain features, such as the use of light or theme, which may provide some clue as to the identity of the artist. When we bend over, thoughtlessly, in picking up a scrap of paper we may be said to act "willfully," but when we perform an action such as pumping with the intention of there being some consequence, then our action of achieving this consequence may be called "an act of will." This distinction should be kept in mind throughout our discussion. It is not a distinction that Anscombe makes, explicitly, but it figures in how we will come to regard, e.g., the relation of volition and intention.

## SECTION 2: *PREDICTION, COMMANDS AND THE FALSITY OF EXPRESSIONS OF INTENTION*

It is important to distinguish what appear to be obvious statements of intention, such as 'I am going to take a walk', from predictions, such as 'I am going to catch a cold'. Both are essentially tied to the future; but what is the difference? J. A. Passmore and P. L. Heath observed, a few years before the publication of Anscombe's *Intention* that a statement of intention differs from a prediction in the sense that an intention may be truthfully avowed, even if it is never fulfilled (Passmore and Heath [1955] p. 144). Anscombe, however, addresses the difference between *expressions* of intention and predictions but not that between intentions and predictions *per se*. Even if Passmore and Heath are correct, this will not resolve the question as to how it is that I am able to distinguish an expression of intention from prediction when I say "I am going to fail this exam?" As Anscombe observes, I may, actually, be expressing my intention to fail the exam. If I were to say "I am going to be sick," the ambiguity remains a possibility. But not so in the case of "Gravity is going to hold me to the surface of the earth." Thus the possibility of an intentional reading is related to what is within the means of the agent to cause. What we, really, want to know is what the difference *is* between an expression of intention and a prediction in connection with action. On those occasions where one might say 'I'm going to the store' is a prediction, it must be kept in mind that what we have is not a prediction in the sense of predicting the weather. In the case of predicting the weather, it makes sense to consider whatever likelihood there is of the event taking place as a function of the weight we place on certain evidence, given past data. Ordinarily, we do not consider such "weight" with respect to our predictive capacity when it is our own future actions which are being predicted. This is not to say that no such property as "weight" is at issue, but only that we do not, ordinarily, consider it when we predict our own actions. There is a sense in which in the case of our own actions "weight" never varies, unlike overt cases of prediction where "weight" is relevant, such as predicting the outcome of an election.

If we rely on our common sense intuition—itself a common-sensical notion irreducible to notions even more commonsensi-cal—then we are inclined to say that an expression of intention is an expression of some inner state. But if so, the relation of inner state and future facts requires clarification, even though it is its connection to the future that results in uncertainty over whether an utterance is an expression of intention or prediction. There is little reason one might give for distinguishing how an expressions of intention and predictions *relate* to the future. But one thing seems to be certain: without, at least, a belief that we can make successful predictions, no intention will be formed. We believe that we have the power to change the facts so that what we want is realized; this belief is at the root of our belief in our ability to predict. We do not infer our intentions from our predictions. Without the ability to make any prediction, right or wrong, about the outcome of our actions, deliberation and, therefore intention, is a concept with very limited application.

It would be unproductive, to say the least, to locate the connection between intentions and the future in a property, or properties, of a state of mind. Such relations, Anscombe suggests, are not psychological in nature. But what about predictions? If I say 'I *will* catch a cold', and soon, thereafter, I say, truly, 'I *have* caught a cold', then my first statement is true by virtue of the very fact that makes the second sentence true, distinguished as it is from the first by tense alone. Is this what is characteristic of predictions; that is, this change of tense? If so, then commands and statements of intention are predictions; but also, if so, this fact will supply no objection to the belief that predictions are expressed by sentences related in this way to change of tense, as the facts come about allowing a judgment on whether the intention (or command) is satisfied.

Wittgenstein, Anscombe reminds us, regarded commands and expressions of intention as predictions in some sense. (Wittgenstein [1953] 630) What Anscombe suggests is that estimates (pertaining to the future), commands, expressions of intention, etc. may be species of predictions. She cautions, however, that an utterance may serve the purpose of making more than one sort of prediction. Her example is where a doctor says to a patient in his presence "Nurse will take you to the operating theatre." Exactly the same case can be found in Peter Geach, (Geach [1957-58] p. 273) Geach makes the point that the statement does three things at once: it is an expression of the surgeon's intention, a piece of information given to the patient, and an order to the nurse. Geach and Anscombe do not differ in how it is to be regarded, but she notes that the fact that the sentence 'Nurse will take you to the operating theatre' is in the indicative and will not, as such, afford us any basis for distinguishing expressions of intention from predictions.

It is easy to think of the conditions for the satisfaction of a command as being like the truth conditions of a sentence. So why is it that we do not speak of an obeyed command as true? Without giving a straightforward answer to this question, Anscombe provides some elements of contrast between the two. There are two aspects one associates with commands but not with ordinary indicative sentences. One is that an imperative takes a form serving to induce some agent to act in a certain way. Second, there is the future tense feature indicative of many such constructions. In addition, unlike predictions, the basis of which is the evidence which supports them, commands (somewhat like intentions) are sound in the sense of being worthy. While it can be said that commands lack a requirement of future tense, expressions of intention seem to involve future tense, essentially. While this may align expressions of intention more closely to predictions, there are deeper objections to identifying expressions of intention as a species of prediction.

If I do not fulfill my expressed intention, it neither follows that I have expressed a lying intention nor that I was mistaken in what

I said when I said such and such would take place. If my prediction fails, then what I have said is false. A falsehood may be regarded as in some sense a failure of one's judgment. Failing to act on an intention may result, simply enough, from a change of mind. This is a different kind of "failure" than a failure of judgment. Where I fail to fulfill my stated intention, the fault, if there is any to be had, is owing to the facts not coming to conform to the word, rather than, as in the case of judgment (or prediction), the words not conforming to the world. The former is, unlike the case of judgment, or prediction, an error in "performance" not judgment. Although she cites Theophratus in this regard, readers may recognize her example as being very much like one proposed by her contemporary, H. A. Prichard who remarked in an essay well known at the time of her writing:

> *But we have to bear in mind that the change which we willed may not have been the same as the change we think we effected...where I willed the existence of a certain word on a piece of paper, I afterwards find that what I caused was a different word."*
>
> — (Prichard [1949] p. 192)

Anscombe points out that we speak of *expressions* of intentions but not of expressions of commands. A command requires symbols. It is performative; but an expression of intention suggests that there is something that is expressed that may exist independently of its being expressed, something internal that may remain unexpressed or covert. But, if an intention is something internal, how then are we to relate the intention to facts concerning the future? We face something very much like the egocentric predicament. This is problematic and implies the need to look beyond prediction as the basis of our understanding of intentions. At this point, Anscombe makes a crucial move in an entirely different direction.

She will admit that intentions can be had by both humans and animals, but it is only in the case of humans that there are expressions of intentions. Such expressions are linguistic and are to be distinguished from the "natural expressions of intention" we find affirmed in Wittgenstein (Wittgenstein [1953] 647). This move, away from intention and towards the *expression* of intention, is at the center of Anscombe's revolution in philosophical psychology.

## SECTION 3: *EXPRESSION OF INTENTION, PREDICTION AND LEAVES THAT TALK*

If I don't know what you are trying to do, I am limited in what to expect from you next. But, if *I* am trying to do something, then I know what it is I am trying to do, and once I've resolved to do something, I know what to expect next, assuming, of course, that I anticipate no external constraints on my execution of the resolve (intention). But why should my expectations be so high in my own case but not so high in that case where I am observing someone else, someone, that is, seemingly intent on doing something I know not what; and what is it to believe on observation that someone else is intent on doing something, if they are silent, and if there is, as Anscombe says, no natural expression of intent, nor a clear idea of what he needs to be doing in order to do what he wants? If someone has been working quietly and I say "He is going to lift that stone," I would be making a prediction; but if I say "I am going to lift that stone" this will be, immediately, construed as expressing an intention, and from this assertion the hearer may predict what it is I am going to do.

Philosophers have, frequently, preoccupied themselves by entertaining such asymmetries in attempting to get a linguistic handle on such matters as our self-attribution of pain—which often seems in some sense "direct"—and the attribution of pain to others. But there is an asymmetry among asymmetries when we are talking about the attribution of intention. An attribution of pain does not depend on whether the subject of the attribution is oneself or another: saying "John is in pain" may be based on different considerations than "I am in pain," yet both are attributions of pain. But there is something different going on in the case of attributions of intentional action. Again, if I say "He is going to go to the store" that is not a statement *of* intention, even if it implies an intention; but if I should say "I am going to go to the store," then the preferred interpretation is that I am stating my intention and not, merely, saying something from which an intention can be inferred. In other words, the difference between first and third person attributions does not affect *what* is being attributed, whereas the difference between first and third person may indicate *that* it is an intention being attributed. If there is no natural expression of intention, then there is no, clear, outer criterion for the inner state, if such there be, of having an intention. We are dependent, here, on the conventions of language. The same cannot be said in the case of pain. If we attempt to examine our intentions by examining what a statement of intention is an expression of, then according to Anscombe we fall into the errors of introspective psychology and its assortment of confusing mentalistic associations.

If Anscombe is right we need to do better than we would by either approaching the concept of intention by examining its verbal expression, or probing, introspectively, mental elements that may be thought to accompany our intentions. How, then, does someone know that he has a, certain, intention when he says: "I am going to the store"? If we say that there is something in his mind, an intention, and that he knows his intention by examining this inner state, there will be a possibility that he is in error. But it would make no sense for him to say, "I am going to the store, but I'm not sure that this is what I intend to do," that is, unless he anticipates compulsion by some agency outside his control. Likewise, if I suddenly remember that I intended to do something, but didn't, there is no inner state, the intention, that occurs as an element of my recollection. Neither introspection nor grammar reveals the difference between prediction and a statement of intention.

One way of describing the distinction between expressions of intention, and prediction, is first to regard the agent's reasons for acting in such a way as to understand them as involving some description of the future. If we talk about prediction as constitutive in some sense, although not exhaustively so, of an expression of intention, we might relate the description of the future to the expression of intention, or to the intention, itself, by way of the *evidence* available to the agent, *qua* "predictor." But this is not the case when we give *reasons* for our intentional behavior. In this case the future is not related to our resolve to act in virtue of our having cited evidence that we will in fact fulfill our intention. Thus there is a contrast of evidence and reason, one that has been, closely, tied to another contrast, viz. that of causes and reasons. This distinction between reasons and causes will be basic to Anscombe's discussion. At this stage of her discussion this contrast provides us with no respite from our effort to distinguish expressions of intention and predictions. She introduces, however, an analogy, one that we will consider in some detail, partly because it has an interesting history and, partly, because Anscombe may not have gotten the original point of the analogy, exactly, right.

Anscombe remarks that she saw some notes on one of Wittgenstein's lectures wherein he describes leaves being blown in various ways by the wind. These are talking leaves, and what they say is "Now I'll go this way... now that way." The question, then, is whether our situation is like that of the talking leaves. It is interesting that the analogy would be one of talking leaves. H. H. Price had, much earlier, discussed talking leaves in connection with other minds. (Price [1938]) Whether there is an historical connection to Price is difficult to tell. However, there is a remarkably similar analogy drawn by Hans Reichenbach much later, circa 1951. The original point of the analogy is in doubt, however, although Anscombe says that Wittgenstein was certainly engaging in a denial of freewill. Close examination reveals, however, that in all likelihood it was devised to illustrate how it is that distinguishing intentions and predictions, rather than assimilating them, creates an illusion of freedom. This, I think, was Wittgenstein's intent, although this writer has been unable to locate the original source in Wittgenstein.

As we said, Reichenbach employs a very similar analogy to illustrate how the illusion of freedom might arise.

> *Accordingly, the feeling of freedom is merely an epiphenomenon. By analogy, a stone which was moved by an externally caused impact and which continued to move after the impact had ceased would feel itself free if it had the capacity to think and if its motion coincided with its wishes to continue on its path.*
>
> — (Reichenbach [1959] p. 152)

If we take it that the talking leaves are analogous to the human agent, we need to relate "evidence" and "cause." Evidence is provided for a causal relation, and causation in some sense is related to prediction. Anscombe believes the analogy fails because there is nothing corresponding to prediction in the case of the leaves. But it's not so much a failure of the analogy as the application by Anscombe of the analogy to a different set of circumstances. The issue that both analogies address is how a belief in free-will arises from an illusion. There is no reason to believe that they were intended to clarify the distinction between prediction and expression of intention. The analogies of Wittgenstein and Reichenbach are deliberate in not distinguishing causes and reasons in the following sense. The leaves (or stone) experience their actions as free, precisely owing to their inability to identify the causes of their actions. The reason such causes are "invisible" to them is that their intentions coincide, perfectly, with the determined effects of physical causes. Because the "predictions" predict what the "reasons" justify, the two are difficult to distinguish if, indeed, they can be distinguished. It is not essential, as Anscombe appears to suggest, that predictions by the agent are an "unnecessary" accompaniment of the actions themselves. Rather, what is the case is that, for the agent unaware of the causes of his action, there is awareness only of his action being in compliance with his intentions. Causes drop out, epistemologically, not ontologically. It should be kept in mind that Wittgenstein was among the first to regard causes and reasons as providing an important contrast, and that in the case of this analogy he is remarking on what happens when we think we are free when in fact we are not. While Wittgenstein may have believed in determinism, his intent was to provide an insight into our *sense* of freedom, not to argue *for* determinism. A final comment on Reichenbach is in order.

Reichenbach's discussion of free-will is informed by the views of Spinoza. He doesn't cite, precisely, where his Spinozistic ideas originate, but we do find in Spinoza positions that cohere with Reichenbach's position, such as when Spinoza says:

*Experience teaches us no less clearly than reason, that men believe themselves to be free, simply because they are conscious of their actions, and unconscious of the causes whereby those actions are determined...*

— (Spinoza [1960] p. 268)

When we give reasons for our predictions, typically, we give reasons for *belief*, not reasons for making the prediction. When we give a reason for action, typically, we are not giving a reason for belief but, rather, justification for doing what we are doing. At this stage of the discussion, while the distinction between predictions, and expressions of intention, is difficult to make, if not impossible, we have gained an insight into one approach, one having to do with reasons for action, rather than evidence for the coming about of the actions we predict. Consider the talking leaves. The leaves say "Now I'll go this way..." When is this a statement of intention, and when is it a prediction? Anscombe next turns to the question of whether we can ever be certain of the truth of such statements as "A intends *X*."

## SECTION 4: *THE AGENT AS SOLE AUTHORITY IN KNOWLEDGE OF INTENTIONS*

A report on someone else's intention is more likely to be useful if you report what that someone is in fact doing. I have a good chance of figuring out someone's intentions if I know what he is doing. The more I know of what he is doing, the more likely I am to know what he intends; for what a person does is, typically, what he intends. As long as I have reasonable assurance that he is aware of what he is doing, and there are no obstacles in his way, I am, usually able to deduce his intentions within a certain modulus of time. If this were not the case, under ordinary circumstances, communication would be impaired. If I came into your room I would know that you were sitting. You would know in all likelihood that you were sitting. There would be a strong "chance" of my being correct in saying that sitting was your intention. If I were a strange sort of being who upon entering the room became aware not of your sitting but, rather, of your effect on the acoustics of the room in which you are sitting, then you and I would have some difficulty in communicating. Anscombe does not appear to think it is worth mentioning, however, that the "chance" of your being wrong is considerably less than my chance of getting wrong what it is you intend. But *why* is it that we take the authority of the one whose intentions are in question to be the final word? Anscombe gives three reasons.

First, Anscombe says that we may have a good grasp on the intention *of* one's doing something without knowing his intention *in* doing something. She doesn't explain the difference. Let's make an attempt. Perhaps the difference is that having a hold on the intention of one's doing something will not reveal the intention with which this action performed. We know the action a person intends but we might not know with what intention he performs this action. I see a man wave. The intention *of* his doing so is to catch a cab, but his intention *in* waving may be to make an important dental appointment. We see that he turns towards the cab; he looks straight at the cab and, then, waves. We can, pretty much, figure out the intention *of* his waving; however, we don't know a thing about his teeth; his dentist, or why he is anxious. In order to know his intention *in* waving down the cab, i.e. meeting the appointment, it seems we must make some inquiry, typically appealing to some avowal of intention on the part of the agent himself. This is not like seeing someone sitting in a chair and, thereby, arriving at a good idea of what she is doing, i.e. sitting in a chair. Another sort of example, where we rely on the authority of the agent, is where there is no question of his intentions, since they are so obvious. It isn't clear what Anscombe means here. We can only speculate that in doing things with obvious intention we do not preclude the agent's testimony as decisive on that occasion. Even though it is obvious that a man is flipping the switch in order to turn on the light, the authority of the agent is in such cases, naturally, believed to be ultimate in determining his intention. The third explanation for why people take the agent's testimony as decisive is that it is easy to believe that someone may have formed an intention, but as yet has not carried it out; or that he has changed his mind as to what he intends to do, although so far he may have done nothing to indicate what this change of mind might be. It is regarded as "an interior thing." All three of these reasons for taking the agent's authority as ultimate depend on the idea that that the agent has privileged access to something interior to his own mind. What the agent does is not the first consideration; what is in his mind is. Anscombe inverts this picture, and takes what a man actually does as fundamental in arriving at what intentions are involved in a person's acting. John Macmurray, some years prior to the publication of *Intention*, had taken a stand quite opposite of Anscombe's following consideration of similar examples. Before moving on to discuss Anscombe, a word is in order about the state of the issue as she found it at the time she wrote.

Macmurray had raised the question as to how we distinguish mere *events* from *doings* (Macmurray [1938] p. 79). The difference between the two, he alleged, was that doings involve intention. Take Anscombe's case where that "special" person notices acoustic effects. What makes this a strange case, for someone taking Macmurray's position, is that such acoustic effects appear to be mere events and not, really, *doings*, (compare, here, Melden's happenings vs. doings). Macmurray, in fact, brings in trial testimony, just as does Anscombe; but Macmurray's focus is not on the witness but, rather, the defendant. The jury is faced with the question whether there is sufficient evidence to establish intent. Ultimately, the only one who can know for certain is the defendant, nothing a witness may provide being of equal value for the purpose at hand. Anscombe takes the very opposite position, arguing that the first thing we must consider is what the person in question actually does. It can be reasonably argued from Macmurray's point of view that the authority of a sincere speaker with respect to his intentions is not, merely, a matter of chance, as it would be in Anscombe's case where we chance to be right when we infer what the defendant intended by what he was "seen" to be doing.

# PART 2:
# Reasons, Intentions, and Knowledge

Even if it were the case that the ultimate authority as to what the intentions of action are is located in the inner life of the agent and not his behavior, this would not provide an answer to the question, "What is intention?" Anscombe submits for our consideration a proposal that will afford us a better understanding of how to go about resolving this question. Up to this point, intention has been regarded as predictive in a certain sense; Anscombe has spoke of evidence relevant to the prediction in contrast to reasons for action. However, when she proposes an answer to the question just raised, "What is intention?" she will contrast causes and reasons. This contrast will remain thematic throughout her discussion, and taken together with the idea of a "mental cause" will set the stage for much, if not all, of what is to follow.

### SECTION 5: "... A CERTAIN SENSE OF THE QUESTION 'WHY?'"

What distinguishes intentional actions from other behavior is that in the case of intentional actions we can raise the question 'Why?' in the sense of inquiring into *reasons* for acting. Anscombe will not, at any stage in her discussion, attempt an *analysis* of the why-question used to elucidate intention, nor was she the first to recognize its special place in discussing action. Anthony Kenny locates a, very, similar idea in Aristotle. Answering the question "Why?" may entail a *causal* explanation or, depending on the sense attached to it, a *rational* explanation. In order to exclude from a 'why' question the imputation of a requested causal explanation Kenny suggests 'wherefore'. (Kenny [1979] p. 114). Before Anscombe made crucial use of this why-question, others had remarked on the differences between the causal and rational explanation, where "explanation" referred to an answer to some why-question.

One noteworthy example is Wm. Dray, who took a number of cues from his predecessors, among them Collingwood and Braithwaite. Dray is, particularly, interesting because for him—contrary to what Davidson implied when he acknowledged a categorical distinction between causal and rational senses of the why-question (Davidson [1963] p. 3)—the difference is one, mainly, of perspective. The causal why-question belongs to the "spectator" perspective, whereas the rational why-question belongs to the agent's perspective. (Dray [1956] chapter V) Such considerations would ramify through Anscombe's views on the epistemology of actions "in-intention." Observational knowledge belongs to causal explanation, whereas explanations in terms of one's own intentions, insofar as they are possible, are not acquired *via* observation. In this way what we shall call the "relevant why-question," i.e. the why-question definitive of 'intention' becomes assimilated to nonobservational knowledge, a move which in historical perspective is not as radical as it may first appear.

Even though answering such a question as "Why did you act so?" will provide an answer to another question, "What was your reason for acting?," this would fail to bring us much closer to understanding intention, since understanding the, relevant, sense of 'Why?' would be, merely, postponed until we could arrive at some understanding of the meaning of the question "What was your *reason* for acting?" I knock over a cup; I caught my knee, say on the edge of the table while standing up. I may be asked by someone who wasn't watching my knee, "Why did you knock over that cup?" I am not being asked for evidence that may have allowed me to make the prediction that I would knock over the cup. What is in play is not evidence, but reasons. Nor is the cause of one's knocking over the cup in question.

Although in the case of the cup we speak of being "caused" to knock it over, the agent does not infer the cause from some evidential basis. Just as a person knows without looking how the limbs of his body are oriented with respect to his torso, or knows where he is feeling a certain pain, he knows that the sudden appearance of a face in the window is what caused his sudden start without examining evidence for the theory that this is what caused it. Not all actions of this sort are involuntary, as was the case in knocking over the cup. Let's take an example Anscombe doesn't use, since hers is not as convincing. Children will sometimes hear a siren and, without thinking, mimic the sound. The action is voluntary and, yet, they are caused to do so in the same sense of "cause" that applied to knocking over the cup, although the action is voluntarily performed. Before proceeding to give a more precise account of Anscombe's selective employment of 'why', it will be useful in evaluating her overall strategy to consider intentional withholding of action in order to see how it accommodates different cases. In the next section she will introduce, for the first time into the theory of action, the notion of 'falling under a description." She would later critique Davidson based on her doubt that its employment suffices in cases of omissions for the purpose of distinguishing intentional and non-intentional actions. (Anscombe [1982] p. 208) Although we will not discuss omission at any length, a word on its special status in action theory will prove to be a worthwhile digression.

What events are, and how they are individuated is a subject with a long history. What we have to say about omissions must be said without resolving more general issues such as the nature of events. Whatever theory of events one chooses it is difficult to assimilate omission to other events, especially if events are regarded as changes in a substance or substratum. The contrast between omissions and other actions is not as evident if we consider events properties of objects at a time, a theory which, while quite commonly held, is probably inadequate. Without pursuing the matter, it should be noted that events understood as properties at a place at a time, say, would be without duration and, so, "events" only in some pickwickian sense. On our view, events must possess duration.

Omissions are not changes; they are not happenings in the way an eclipse is an event that happens. However, events are supposed to have causes. My omitting to sign my middle name on a document may cause confusion in some circumstances. If so, an omission *can* be a cause. If so, causation is not, necessarily, a relation between events, merely, that is, as long as omission is not an event or is an event of a very special sort. Still, an omission occurs in time with causation occurring only between things *in* time. Further, an omission may not only be a cause; it may be an effect. I may deliberately omit something, such as my middle initial, or the omission may come about accidentally. There are no acts of omission in, precisely, the same way that there are willful acts that are not acts of will. Scratching one's nose without thinking is not an act of will, as raising one's broken arm on doctor's orders would, certainly, be. Suppose I don't call the mayor's office. In fact, I've never called the mayor's office. But doesn't not calling him constitute an omission only as long as I mean that, had I called, it would have been intentional? Since the situation is one where I would not have had any intention of calling the mayor, I cannot conclude that the call *would have been* intentional; therefore, not calling was not an omission. Had I such an intention, but for some reason not called without changing my mind, then I would have omitted the call since it was my intention to call. When a non-occurrence is an omission, it is backed by an intention but not the intention to omit performing the action. By contrast, if I make something happen there may be the intention to make *it* happen but no other intention is necessary in order for it to be an action. But in order to be said to omit an action some pre-existing intention is necessary besides any intention to omit the action. We see, then, that omissions present an exceptional case in some respects.

We feel the compulsion, at some point, to ask: what must be added to an event that never happened in order to make it an omission? An omission, unlike a bodily movement which had it happened would have been just that, viz. a bodily movement, is such a nonoccurrence of an event that had it occurred that event would have been an action and *would* have been intentional. Omissions, as we have said, constitute a special class, or category. Although Anscombe may be right to criticize Davidson on this matter, no one, including Anscombe, has presented a satisfactory theory of its nature and implications.

Anscombe does not address the difference between reasons for acting and reasons for not acting. Where there is a reason for not acting, my not "acting" is acting, nonetheless. 'Acting' in 'not acting' may refer to an action or it may not. If I am asked why I didn't raise my hand, I may say that I didn't want people to know I was present. In saying this, I am offering a reason; in this case, that I do not raise my hand is an action. Do we want to say that not acting is an action only when the agent holds that there is a reason for not acting? What would make little, if any, sense would be to say that inaction is a, mere, event. Inaction makes *sense*, as an event, only if it is an action. In this instance being an event depends on being an action, not the other way around. However, if I am asked why I didn't raise my hand, I may say that there was no reason to; in this case, if I describe my inaction as 'not acting', the word 'acting' is being used in a different sense. It conveys a sense of behaving which is to be distinguished from not acting; that is, one which is caused, but for which there may be no reason, such as a heavy weight's having been placed in my hand preventing me from raising it. In this sense there is no *mental cause*, as when I jump because I am startled by a face in the window. If I say I nailed the hammer to the wall, and someone asks why, I may say "no reason." But if I am asked why I didn't nail the hammer to the wall and reply "no reason" I may mean only that there was no reason to do such a silly thing. 'Acting' in 'not acting' is, therefore ambiguous. It may mean an abstinence, or simply not doing something, but in the latter case it does not apply to weighing down my hand preventing action.

There is no simple distinction between reasons and causes that can be used to make the distinction between the two sorts of abstinences we have discussed. In other words, having a reason not to do something may be unrelated to intention, even when it contrasts with 'cause'. I had no intention not to raise my hand; I had no reason not to raise it. But I was not caused not to raise it.

## *a) Some Gricean Points*

The literature on action theory that followed publication of Anscombe's *Intention*, rarely, mentions her predecessors, although H. A. Prichard and Aristotle do receive a fair amount of attention. However, others who published on the subject about the same time as did Anscombe, people such as Stuart Hampshire have been, largely, forgotten. Few, if any, historical commentaries on action theory have delved into the influence of H. P. Grice. J. L. Speranza, who knows a great deal about Grice, has pointed out to me that Grice appears to have mentioned Anscombe only in a minor way; and Anscombe, it must be said, reciprocated. Nevertheless, several years before Anscombe wrote, Grice was applying the concept of intention, not "intension," to understanding 'meaning' and the way he went about it had, definite, implications for subsequent discussion of the topic.

Anscombe's approach to the problem of understanding intention was predicated, largely, on the idea that intentions are not entities. This approach extended to regarding ideas, themselves, as grammatical rather than ontological. Following the publication of Wittgenstein's *Philosophical Investigations* there began a trend towards dispensing with entities, or ontology, more generally, in favor of linguistic distinctions which made positing their existence unnecessary. The idea of a voluntary action was viewed by Ryle, to take one example, not as referring to some special entity, or event, such as a volition but, rather, as being a way of describing actions which "ought not to be done." (Ryle [1950] p. 69) Similarly, Grice dispensed with the need to recognize "special objects," such as sense data, in favor of speaking of statements limited to what can be "doubted or denied." (Grice [1961] p. 226-227) Ayer had spoken, as well, of the "sense data language" *in lieu* of entities, as such. Furthermore, Grice took the step of dispensing with semantical entities, such as intensions, theorizing that 'meaning' in the sense of 'A means something by x' could be given an account in terms of intentions, where the relevant intention is what the speaker induces the hearer to believe is "behind the utterance." (Grice [1957] p. 217). It is the view to be taken, here, that Anscombe's use of the notion of the why-question serves very much the same ends as were served by the use of circumstances of utterance we find in Ryle and Grice, viz. to eliminate the need for reliance on "special objects." Such a procedure was became an integral part of what Gustav Bergmann, first, referred to as the "linguistic turn." (Bergmann [1953] p. 33).

## SECTION 6: *INTENTIONAL 'UNDER A DESCRIPTION'*

Intentional acts, as we have seen, are actions to which the question 'Why?' applies when that question is taken in a particular sense. Anscombe continues to explore this sense. One way of doing so is to ask when the question does *not* apply. Suppose a man is asked, "Why are you sawing that board?" He might, very well, reply "I didn't' realize I was sawing a board." He may not understand 'board' but then, again, he might not realize he was sawing a board. He may have been sawing something else, and there might have been a board underneath. On another occasion, a man may be asked "Why are you sawing that oak plank?" He might reply that he didn't know that that was what he was doing; he thought the board was maple. What he was doing, sawing, he knew he was doing; but he didn't know he was sawing an oak plank. He may know he was sawing *under the description* 'sawing a plank' but not under the description 'sawing an oak plank'. A difference in description does not imply a difference in the action. The man is not doing one thing under the description 'sawing a board' and another under 'sawing an oak plank'. Because this idea of 'falling under a description' has become an important topic, we shall examine it in greater detail.

### *a) Anscombe's Later Discussion of 'Under a Description'*

In 1979, Anscombe published an essay defending her use of the idea of 'falling under a description' in action theory against a number of criticisms. (Anscombe [1979] pp. 208-220). We will not discuss these criticisms at any length, only her response. Next, we shall enter into a critical discussion of how she, and Donald Davidson, make use of this idea. With respect to '*x* under the description *d*', she says that the subject of the sentence in which it occurs may be '*x*', but never '*x* under the description *d*'. In her reply to criticisms, she informs us that in '*x* under the description *d*' '*x*' is the subject of a sentence in which the entire expression occurs, while '*x* under the description *d*' is never the subject of the sentence. (Anscombe [1979] p. 208) That is, to take a simpler example than the one she provides, in say "Ortcutt under the description 'possible double-agent' became an object of interest" the subject of the sentence is 'Ortcutt' and not 'Ortcutt under the description 'possible double-agent''. Moreover, she claims that "under the description *d*" means the same as '*qua d*'. She cites Aristotle (Aristotle [*Posterior Analytics*] I:38, 49a11), as claiming that '*qua*' "belongs to the predicate." But this is an oversimplification of the facts, and may be misleading. A closer look at Aristotle reveals a somewhat different situation.

Consider the syllogisms (as we have reconstructed them from Aristotle's description) in the passage Anscombe cites from the *Posterior Analytics*.

Of the good there is knowledge (*qua* good)
Justice is good
Therefore, justice is knowledge (*qua* good)

Of some particular thing there is knowledge (*qua* some particular thing)
The good is some particular thing
Therefore, of the good there is knowledge (qua some particular thing).

'*Qua*' sets forth a *qua*lification. Aristotle is making a proposal concerning where, in the first, syllogism, to put the second occurrence of 'good'. He puts it with the Major term, because if he puts it with the Middle term, the predicate of the conclusion will not hold of the minor term. Further, if you put it with the Minor term, then you get pointless redundancy ('good (*qua* good)'). So it goes with the Major term. Anscombe claims that Aristotle puts '*qua*' with the subject rather than the predicate, and, then, she draws the conclusion that there are no things, *A*, such that they are "*A qua B.*" In the first place, Aristotle is not making a general claim in the passages cited that '*qua*' always goes with the predicate, only that when there are two occurrences of the term, that *in the context of a syllogism* the term belongs with the Major term. At most, Aristotle is saying that sometimes '*qua*' belongs with the predicate. Whether it always does is another question. The question is this: Does 'under the description *d*' always mean '*qua d*'? We suspect the answer is no.

If I say, "I was allowed on stage under the description 'stage manager'"? This is ambiguous; this is the first claim we would make. If "under the description of stage manager" means "being stage manager so-called," that would be one reading, one where I am, merely, referred to as such, that is as stage manager. I may not be the stage manager. In this case the sentence means one thing: I was allowed on stage as the so-called stage manager. But suppose I mean by "under the description of stage manager," rather "*qua* stage manager," that would be something else. Then the sentence would mean that I was allowed onstage because I was the stage manager. We cannot exclude, therefore, two possible readings of 'under a description' only one of which is '*qua*'. The situation is a bit clearer if we take 'authority' instead of 'manager', so that our sentence becomes: "I was allowed on stage because I was the so-called stage manager," as opposed to "I was allowed on stage *qua* stage manager." In addition, one cannot construct cases where I am on stage *qua* stage manager, although I am not the stage manager, without reliance on performance factors unrelated to "competence" in Chomsky's sense (Chomsky [1965] pp. 208-210). It may not even be the case that I am a so-called stage manager; no one may have ever understood me to be the stage manager. It may have been the case that my being let on stage *qua* stage manager implies that I was also called the stage manager, but in order to draw the conclusion that the cases were the same, and that there is no ambiguity, it would have to be added that one might in the very same sense be both the stage manager and the so-called stage manager. The reader will not experience the contrast unless the contrast between being a stage manager and being a so-called stage manager is part of one's dialect (or idiolect). So it would appear that there is a difference between two possible readings of 'under a description'. But now the important question: In the sense in which 'under a description' does not mean '*qua*' is 'x under the description d' a subject term?

If in "Bob under the description 'stage manager' Ved" (where 'V' is a verb) we have it that" "under the description 'stage manager'" can be read as "the so-called stage manager," then in "Bob as the so called stage manager fired Ruddy" the subject is not "Bob" but "Bob as the so-called stage manager." But how can we tell? Isn't 'Bob' the grammatical subject with the 'as' clause simply an expression in the predicate? If we take the passive of "Bob as the so-called stage manager fired Ruddy," we might get "Ruddy as the so-called stage manager was fired by Bob." The sentence 'Bob was fired by Ruddy as the so called stage manager' seems, marginally, degraded. Syntactically, the first sentence is a non-degraded passive, and one might want to argue that, therefore, 'Bob' not 'Bob as the so called stage manager' must be the subject of the original sentence. *But* what we need to do is distinguish the logical subject and the syntactic or grammatical subject, somewhat in the way Russell distinguished the logical subject of 'Pegasus exists' from its grammatical subject. This becomes an issue when we attempt to analyze the constituent structure of a sentence.

Sometimes in analyzing the constituent structure of a sentence we make use of certain tools. One such tool is to observe the possible ways in which constituents, and sets of constituents, can be "moved" about in a sentence without disturbing its grammaticality. Let's make use of this tool in examining the sentence 'Bob as the so-called stage manager fired Ruddy'. Our judgments will take into account some semantical as well as grammatical considerations. When we passivize a sentence we, typically, move the object of the verb to the front; change the verb's inflection; and adjoin a prepositional phrase with the original subject as its object. (Chomsky [1957] p.112) So, from 'Bob as the so-called manager fired Ruddy' we might get 'Ruddy as the so-called stage manager was fired by Bob'. But depending on whether we include the phrase 'as the so-called stage manager' in the noun expression constituting the subject of the original sentence we might passivize, somewhat differently: 'Ruddy was fired by Bob as the so-called stage manager'. This sentence, unlike our first passive form seems, marginally, degraded; but the semantics of the original active sentence has been utterly destroyed inasmuch as Ruddy was not described 'as the so-called stage manager' in the active form. For our purposes the constituent that "moves" will be the subject of the sentence. Setting aside what the *linguists* might say about the relation of syntax and semantics, for the time being, let us suppose with philosophers such as Russell that there is a distinction to be drawn between "logical form" (in a broad sense) and grammatical form (syntactic structure).

If we make this distinction, we can see that in the passive sentence, above, the truth value as well as the meaning is changed, but, if the passive were in fact "Ruddy was fired by Bob as the so-called stage manager," then these problems do not arise. This is not to say that this latter construction is, entirely, acceptable. Its not being syntactically as acceptable suggests that the passive where 'Bob' is moved *qua* subject is the correct result of passivization, and Anscombe's view that 'Bob' not 'Bob as the so-called stage manager' is the subject of the sentence is confirmed. What is most important, however, is that there is a *contrast*, one that reveals the radically different semantic consequences of taking 'Bob' rather than 'Bob as the so-called stage manager' as logical subject. To be sure, Anscombe is correct in noting that passivization is possible where, certain, semantic features are not preserved, but if we make it a condition of being the logical, not merely the syntactical, subject that all semantic features of the sentence be preserved under passivization, then although it is marginally degraded, grammatically, its meaning is preserved under passivization only if the subject is taken to be the entire expression 'Bob as the so-called stage manager'. If we are allowed this, then we can say that contrary to what she has said '*x* under the description *d*' need not be rejected in all cases as the logical subject of the sentence in which it occurs. This is not to say that in *nature* there are kinds which include *being the so-called stage manager*. But we can attribute to "Bob under the description 'stage manager'" certain properties as in "Bob under the description 'stage manager' was unfair," meaning that under some other description he might *be* fair, such as "Bob under the description 'father' was fair." There is another important issue connected with Anscombe's introduction of the notion of 'under a description' related to action theory, as we shall soon discover. While Donald Davidson made significant use of her proposal, Anscombe, however, took exception to the way he went about it. We turn next to some of the details of Davidson's position and Anscombe critical commentary.

## b) Davidson's Use of 'Under a Description'

Davidson made important use of the idea of a thing's being taken "under a description," claiming that attributions of agency depend on there being some description under which what someone did can be said to have been done intentionally. A man may be doing something when he saws a board, but that action is intentional only relative to a description. Under the description 'sawing an *oak* board', the action may not have been intentional; but under the description 'sawing a *maple* board' the action may have been intentional, and, even though there may be only one such description, the action is intentional, and the man is considered the "agent" of that action. Anscombe, also, saw a connection between the intentionality of action and the intentionality of sensation.

Knowledge by observation is impossible without sensation, and sensation, if Anscombe is right (Anscombe [1965b] p. 4) is like action in being intentional in three respects: first, the case of action where the intended act doesn't occur is analogous to a sensation (or thought) that something exists when it does not. It is worth mentioning that if the reader is perplexed by the move from sensation to thought, little explanation is to be found in Anscombe introductory remarks. Second, much in the same way that an action may be intentional under one description but not another, we cannot substitute one description of an object of an intentional verb (presumably including those expressing sensations) for another, where the object of the verb does not exist; and, third, analogous to the way a description of an action may be vague, the object of an intentional verb can, be indeterminate. It is a curious fact that, even though intention in action, and in sensation, or thought, are analogous, Anscombe does not appeal to the 'Why?' question in describing what makes a *sensation* intentional. She has, already, distinguished an *intention* from *being intentional* (Anscombe [1957] p. 1) but one would suppose that the two might be related in some important way. We never ask of a sensation "Why?" in the sense of the why-question associated with intention, and this marks a significant difference; setting psychoanalysis aside, there is no *reason* we experience a sensation, only a cause of the sensation, and here we restrict ourselves to sensations of the cognitive sort. The question, however, remains: If sensations are intentional, merely, analogically, to action, and we cannot raise the why-question in regards to sensation, then what entitles us to speak of the "intentionality" of sensations at all? The idea 'under a description' links sensation and action to intentionality; the 'Why?' question, hardly, suggests a connection.

We can mention only in passing that Anscombe's discussion of 'under a description' are informed by Geach's views on "relative identity" and Quine's application of the concept to opaque domains.

### c) The Intentionality of Sensation

An intentional verb is one taking an intentional object, and intentional objects belong with direct objects. What, then, are the direct objects, i.e. intentional objects of intentional verbs? The alternatives are, basically, these. Either the intentional object is an idea, or it is a grammatical object. In the sentence 'John sent a book to Mary' the grammatical direct object is 'a book'. If asked what John gave to Mary, I would not expect the answer: "a direct object." Similarly, if I were asked what the object of my thinking is when I think of Zeus, I would say neither a direct object nor an idea. The thought is not about an idea. It is about Zeus. The common sense view of such thoughts carries a number of pertinent implications.

What makes a thought a thought *about Zeus* and not a thought about Athena? In order to think of Zeus, and not Athena, I must have an idea of Zeus. That is the common sense belief. To say this is not to say I have to think of an idea of Zeus in order to think of Zeus, only that the idea must be present. If we say we are thinking about a direct object we find ourselves in some difficulty, since Zeus is not a noun phrase. If I am thinking about a nonexistent object, am I thinking about nothing? No. I am thinking about something that doesn't exist. What is the difference, then, between thinking of something that doesn't exist and thinking of nothing? Still, the puzzle is an ancient one. If I am thinking of nothing, there is a sense in which I may not be thinking at all. When I say "I am thinking about Zeus" I am saying that I have a thought which is of the Zeus sort; the idea of Zeus is not the object of thought but a property of thought. There is no description under which a thought is about Zeus, while under another description it is a thought about something else, or another thought. In this respect a thought may not be like an intentional action although a thought may be intentional. What, then, is the relation of intentional objects and direct objects? This is the question we must answer.

According to Anscombe (Anscombe [1965b] p. 9), an intentional object is given by a *description under which*. This idea provides a link between 'under a description' and objects of thought. But what, exactly, is it? She does not exclude ideas, as such, but she does insist that insofar as they are pertinent to the intentionality of thought, and sensation, they are to be regarded as "grammatical notions," not entities. Pursuing the analogy between action and thought illuminates crucial features of the problem as Anscombe sees it. Let's consider one example she discusses. Anscombe has said that an intentional object is given by a direct object, but not all direct objects supply intentional objects. If someone says "They worship the Sun," the direct object is 'the Sun." Taken under the description 'big ball of hot gas' this direct object does not give the intentional object, since the worshippers do not accept the idea that they are worshipping a big ball of hot gas. A more obviously intentional verb is 'aim'. Suppose a hunter aims at a deer, fires, and discovers that the patch of brown he aimed at was not a deer at all but, rather, his father. An observer reported that he aimed at his father; he reported he aimed at a deer. Anscombe alleges an ambiguity in 'He aimed at his father'.

Although there is a sense in which 'He aimed at his father is true', 'his father' does not give the intentional object, even though it the only morphologically realized grammatical object in the sentence. *What* is aimed is the gun; 'his father' is the object of the preposition 'at'; the preposition links the subject of the verb and the preposition's own object. At this point, Anscombe makes a surprising move: she introduces talk of *material objects*. (Anscombe [1965b] p. 10). We now have to contend with two sorts of objects": intentional objects and material objects. The gambit is familiar. C. D. Broad had attempted what he called the analysis of the "perceptual situation." In the course of dealing with illusory situations he invoked a distinction between "epistemological objects" and "ontological objects." (Broad [1925] chapter IV) An intentional object in Anscombe's sense may be regarded as an "epistemological object" on Broad's approach. Similarly, the material object in Anscombe is the "ontological object" in Broad's case. In the sense that the sentence 'He aimed at his father' is true, the *verb* is said to take a material object, but in the sense in which the sentence is false, the intentional object is the deer. But the deer does not exist, so was the hunter aiming at a deer or his father? Anscombe's answer is a curious one, indeed. She says that what he was aiming at was a patch of color, and that the patch of color "in fact" was his father's hat. Now we cannot say that the intentional object was his father's hat; that would return us to the original problem. The intentional object is the patch of color. What are we to make of Anscombe's analysis of the situation? Without pursuing it much further, I will entertain one possible alternative.

We might avoid the encumbrance of introducing the distinction between intentional and material objects, if we can circumvent the problem of ambiguity. One proposal would be to deny that 'He aimed at his father' is ambiguous. How might this be justified? Recall the "brown patch" mentioned in Anscombe's account. Set aside the fact that this sounds very much like a commitment to sense-data. The situation is one, really, where two sentence types are at issue, exemplified, respectively, by 'He aimed at his father' and 'I aimed at a deer'. According to Anscombe, the first sentence is ambiguous. But is this, actually, the case? Is this the locus of "ambiguity"? Suppose one were to say that in the first sentence the intentional object belongs not to the agent, but the witness. What the witness witnesses, although it may not resemble the brown patch given to the agent, is given under the description 'his father' and differs from the intentional object of the agent, i.e. the brown patch under the description 'a deer'. In this case, there is no ambiguity; only are two intentional objects! Not two senses of 'He aimed at his father." This is not to say that the analogy between the intentionality of action and thought, or sensation, would collapse; but it would suggest a weakening of this comparison. It will, surely, be asked, "Isn't there *some* sense in which 'He aimed at his father' is ambiguous? Perhaps not.

The sense in which 'He aimed at his father' is false is the sense in which the sentence refers to an action; the sense in which it does not is the sense in which what is being reported is an event. "He aimed at his father' is true, where 'aim' is not being used as an intentional verb; but 'I aimed at my father' is false where 'aim' unlike 'see' is an intentional verb. If this is the correct approach there need be no ambiguity in the verb, only in whether it is being used as an intensional verb in the report. Where there is only an *event* reported, we would say, equivalently, 'He pointed the gun at his father'; but where an *action* is at issue, it is most obviously reported in the first person as 'I aimed the gun at a deer', and the verb must be intensional.

If there is ambiguity, as she suggests, here is where it belongs: the witness's sentence, 'He aimed at his father', may report what happened, not what was "done." What is done may be what happens but the converse need not obtain, since what happens may be caused but happen for no *reason* at all, whereas in the case of something done, even if it is done for no reason, we can intelligibly raise the why-question Anscombe regards as definitive of intentional behavior. Even if we were to forgo taking advantage of the difference between happenings and action, we could locate the difference between 'He aimed at his father' and 'I aimed at a deer' in something besides an ambiguity in 'aim' or its use. The difference between them may be that asking the why-question of one, 'Why did *he* aim at his father', is different from asking the why-question of one's self, 'Why did *I* aim at a deer'. It is reasonable, however, to suppose that there are occasions where the witness may think he is reporting an action; but that he would be reporting an action, rather than a mere event or happening, does not follow from the fact of what *he* says, 'He pointed his gun at his father', in the way '*I* aimed at a deer' *would* be the report of an action.

We have discussed intention, mainly, in connection with intentional objects. We moved away from the ambiguity of "aiming" at his father as opposed to "aiming" at a deer. We spoke, instead, of a difference in what is being reported, events vs. actions, where in the case of the latter the verb I used I used intensionally. There is reason to believe Anscombe would have resisted this approach at the time she wrote *Intention*. But later on she emended her views in such a way that makes our proposal more reasonable from her point of view. This came about in part in response to a perceived weakness in Davidson's account of agency. There are two weaknesses in Davidson's account which we believe to be, highly, significant. One Anscombe discusses and the other bears on the attempt by Davidson to distinguish agency on the basis of a claim that depends, essentially, on the concept 'under a description'.

### d) Anscombe's Criticism of Davidson on Agency

Up to this point, the fundamental distinction has been between intentional action and non-intentional action, any "middle" being excluded. Later, however, Anscombe distinguishes what she calls "human action" and "intentional human action." (Anscombe [1982] p. 213) Human action may be voluntary where no intention is at issue. Donald Davidson had maintained that an actor is an "agent" if what he does is intentional under *some* description. (Davidson [1971] p. 46) Anscombe points out in the essay cited that this does not include tripping, nor does it include omissions within the category of actions. Consider the occasion of someone tripping over the rug as he walks to the other side of the room. Walking across the room is an action, but what about events constitutive of that action? Is tripping constitutive of such an action? Suppose it is. Does the walker trip over the rug *qua* agent on Davidson's characterization of agency? How might we decide on this?

Davidson restricts the term 'action' to those events which are intentional under a description. Understood one way this amounts to a denial that there is a natural class of intentional actions, as such, since being intentional is relative to a description and not in the "nature" of the event. Hamlet may have, intentionally, killed the man described as 'the man behind the arras' but he did not intentionally kill, who he killed, under the description 'Polonius'. Davidson is explicit: "a person is the agent of an event if and only if there is a description of what he did that makes true a sentence that says he did it intentionally." (Davidson [1971] p. 46) Is it, then, that descriptions, rather than facts, as such, make an event an action? Is there no "fact of the matter" in venturing to describe an event as an action? What he appears to be driving at is that if being helium, say, were a natural property, then what "makes true a sentence that says" something is helium would *not* depend on how the subject to which the property is attributed is described. Behind this is the notion that description relative attributions are attributions that depend on decisions rather than properties of objects in the world. The class of actions cannot be a natural class because membership in such a class depends on how the events classified as actions are described, not on what they are. However, there do appear to be natural classes where membership is relative to a description. Under the description 'alpha particle' an atom may not be regarded as helium, but under the description 'doubly ionized helium atom' that same object can be understood as nothing else. The example is taken from P. K. Feyerabend who makes use of it in a different context. However, we would not say that the class of helium atoms is not a natural class, because membership is relative to a description. Just because subsumption under a class is relative to a description, in the way Davidson describes, does not entail that the class is not a natural class. Similarly, just because the class of actions is description relative this is not to say that the class of actions is not a natural class.

When we count a substance as a subatomic particle rather than an ionized atom this may depend on our choice of descriptions, but this fact does not supply a *sufficient* reason for believing that when a substance *is* regarded as one or the other this does not depend on the intrinsic properties of the substance at issue. Similarly, if we count an event as an action because under some description (say 'killing the man behind the arras') it is intentional, this does not entail that what makes the event agentive is not a *property* of the agent. Now it is true that some descriptions are ruled out as descriptions under which an action can be *said* to be intentional, whereas there are no descriptions that rule out a substance's being a subatomic particle even though we may correctly describe it as an atom with a certain property, but this is related to the fact that it is a contingent property of the object that the description attributes, whereas having the properties that helium, say, has is not a contingent matter: an element with a different atomic weight would not be helium. Even if one supposes that actions, unlike elements, lack these "essential" properties, and are not, strictly speaking (on one definition) constitutive of a "natural class," this is not to say that membership in the class does depends on *some* property the correctness of the attribution of which depends on a decision as to which description to use in talking about it. After all, we have not defined a "natural class" as a class which is selected on the basis of the essential properties of its members. The class of animals with four legs is a "natural class" in a sense in which the class of interest rates set by the Federal Reserve between 1980 and 2009 is not; the first depends on properties occurring in "nature," whereas the latter depends on decisions. Ultimately, a Davidsonian approach to agency depends on the semantics of propositional attitudes connected with the beliefs and desires of the agent. Properly regarded, it is yet another instance of what we find in much analytical philosophy: trying to do too much with too few ideas. But how it may asked, does this relate to Anscombe? She focuses on one example raised by Davidson, one that proves to be more complex than one might first imagine.

Davidson, himself, was concerned that his criterion of agency (intentionality under a description) might include too much. So, e.g., as part of my intentionally walking across the room, I trip over the rug, and it might be thought that on his criterion this tripping is an action, when in fact it appears not to be. Davidson says that this ought not be included as an action. Anscombe (Anscombe [1982] p. 207-208) argues against Davidson, saying that *if* every part of our intentional "progress" across the room is intentional under *that* description—i.e. 'walking across the room'—then tripping will be intentional, but that, since Davidson denies that the tripping is intentional, his position is untenable. However, a look at what Davidson actually says weakens Anscombe's criticism. In the first place, Davidson denies that the tripping *is* part of one's intentional "progress" across the room. (Davidson [1971] p. 47) Who is right? The idea that tripping, even if it is in the direction of the other side of the room, is part of my "intentional progress" is dubious. It is neither "progress" nor intentional. So, it would appear that the argument needs supplementing; in particular, Anscombe ought to have told us why Davidson was wrong to deny that tripping is part of my intentional progress across the room. But there may be a problem for

Davidson, as well. After all, tripping does not require a cause *qua* agent. Anscombe will argue that, while tripping is not intentional, it is agentive in the sense that it is a "human action" and not a, mere, event. This is a radical move by Anscombe. It ties in with her ethical theory, which we shall not examine in any detail. First, however, let us examine whether Anscombe is correct in her belief that on Davidson's criterion of agency tripping is part of the intentional action. We may not resolve the matter to our complete satisfaction, but we will benefit by exploring what is available in Davidson's defense.

One thing we want to ask is whether every part of an action that is intentional under a description is, itself, intentional. It is intentional, according to Davidson, if under some description it is intentional. But what about tripping over the rug? Every part of the *progress* in walking across the room is intentional under the description 'walking across the room'. If the only warrant for saying this is that tripping is part of some action that is, itself, intentional under a description, then the question can continue to be raised whether tripping over the rug *is* part of an action that is intentional under the description, 'walking across the room'. But is tripping part of this "progress"? If a parachutist jumps without his parachute is he making "progress" as he approaches the spot which was his intended destination? One is inclined to think not. The comparison is not exact, but it is sufficient to raise serious questions.

One might say that being a part of some intentional action depends on there being some description under which it *is* part. Under the description 'hitting a double' breaking the bat need not be regarded as part of the action, but making sufficient contact with the ball, clearly, is. One aspect of this issue might figure, prominently, if pursued in a somewhat different direction. Later we shall contrast Anscombe's view of causation with "regularity" theories. Anscombe will "thump" for what is, essentially, an alternative view, viz. a "singularist" position. If we regard hitting the double in its "singularity," then breaking the bat may be part of the action, but the bat's breaking can, only, be dubiously regarded as the cause of making the double. I set such issues aside, until later, although these considerations might materially affect the course of discussion. Let's return, then, to the discussion as presented, keeping in mind that Davidson, himself, is neither a singularist nor a regularity theorist, strictly speaking.

The question, at this stage, becomes: Is breaking the bat just as much part of making the double as making contact with the ball? What transpires in the course of an action may not be an action itself. Only actions can be intentional, here I include mental "acts." He made a double in that he made sufficient contact with the ball etc.; not "He made a double in that he broke the bat," etc. Anscombe's description included the term 'progress' ("progress across the room"). But 'progress' is a strange description of the "act" of tripping. Even if he batter knows how to break bats while making doubles, and even if that action were intentional, we would not say "He broke the bat as part of his intentional progress in making a double." Breaking the bat may have been intentional but it was not "progress in making the double." Even if the batter knows that only when he breaks a bat can he get a run and, so, attempts to break the bat in making the hit, the ball has already been hit and the action, as such, does not include breaking the bat. It may have been part of what happened in the course of making the double without being part of the action. Breaking a bat in the course of hitting a double may not only not be an intentional action, it may barely qualify as a "human action."

Anscombe will argue that all "human action" is moral action. (Anscombe [1982] p. 209). The issue of intentional action is, thereby, moved, somewhat, from philosophical psychology to ethics. Historically, this is significant. Her predecessors in the discussion of intentional, or voluntary, action were, primarily, psychologists and not ethicists, e.g. James, Stout, Ryle, etc. Voluntary action in the interim became linked more firmly to the free-will issue. To be sure, this always had a place in the discussion of "free-action," but Anscombe's *Intention* is less an essay in ethics and more an essay in philosophical psychology, notwithstanding the attention paid to Aristotle practical syllogism, which we shall examine in due course. A second reason Anscombe's emended view is important is that a distinction is drawn for the first time in her own work between "intentionalness" of an action and an action's having an intentional object. (Anscombe [1982] p. 223) Recall that an "intentional object" is given by a description under which an action is performed. (Anscombe [1965b] p. 9). But what is the status of 'under a description' now that we are talking about "human action" and not the more special notion of intention? Do we say that a *human action* is distinguished from other actions in being such that there is an appropriate use of the why-question? We can't say this if the appropriateness of the question is reserved for a *species* of human action, viz. intentional action.

There are no easy solutions to the problems such questions raise. In some way the notion of responsibility, must, enter; one may be responsible for not taking care in crossing the room and tripping as a result. Further, we have seen that the why-question doesn't enter in the case of the intentionality of sensation. Well, then, what *is* its status with respect to human action? Since at this stage of her development all human action, intentional or otherwise, is of a moral character, we must ask "What gives moral character to the action?" The clearest answer, if there is one at all, is contained in her discussion of 'pre-moral evil'. What supplies the action's moral content is "what you do it for." (Anscombe [1982] p. 217). In other words, it is not the question "Why?" taken in a particular sense that is definitive, it is the question "What for?" We shall pursue this ethical aspect no further. Instead, a closer look at Davidson's employment of falling 'under a description' reveals certain weaknesses associated with extending its significance to the wider discussion.

## *Davidson on Tying Our Shoes 'Under a Description'*

Davidson distinguishes two sorts of actions, sorts we shall continue to describe as "basic" and "non-basic actions." Considerable use will be made of this distinction. When we speak of "basic actions" we mean those actions which, following Arthur Danto, are such that "a man performing one does not cause it by performing some other action that stands to it as a cause to an effect." (Danto [1965] p. 257) Wittgenstein describes what we call "basic actions" even more succinctly. (Wittgenstein [1953] 614) Intuitively, a basic action is said to be a bodily movement which we cause without having to *do* anything else in order to make it happen, such as when we raise our arm or tighten our fist.

Davidson follows Anscombe's lead in holding that there is a special status owed basic actions. Such actions, according to Davidson, are "all the actions there are." (Davidson (1971) p. 59) The question we want to raise is this: Can basic actions be ruled out, as a natural class, for the same reasons Davidson gives for ruling out intentional actions, generally, as such a class? We continue to use "natural" broadly, excluding mainly decision relative attributes and most monadic properties that do not inhere in an object. As we have seen, Davidson has denied that there is a natural class of intentional actions, since behavior may be intentional under one description but not another. Killing Polonius or the man behind the arras is not, however, the *real* action; the real action is the basic action. "The rest is up to nature." (Davidson [1971] p. 59) Making a thrust motion with one's arm (an arm connected to a hand holding a sword) is a basic action. But what makes it an action? Is it because it is intentional under the description 'killing the man behind the arras'? And, yet, the very same basic event would have been possible without the arras, without Polonius, or even the belief that there is a man behind the arras. If the *basic* action is intentional must it be intentional under some description? Let's examine the example of tying one's shoes.

Tying one's shoes is not a basic action. It is easy to imagine that the movements required in order to tie my shoes are, precisely, the same movements required in order to make a statement in some unspecified sign language. Suppose because I have my eyes closed, etc. I don't see that my finger movements do not have the result of my shoes being tied. As it turns out, they are, however, an assertion in some sign language. Shoe tying is one thing; signing is another. These are two different actions, although not two "real" actions in Davidson's or Anscombe's sense. How do we describe what these two actions, i.e. the assertion and the shoe tying, have in common? If I describe the movements in terms of shoe tying, I say "I move my fingers in just the way required in order to tie my shoes"; alternatively, if I describe the movements in terms of signing I say: "I move my fingers in just such a way as is required in order to assert such and such in sign language." I can even say "When I want to state such and such in this sign language I move my fingers in just such a way as to tie my shoes." This state of affairs may have implications for whether we can regard basic actions as constituting a natural class. Consider a less complex action, flicking the light switch.

If Davidson is right, flicking the switch does not belong to a natural class, any more than being a paper weight, since under one description, 'illuminating the room', it may be intentional, whereas under the description 'waking up that mean dog in the corner' it is not. But in the case of basic actions, how would I rule these out as constituting a natural class of intentional actions? This is problematic since I can't come up with a description of such actions, such as 'the finger movements required for tying my shoes', without relying on some description of the result of those actions rather than a description of the bodily movements themselves. Trying to describe my bodily movements without relying on descriptions of their effects is impossible without such reliance. If we attempt describe to someone how to tie their shoes, there is a point beyond which we fail to communicate because the action eludes description. But, if I can't even give a description of my intentional finger movements that is separable from other actions, how can I deny that such actions constitute a natural class because under some *descriptions* they are not intentional? The argument against intentional acts constituting a natural kind may retain some hope of validity when it comes to non-basic actions, but when it comes to the only "real" actions, basic actions, there are, it seems to get hung-up by the fact that there is no available description at all of the action itself.

The issue of how we describe basic actions, such as motion associated with tying one's shoes, is very much related to that of knowing the position of our limbs without observation, something Anscombe discusses at some length. There are a number of important respects in which this discussion relates to sensations and our descriptions of them; i.e. the notions of 'sensation' and 'basic action' are epistemologically speaking close cousins. Let's examine in greater detail, however, how the inseparability of descriptions of basic actions such as shoe tying becomes a problem for attributing intentionality to basic actions.

Davidson tells us that when we tie our shoelaces there are two things going on: first, the movement of the fingers; and, secondly, the movement of the laces. He asks if it is possible to separate these two. The difficulty is that we are unable to describe, or even think, how we are moving our fingers without describing the movement of the laces. (Davidson [1971] p. 51) We have seen that according to Davidson there is the real action and, then, there is what follows; and what follows does so in accordance with natural law. This is what is meant by saying that there is the basic action and "nature does the rest." At this point, our question becomes: Besides "the rest," what is left, if anything, that we can call an action?

What entitles me to call the only "real" action, the basic action, intentional? If we cannot reach beneath the effects of the action, "to tie my shoes," in describing the action, itself, how can we say that the *real* action is intentional because it is intentional under a description of something else, viz. the laces being moved with such and such a result? Any description involving the locution "in just such a way" is vague. There are any number of ways of moving one's fingers that result in the shoes becoming tied; thus, the description fails just as the description 'the present Chief Justice Supreme Court justice is bald' fails inasmuch as there is more than one Supreme Court justice. Davidson cannot supply a description of *this* action and so cannot provide a basis for the intentionality of *this* action in terms of *some* description under which *it* is intentional.

If I say that an intention consists in a belief and a positive attitude, perhaps a desire, then what "pro-attitude" do I have in *moving my fingers* in just such a way as to tie my shoes? My pro-attitude towards tying my shoes is one thing; my pro-attitude towards moving my fingers in *this* way is something else, altogether. If the descriptions of tying ones shoes and moving one's fingers in such and such a way are not "separable" then are we to conclude that the basic and non-basic actions are one and the same under any description in which they are intentional? Surely not. But if I cannot separate in description what I do and what nature does, then what entitles me to say that it is I who act and not nature? In this case *doings* would collapse into *happenings*. And wouldn't this, also, entail a denial that there are basic *actions* and, by extension, that there are no *real* intentional actions? Moving the laces introduces nature: the entrainment of the laces by torque associated with the grip I have on them, torque resulting in a vector of a particular sort. Such entrainment is an event in nature, while the finger movement is, presumably, a deliberate action.

Anscombe is comfortable with the idea that my actions may be intentional under a vague description. (Anscombe [1965b] p. 4) We shall, now, examine this vagueness in light of Davidson's remarks on shoe-tying. (Davidson [1971] p. 51) There is no problem in giving a description of what I am doing with the sword when I stab the man behind the arras, since the description of what I am doing with the sword need not include reference to stabbing the man behind the arras in the way alleged description of what I am doing with my fingers *must* include reference to tying my shoes (or some other such description such as making an assertion in sign language). Contrast the basic action case where "separability" is an issue to cases where it is not. Here, it would appear that the *only* description of my action Davidson can make available is the very description under which he would assert that my behavior is intentional. In the shoe tying case, although there may be alternative descriptions, such as "I move my hands in just such a way as to say 'thank you' in sign language Alpha," this need not be the case, and even here my finger movements, themselves, would not be described, only their consequence. In the case of moving the sword in just such a way as to stab the man behind the arras, there are plenty of descriptions of moving the sword that do not refer to its consequences.

Trying to come up with an equivalent description, owing to its vagueness, is, to use a metaphor out of Wittgenstein, like trying to draw an outline of a cloud. But what makes the description so vague? Why can't we do better than restate our intention? Problems of vagueness with respect to the descriptions of actions tend to merge with ontological issues surrounding individuation. Without attempting to resolve this issue, let's examine where the issue of individuation and intentionality are tangent.

Where one might think of an event as any change, each of the minimal events which, collectively, constitute the events that make up the process of tying one's shoes fall within an interval so brief as to belong, entirely, within a "specious present"; that is, they fall within an interval no greater than the duration of "now." Anscombe sometimes speaks of "forming an intention." The interval of time required for forming an intention, almost, certainly rules out there being an intention for each event involved in tying one's shoes; the action is continuous although it need not be. We may form an intention to tie our shoes, but we do not form an intention for each event we cause in tying our shoes—moving this finger in such and such a way, moving that finger in such and such a way, etc., although each such event is a willful act. This is true even when we are tying our shoes for the first time. Maintaining that tying one's shoes is a single event, merely, raises another problem: the difference between processes and events; and, along with this, the problem, as we have said, of the individuation of events.

Gustav Bergmann observed that we cannot name an individual within a specious present and, even though he spoke of "things" and not events, as such, we can apply his philosophical point to action and say that since we cannot in principle name the action, neither can we describe it utilizing what Anscombe called an "external" description, i.e., a description that depends on a feature "external" to the specious present. (Bergmann [1964] p. 104) If so, vagueness is unavoidable in the best possible case. The reader will notice that Bergmann's making the individual unnamable within a specious present excludes a "subjective" language containing names of such individuals entirely within a specious present. This raises questions about privacy, subjectivity and private languages but, for now, let's restrict the discussion to the relation of agency and "basic actions." Before going any further let's examine why this is so important.

We repeat, once more, Davidson's criterion (what else would one call it?) of agency: an action is agentive if there is at least one "description under which" it is intentional. Some descriptions may not render the action intentional, but at least one must. Recall, also, that in Anscombe's discussion of the intentionality of sensation she remarked that one respect in which a sensation is intentional is that different descriptions of the same object are not substitutable. (Anscombe [1965b] p. 6) Davidson's example of shoe tying is in a sense a "dialectical" bridge between action and sensation for describing exactly what we do with our fingers presents some of the same difficulties we encounter in describing vague concepts like those associated with colors. The claim we should like to make is that basic actions are more like sensations than non-basic actions and, as we have argued, Davidson's criterion fails in the case of such actions. There is a vagueness associated with actions as well as sensations, one that tends to confirm this assimilation of basic actions and sensations in a number of respects.

Anscombe notes that while I can count kisses, explosions etc. I cannot, however, count actions, as such. (Ancscombe [1979] p. 213) But in the case of colors I may count them, even without being able to answer the question: "What do you take color to be?" A decision is required as to what we should take to be actions, however, if actions are going to be counted. An event under a certain description may qualify that event as an action, perhaps even one that is intentional; but color requires no similar warrant. However, we do not require a decision in determining whether an event qualifies as a sensation, at least not in the same sense. Blue is not, like kissing, such as to require some description under which it can be described as a color in the way some description *is* required in order to regard, certain, bodily movements as kisses. We do not have to select a description under which something is blue in order to justify calling it blue. Blue, therefore, is in this respect more like a natural kind than an action.

Being a sensation of blue is not relative to a description. Being an intentional action is relative to a description, if Davidson is right. A basic action, it should be maintained, is more like a sensation than a non basic action, in this respect: it does not, as Davidson would have it, require a description under which it is to be considered an action, as opposed to an event, or mere "happening." Contributing to our realization of this fact is that there are no two descriptions of a state of *mind* such that under one an experience is a sensation, but under another it is not. I have been maintaining in opposition to Davidson that on his criterion one's basic actions are not actions of an agent and that, since this is absurd, he cannot be correct *in the way he describes* what it is to be an agent. Since basic actions are the only real actions, according to both Anscombe and Davidson, no action, on this account is, really, that of an agent. What, then, is the description of my finger movement in shoe tying? As we have seen, Davidson retreats behind the "under a description" gambit.

In considering possible alternatives to Davidson's description of shoe tying, why not say 'I move the air surrounding the laces in just the way required to tie my shoes'? It might be replied that this is not the description under which the agent "knows what he is doing." But this is insufficient basis for rejecting the description. What about tying my shoes in the dark? In this case, I can't know what I am doing. I may know without looking what the orientation of my body is, but I can't know what I'm doing *with* my fingers, if I can't see them. If I compare descriptions of the movement of the laces and descriptions of my fingers, I seem to get the same description. I move my fingers 'in just such as way as my shoes get tied, and the laces move 'in just such a way that my shoes get tied'.

There appears to be no way of describing my finger movements as such. In addition the description Davidson offers is not individuating; it pertains only to the entire action involved in tying the shoes. How do I describe the first couple of seconds of finger movement and, then, the next couple of seconds? Is it the same description in both cases? Then what is the significance of a description in the first place, if it fits numerous actions? But even if each and every objection can be met, what is beyond dispute is there is a *contrast* between describing basic actions, like finger movement, and describing non-basic actions. There may be no description of my finger movement as such available to the agent. Saying that I moved my fingers in just such a way as to have the effect of my shoes being tied tells me nothing about my finger movements, but, only, what happens when I move my fingers. Similarly, but with a different effect, I might say "The acorn fell in just such a way as to set off the trap" without describing the *movement* of the acorn.

In summary: we might argue, as Davidson does, that the intentionality of Hamlet's killing Polonius is relative to a description, and so not an event of the natural kind, intentional action, but we cannot argue that basic actions such as moving our fingers in such and such a way do not constitute a natural kind *for the same reason*, simply because there is no description *available*! So in the case of the most fundamental of actions, by Davidson's own admission, relativity to a description is not a signature fact of attributions of intentionality, assuming that tying one's shoes is an intentional act. Intentionality in this instance, even if we accept Davidson's proposal, cannot be ruled out as a defining property of a natural kind.

## SECTION 7: *THE INVOLUNTARY*

The why-question Anscombe has made use of in discussing intention cannot be, intelligibly, raised when an action is involuntary. But the notion of some action's being involuntary presupposes an understanding of the very subject of our inquiry, intention. We cannot say an action was involuntary without presupposing that it was in some sense unintentional. The meaning of 'involuntary' is, however, not very clear.

There is one sense of 'involuntary' that Anscombe wishes to reject in particular. Ryle had maintained that, ordinarily, 'voluntary' and 'involuntary' apply to actions "which ought not to be done" (Ryle [1949] p. 69). We are said to make use of these terms only in placing, or absolving from, blame. For example, if someone makes a noise, and he ought not to have done so, he may say "I didn't do it voluntarily; someone pinched me." Although Anscombe doesn't mention Ryle, it is his position she is criticizing when she discusses the physiologist's use of 'involuntary', a use carrying no imputation of error or infelicity.

Suppose I am looking for a ring I believe a squirrel has carried into a hole in a tree. I reach in and feel a swarm of bees. I quickly withdraw my hand. In doing so, I bump my friend standing behind me. He asks me why I did what I did. I reply that my bumping him was "involuntary." Still, it was not involuntary in the sense of a reflex action, although it might have been had I, say, been stung. I withdrew my hand on purpose, although my bumping my friend was not on purpose. There is a distinction to be made between involuntary actions of this sort and knee jerks the doctor evokes in his office. Unlike the knee-jerk, this action has what Anscombe calls a "mental cause." The question Anscombe will, therefore, turn to is the question of what distinguishes the class of actions described as "involuntary," which implies an understanding of 'intention', from those that don't.

## SECTION 8: *NON-OBSERVATIONAL KNOWLEDGE*

The sense of 'involuntary' that is not infected with any presupposition of the meaning of 'intention' is the sense we are looking to isolate in understanding when the why-question is applicable. As we have, already, discovered, there are actions, such as the movement of the gut in digestion, which are involuntary and which require observation in order to know. But there are other actions which are, also, involuntary, actions we know without observation. Central to making explicit the differences between the two classes is what Anscombe means by 'separable' as applied to our description of these, respective, events. What she means by 'separable' was best described in her essay "On Sensations of Position."

According to Anscombe, I can know something by observation only when the sensation which goes with the observation is "separable." A sensation is said to be "separable" when its "internal" description can be distinguished from the description of the very fact, purportedly, known by observation. (Anscombe [1962] p. 72) I can offer no description of any *sensation* of the position of my limbs without using a description of *the position of my limbs*. The reader is encouraged to compare this state of affairs to the difficulty in Davidson's case of providing a description of the basic action(s) associated with shoe tying which is inseparable from a description of the *results* of such basic action(s). In the case of sensations of the position of my limbs, since there is no independent description, I cannot make use of the sensation as a clue to the position of my limbs. That is Anscombe's view. In fact, arguably there is no sensation at all which connects up with my *knowledge* of the position of my limbs.

Sensations do not "inform" me. That I do not know what sensation to expect before I intentionally, say, raise my arm, also, suggests that sensations play little, or no, role in my knowledge of the movement of my limbs. In our discussion of Davidson, we had occasion to discuss sensations and descriptions as they relate to movement of the limbs; if we take movement of the limbs as change in the position of our limbs, we might want to raise the question "How do I know the change in position of my limbs without observation?" After all, this is what is more closely tied to action than position alone. Our intentions relate to *changes* in position more than to the position of our limbs. For now, we leave the issue at that. For our purpose, what is important is that knowledge by observation requires the separability of sensation, and in the case of our knowledge of the position of our limbs this separation cannot be achieved with respect to any sensation that may accompany our knowledge of position. There is another argument favoring Anscombe's view that one might add.

When a doctor asks if I have feeling in one of my limbs, I need to have something touch that limb in order to answer, unless, perhaps, I report a preexisting sensation, such as a pain. However, even in those cases where I neither have such a pain, nor anything touching the limb, I can tell the doctor whether my leg is raised or bent etc. My knowledge of the position of my limbs is in this sense not a matter of sensation, in particular where a sensation is caused by some object external to the body. This latter point is raised in reply to some astute criticisms by Braybrooke. (Anscombe [1962] pp. 71-72) Although Anscombe doesn't, explicitly, raise the point, before proceeding we should note that, even though knowledge of the position of our limbs is not observational, it is possible to err; otherwise it would not be knowledge. (Anscombe [1957] p. 14). Suppose I am an amputee with the experience of a "phantom" limb. The position of the limb may be "felt" just as in the case of an existent limb and, yet, I must be wrong. It is not the evidence of position that misleads me, but what, then, is it? Do we want to say that there is empirical knowledge which is not direct and, yet, does not require sensation? If so, what makes it empirical?

At this stage in her discussion, Anscombe is compelled to examine what defines one class of involuntary actions—one, in particular, which does not depend for its specification on properties that are presupposed by actions for which the relevant why-question is suitable. Those actions which can be known by the agent without observation are said to meet this requirement of non-circularity. Anscombe's view that knowledge entails the possibility of err leads her to an interesting contrast between what we *know* and what we *can say*. I can be said to know the position of my limbs, but I can only say where I feel pain. This is an odd position to take and, while she is driven to it, willingly, by her belief that err must be possible where knowledge is possible, it seems difficult to deny that I know that I feel a pain in, say, my foot. Her reasoning goes something like this: If I say I have a pain in my foot but bandage my hand, not my foot, and furthermore allow grasping and pulling on my foot but wince when you touch my hand, then I don't know what you meant by your claim that you have a pain in your foot. But if I should say that my leg is bent and you can plainly see that it is not, then, while what I say may be mistaken, it is not confusing or, otherwise, unintelligible. She remarks that, while I can *say* where my pain is, I do not *know* the location of my pain. What Anscombe does, at this point, is argue that our knowledge of our intentional actions, *qua* intentional, as opposed to other actions, is not observational knowledge; it is like our knowledge of the position of our limbs. She appears to feel no discomfort in moving from what she says about knowledge of a state of our body to knowledge of actions. Let's consider an action which we can, rightly, in some sense call "involuntary."

Suppose my approaching a stop light causes it to go green. On every such occasion I may know this fact only by observation. Suppose, further, that in such cases, what I do I do *not* do voluntarily. If so, then "Why did you do that?" is not a question applicable in the relevant sense of 'why', i.e. the one suited for inquiring about reasons. The question is unsuitable in these cases because the term 'involuntary' applied to these cases just means 'unintentional', and we are left with the "circle" of presupposing an ability to use 'intention' in our use of 'involuntary'. The *relevant* sense of the why-question would be the same as the one where we are asked "Why?" in case we didn't know that we were performing the action, and, therefore, did not perform it intentionally. In other words, the sense of 'involuntary' at issue must not entail 'intentional'. This sense *is* applicable to those cases where we know our action, i.e. our intentional action, by means other than observation. At this stage, Anscombe does something very interesting: she reintroduces the idea of a cause.

Recall that she began by discussing our knowledge, without observation, of the position of our limbs; she, then, moved to such knowledge of movements of our limbs (the reflex knee-jerk at the doctor's office); but, now, she moves to knowledge of the causes of action. Suppose the sudden appearance of a face causes me to jump. I do observe the face, but what I don't observe is the face "making me jump." This business of *making* introduces a new move in the discussion. My jumping is involuntary. In this sense of 'involuntary' I *cannot* know the cause of my action without observation, although I know what I'm doing without observation. In such cases the relevant why-question is to be rejected and, concomitantly, any suggestion that 'intention' is implied by describing it as "involuntary." When my leg was made to jump in the doctor's office, here was a case where I could only know the *cause* by observation; here was a case where I could know my leg moved without looking at it; and yet, here, was a case where 'Why?" in the sense relevant to intentional actions was not applicable. Therefore 'involuntary' in this case does not apply to the action, as it did in the case of crossing the street and, thereby, causing the green light to go on, "involuntarily." In this latter case I can, always, say "I didn't know what I was doing," not so in the case of the reflexive knee-jerk.

### *Donnellan on 'Knowing What I Am Doing'*

It may come as a surprise to some that Keith Donnellan, whose work figures, prominently, in the history of the theory of reference, addressed Anscombe's views on our self-knowledge of the actions we perform. (Donnellan [1963] pp. 401-409). His mistakes, as well as insights, illustrate the difficulties in getting a clear picture of her views. Donnellan attempts to show that while we may have knowledge of pain, anger, belief, etc. without observation, as well as of the position of our limbs, etc., knowledge of our intentional actions is of neither sort.

Anscombe, as we have already discovered, rules out assimilating knowledge of our intentions to knowledge of pain sensations. We can *say*, but not know, our pain. Donnellan avers that neither can we defend the notion that knowledge of intentions is like knowledge of the position of our limbs. Anscombe links the sort of knowledge we have of the position of our limbs to that of our knowledge of intention insofar, that is, as neither is observational knowledge. Wittgenstein was inclined to speak of sensations related to the positions of our limbs as informing us in a way similar to the way some would say pain "informs" us of its location. (Wittgenstein [1953] p. 185e). Donnellan rejects linking knowledge of our intentions to the sort of knowledge that we have of the position of our limbs. He reasons by counterexample.

A blind man, says Donnellan, often knows he is approaching an obstacle even without evidence, just as it might be alleged that a person knows his or her intention without evidence. However, the blind man may lose his ability to do this, whereas no one loses the ability to know his intention in acting. There is something essential about knowing our intentions that is not essential to the skills a blind man may possess. A skeptical position with respect to the blind man's ability is in order; that is, Donnellan has not established that this skill really is one based on no evidence, whatsoever. There is some indication that he regards this possibility as not being essential to his case. It is, after all, possible, for example, that someone might, without evidence, pick the winning horse in every race. But if logical possibility is all that is at issue, then Donnellan's case appears to be weakened. It may be *logically* possible to know one's intentions by observation. Donnellan would claim that Anscombe would be committed to denying this based on the assertion that it is essential to our intentions that they be known without observations.

But the constraint, here, is only one of logical possibility and there is nothing contradictory, etc. about knowing by some exotic observational ability yet to be discovered, or evolved, that would allow this. Part of the difficulty with Donnellan's view is that he, correctly, observes a distinction that is easy to overlook, but he doesn't know, exactly, what to do with it. He notices that knowledge of our intentional actions can be analyzed into two components: one subject to our direct awareness, which we can't directly observe, and, another component, which we can directly observe, the physical performance of the intentional action. Anscombe never really addresses this distinction in a lucid way, but later she introduces the distinction in a productive discussion of her ethical theory. To see how, let recall a famous example from Davidson that illustrates how it is possible to do something intentionally without knowing it.

Davidson considered the question whether we can do something intentionally without knowing it. (Davidson [1978] p. 92) One example is where I am attempting to make ten copies of a document using carbon paper. I bear down on the top page, hoping that the bottom page will register the imprint of what I write on the top page. I do not know that this tenth copy will be produced; I may, or may not, however, believe that it will. Nevertheless, if I should succeed, I may do so without knowing it. Whether on Davidson's view I must, in order that the desired outcome be intentional, *believe* that by bearing down in such a way that I will succeed is a matter I set aside. In any case, if Davidson is right, I can intentionally do something without knowing it. This example can be seen to be related to Anscombe's, earlier, example of jotting down something other than what one believes one is jotting down (Anscombe [1957] p. 5), only in Davidson's case I copy something down without believing, perhaps, that I succeed. In both cases there is an intention, but in Anscombe's case I don't do what I intend, although the action is intentional; in the second I do what I intend without knowing it. In one case the intention is not fulfilled, and we know it; in the second, the intention is fulfilled, but we don't know it. In both cases the intention is known without observation, but not the action; so how is it that I do not know my "intentional action"? It is this *sort* of thing that is problematic for Donnellan, and this is why he notes the two components of the action. What are these two components, really? The difficulty is resolved once we get clear on what an "intentional action" is.

As we have seen Anscombe approaches the question of what an intentional action is *via* the suitability of a certain sense of the why-question. She notes that if I didn't know that I did such and such a thing, then the why-question in that instance is inapplicable, nor can I be said to have done *what* I did intentionally. (Anscombe [1957] p. 11) Now one question raised by Davidson's example of the carbon paper is this: If I didn't know what I was doing how, given Anscombe's position with respect to the why-question, can I be said to have done it intentionally. Are we to reject Davidson's example which alleges a case where we do something intentionally without knowing it? This would in effect amount to refutation by counter example.

In order to get to resolve this question, let's compare the Davidson case with, yet, another. Let us suppose that it was not part of my intention to copy what we were writing to a tenth page. Suppose that I simply bore down heavily without this in mind. Someone notices that I in fact created a tenth copy by so doing and asks why I did it. Can I construe this question as the why-question Anscombe believes is definitive of intentional behavior?

In Davidson's case one might argue against Anscombe this way: Anscombe claims that if I don't know what I'm doing I can't be said to have done it intentionally; so, if I can be said to have done something intentionally then I must have known it. But in the Davidson case I did something intentionally without knowing it. Thus by reductio ad absurdum her position is refuted. But now suppose that I want to make seven copies, not ten; and suppose I bear down just so much that I think I only made seven copies. I inadvertently make ten and someone upon examining the tenth copy asks me why I did it. One honest answer would be: "Oh, I didn't know I did that!" Compare this to the case where I set out to make ten copies, but I don't know I've succeeded. I'm asked why I did it. The answer "Oh, I didn't know I did that!" is not the same answer as the first because what I know or don't know differs in each of the two cases. Anscombe is not saying that if I do something intentionally then I must know that I succeed, if the why-question is applicable. In Davidson's case I know "in intention" what it is I am doing whether or not what I am doing in cases where I succeed is something I know I've done. In the Davidson case, I might say "Oh, I didn't know that happened," and not "Oh, I didn't know I was *doing* that. This contrast rescues Anscombe from the sort of criticism that may be lodged against her position based on such cases as Davidson's. Certainly, more can be said about this and related problems.

It is important to distinguish three things: first, the purpose of the action; second, what is actually done in acting intentionally, and third, what Anscombe calls the "intentionalness" of the action. (Anscombe [1982] p. 219). The last is not discussed in *Intention* but it is crucial. My purpose in writing something may be to consummate a business transaction; my intention in moving my hand in such a way may be to write something down, but the "intentionalness" of an action is something, far more, ephemeral. It is this component that suggests what it is that we might be said to know without observation. When we know of an action *qua* intentional action, what makes our knowledge "a knowledge" of the intentionality of the action involves "intentionalness." I will not dwell on the assay of an intentional act in Anscombe. But there is in this something suggestive of a property of immediate acquaintance such as the sharpness of a pain.

## SECTION 9: *A DIFFICULT DISTINCTION BASED ON CAUSATION*

If I announce that my intention is such and such I may be asked why. The answer I give will be a reason for acting. I have told you what I am going to do, and in this sense it is a prediction; and the fact that I gave you a reason makes it a prediction backed by a reason. However, if I state something to be a fact, such as that there is going to be an eclipse tomorrow, then if I am asked why, the question is one concerning reasons for my belief that there will be an eclipse tomorrow. When I give reasons for my intention I am not giving reasons for holding something true. This is something I do when I give reasons for believing there will be an eclipse. But, when I am being asked to give a reason for my stated intention, I give a reason for action not for believing that some statement is true. The distinction between these two cases is not, always, clear and this is what Anscombe wants us to notice.

Someone asks, "Why did you knock the cup over?" I reply, "Because I saw a face in the window and this caused me to jump, knocking over the cup." When the eclipse takes place I can see what is causing it; I observe the moon moving between the earth and the sun. The causing that is going on is visible to the naked eye, and I can see *that* the intervening moon is doing the causing. But when the face appeared, causing me to jump, I did not see the face as a cause of anything. I saw the face and jumped, but I did not observe *that* the face was causing me to jump and knock over the cup. Nevertheless, despite the fact that I didn't observe the causal action of the appearance of the face, I do know that it was the appearance of the face that *caused* me to jump. This knowledge of causation without the requirement of observation is what distinguishes those cases that appear to stand somewhere between those which on the one hand call for causes and, on the other, call for reasons. (Anscombe [1957] p. 16) This category of causes known without observation constitutes a special class, one which Anscombe will explore in some detail under the description of "mental causes."

## SECTION 10: *THE INTRODUCING MENTAL CAUSES*

Where I know some event to be the *cause* of my behavior without observing that it *is* the cause, such a cause is called a "mental cause." The face in the window caused me to jump. My knowledge of *its causing* me to jump is not observational. It is, therefore, a mental cause. Knocking over the cup, as a result of, unexpectedly, seeing a strange face in the window is, precisely, the same sort of behavior James discusses, at one point, only his example is that of a child frightened by an arriving train. (James [1890] p. 488). It is easy to think of Anscombe as forging a revolution in the theory of action in part by dispensing with private entities, such as volitions. Volitions had been thought to be private by some (but not all) volitionists. While "entities," as such, played little, or no, role in James's theory of volition, his reliance on mental activity, such as selective attention was prominent but does not mix, well, with Anscombe's, more or less, Wittgensteinian approach. There is reason to believe, however, that Anscombe had a more friendly rapport with volitionists, like James, than some may suspect.

When she remarks that thoughts may be mental causes, Anscombe is saying something which, on the face of it, is consistent with James's belief that ideas are causes of actions. Certainly there are important differences between James and Anscombe. Anscombe, explicitly, rejects a "mentalistic" approach to intention (Anscombe [1983] p. 98), but "the idea idea" in James is not so far removed from her own position, as can be inferred from the quotation at the beginning of this book. Even so, the suggestion of some sort of "partnership" with James is, likely, to evoke consternation on the part many of her backers, and this would not be an unreasonable reaction. While there may be a place for ideas in her treatment of intentions, ideas are to be thought of as, merely, "grammatical notions." (Anscombe [1965b] p. 9) For the time being, let's set aside her relation to earlier theorists. We now take a closer look at her example of mental causation and, in the case of the example she gives, the important distinction she draws between what may be the object of fear as opposed to the cause of fear.

Wittgenstein had, already, drawn the distinction in a brief remark in the *Philosophical Investigations* (Wittgenstein [1953] 476). A face, Wittgenstein says, may be the "target" (object), rather than the cause of fear. This cryptic remark is clarified, and made useful, by Anscombe. In her scary face example, the scary face is both the object and the cause of the jumping. But not all cases are of this sort. She provides another example, one involving a child who is warned by his caretaker that a bit of cloth is a "piece of satin." The child is fearful, believing she said a "piece of Satan." The cause of his fear is what she said; the object of his fear is the piece of cloth. Here the distinction between cause and object is clear. Her belief, however, that it is *intelligible* to speak of observing causation smacks of an anti-Humean sentiment, inasmuch as Hume denied this, very, possibility. The situation is not just a little puzzling. While she does speak of observing causation, and while she can, as we shall discover, later, be considered a "singularist," rather than a "regularity theorist" with respect causation, she never explicitly sides with others who were adamant in their belief that causation could be observed, people such as C. J. Ducasse. (Ducasse [1924])

Hume had given two definitions of 'cause': one based on a relation between events: where one, the cause, precedes the other (the effect), and where all events resembling the first precede, and are contiguous to, events resembling the second. The other definition describes the causal relation as one in which the idea of one thing brings forth the idea of the other. (Hume [1888] p. 170) Anscombe makes mention of the fact that the idea of mental *causation* fails to cohere with either of Hume's definitions, underscoring the fact that with respect to causation she was not a Humean.

## SECTION 11: *MENTAL CAUSES ARE NEITHER INTENTIONS NOR DESIRES*

What is mental about a "mental cause"? In describing Anscombe's example of mental causation, the scary face example, we said that the face caused the jumping. But what is mental about a face? Or is it a matter of the appearance of the face, rather than the face itself? But she made it seem that what was, really, at issue was not so much whether the face, or its appearance, was the cause of our jumping but the peculiar status of mental *causation*. (Anscombe [1957] p. 16) It is, somewhat, puzzling, therefore, that she says that, even, a knock on the door can be a mental cause. What is it, then, that a face, a knock on the door, and a thought might have in common, if anything, that would qualify them as, potentially, mental causes? In the case of the face, it is my *seeing* the face that is the mental cause; similarly, the knock on the door must be heard. Such mental events, then, are what qualifies such causes as "mental." But what of intentions? Are intentions causes?

If I am asked why I went to get an apple in the basement, I might say "Because I wanted one." This may suggest that the cause of my action was a desire. Anscombe has, however, already dismissed motives as mental causes. (Anscombe [1957] p. 16) Davidson has championed this idea, although few philosophers realize that it goes back further than Davidson, at least as far back as Bertrand Russell, who regarded desires as possessing causal efficacy. (Russell [1914] p. 228) According to Anscombe, an action may take place in the absence of a desire. I may, simply, have had the thought of the apple; felt hunger, without the desire for an apple, and taken action to eat the apple before me. Likewise, if I should hear a knock on the door, I may go answer it without any desire to do so. Thus intention, expressed as a desire will not serve as a mental cause. Our immediate concern is with a single question. In some senses I may want to open the door but to say that that want is a desire would be stretching matters. Davidson had introduce "pro-attitude," a locution we find in P. H. Nowell-Smith, but there is some oversimplification here that we shall not discuss.

Is an intention a mental cause? Isn't it, sometimes, the case that, when I am asked why I did such-and-such, I may say "Because of this-and-that? But doesn't "because," here, suggest some "mental cause"? Anscombe entertains the situation where I answer the why-question in terms of a desire. My intention in doing such-and-such was, I might say, out of a desire to do such-and-such. But a feeling of desire to do what I do, she is quick to point out, is not, always, present; that is, there may have been no felt desire which might be argued to serve as cause of the action. I may simply act out of spite, e.g., in the absence of any conscious thought. If so, there is little sense to the notion of "mental cause," even though the action was intentional. Neither motives, nor intentions, therefore are mental causes.

Anscombe is emphatic that a "mental cause" is not necessarily mental, and she goes on to add some resolution to this, otherwise, murky notion. She remarks that we are dealing with a mental cause when we talk about what *produced* an action, thought or feeling. (Anscombe [1957] p. 18). This does not rule out a feeling being caused by a mental cause, which in turn may lead to action. In this case the cause of a feeling would be a mental cause just as surely as the, sudden, appearance of an image in the window may evoke bodily behavior and, so, action. Anscombe concludes the section by commenting to the effect that the notion of a mental cause is not all that important, and that what *is* important is to distinguish it from other notions, such as intention and motive.

## SECTION 12: *MOTIVES VS. INTENTIONS*

We have seen that mental causes include both intentional and involuntary actions. An example of the first is where hearing the door causes me to answer it. The appearance of the face in the window's causing me to jump is very different. What all mental causes have in common is that we know their efficacy by means other than observation.

An intention is a something we aim at doing or choose to do. Motives may determine what we choose or aim at, but they need not, themselves, be intentions. To take a, specific, example: hatred may be a motive, but only under unusual circumstances would I do something with the intention of hating. Our intentions are, generally, not expressed in terms of objectives which are mental states or actions. Although, according to Anscombe, motives are often distinguished from intentions, in such cases, cases where the objective is to achieve a mental state, it would appear that motives and intentions are difficult to distinguish. Motives, she says, belong within the province of ethics and, as such, are not central to her attempt at understanding intention. They may explain actions, but they do not cause actions; nor are they intentions. Choice is, crucially, linked to intention, not so much motive; although the content of the intention may be owing to motive. A word on choice is in order.

Later in her discussion of practical wisdom, Anscombe will link her use of 'intention' with Aristotle's use of 'choice'. (Anscombe [1957] p. 77) In this section, she identifies an intention with what one may choose. While she does not discuss the issue of free-will, it is pertinent to this discussion to point out that some philosophers held, and hold, that choice is what distinguishes voluntary and involuntary action. Recall that G. E. Moore had remarked, some years earlier, that "it is only choice which distinguishes voluntary from non-voluntary action" (Moore [1898] p. 188). Some may view this as trivial, if not obvious. Yet freedom and freedom of choice, are two different things; and doing something voluntarily is not, necessarily, to do something freely. This will become more important when discuss practical reasoning.

## SECTION 13: *BACKWARD LOOKING MOTIVES AND MOTIVES-IN-GENERAL*

Anscombe sees that there is a distinction to be drawn between "backward-looking" motives and "motives-in-general." Revenge is a good example of motives of the first sort. Someone who takes revenge does so because of some past action by another party. What she calls "motives-in-general" are of a different sort, suggesting a state of mind. Thus, I may be motivated to assist someone out of love; and, while it is almost certain that the loving harks back to some past action, this need not be the case. If I feed the pigeons my action may not be grounded in some past actions, particularly of the birds I feed. Not only are there "backward-looking" motives, there are "forward-looking" motives as well.

Suppose I anticipate being assaulted by someone. I take preemptive action. My motive in doing so is "forward-looking" insofar as it is grounded in some anticipated future action on the part of my enemy. Such cases are of special interest. They are of special interest because, whereas up to now Anscombe has been inclined to distinguish motives and intentions, we are told that if a motive is an intention, then that motive is forward-looking. Of motives-in-general she offers the following characterization: where what is at issue are such motives, we would ask those who seek to understand them to "see the action in this light." She does not pursue the details of motives-in-general much further than this, remarking that the topic is difficult; besides it is not of immediate interest in explicating statements of intention. She does, however, introduce some useful comments on Ryle's view of motives.

Ryle had maintained that motives could be expressed in terms of satisfying certain generalizations. When we say someone "boasted from vanity," we mean, according to Ryle, something like: 'his doing so satisfies the law-like proposition that whenever he finds a chance of securing the admiration and envy of others, he does whatever he thinks will produce this admiration and envy' (Ryle [1949] p. 89). One, rarely, thinks of a lawlike statement as pertaining to a single person, but this is not what concerns Anscombe. What she objects to is that the lawlike generalization suggests that, because it is *lawlike*, we must say that the subject *always* behaves this way, which is simply false, as in the case of man who boasts once in a lifetime. While this may be sufficient as a reply to Ryle, there is, another, issue, one Anscombe doesn't discuss: when does an intentional action *involve* a motive? We don't want to say an intention always involves a motive, but where do motives fit into the picture? This is not an easy question to answer.

Someone throws a ball my direction. I catch it. I do so intentionally. Need there have been a motive? Isn't it possible that I just caught the ball, intentionally, without any motive? The ball came in my direction and I reached out and caught it. I may not even know where the ball came from; I may not have caught it had it been a color I don't like. When speaking of motives-in-general, one might wish to speak of doing something "out of x," e.g. doing something out of hatred, but can I perform an action of this sort and do it with an intention that is not, itself, a motive? There is linguistic evidence that we cannot. To say this circumstance is possible would commit us to the acceptability of such statements as "Out of hatred, I broke his arm with the intention of keeping him from breaking mine." Such an assertion makes no sense.

## SECTION 14: *MENTAL CAUSES AND BACKWARD-LOOKING MOTIVES*

It is difficult to explain why Anscombe, despite having said that mental causes are of little importance, goes on to discuss them at some length. One question she raises is why the fact to which a backward-looking reason points, such as the fact resulting in an act of revenge, should be considered anything more than a mental cause. What strikes her as, particularly, significant is that in cases of backward-looking motives the ideas of good and evil enter the picture. Looked at in a general way, this is a departure from the preceding discussion. It is at this juncture that philosophical psychology meets ethics. Many, if not most, philosophers following the discussion of volition initiated by James, where they were concerned with intentions, at all, were interested, mainly, in ethics. Anscombe's work is, especially, noteworthy in returning the discussion to philosophical psychology. However, we find her moving the discussion back in the direction of ethics. She will, later, say that all human action is moral action.

If I act from revenge, then I believe that, somewhere along the line, I've been harmed; that is, that I have suffered some evil brought on by that agent upon whom I seek revenge. If my attempt at revenge eventuates in good, rather than evil, coming to that agent, this is something done involuntarily on my part. The important thing to notice is that in cases of revenge, and other backward-looking motives, in order to answer the question "Why?" in the sense relevant to uncovering a discernible intention, the idea of good or evil must fit the action from which the attempted revenge arises. This is what is said to distinguish mental causes and backward-looking motives. Where a mental cause answers the why-question, no ethical content is at issue. Neither good nor evil makes the action reasonable. Suppose I seek revenge on someone for killing my brother. Then this fact, and its evil character, enters the explanation of why I acted as I did; but, if it should turn out that the facts are not as the revenge seeker believes, then it is not the fact but, rather, the belief that supplies the rationale. No such revision accrues to a felt need to emend what is purportedly the mental cause of some action. This asymmetry provides the gap allowing a leveraged difference between these two notions; that is, a difference between mental causes and backward-looking motives. In addition, I can choose not to act on a backward-looking motive, as when I refrain from criticizing someone because I believe that my past experience with that person will cause that criticism to be excessive or because I am, presently, in a state of anger or agitation. However, it is not, always, the case that the distinction between these two is, so, easily discerned.

## SECTION 15: *MENTAL CAUSES OR REASONS?*

Anscombe, as we have seen, insists that there is a difference between reasons and causes, but this is not to say that it is always clear that something is a reason, and not a cause, or *vice versa*. Suppose I do something, and someone asks why I did it. Suppose I reply that I did it because I was told to. Is being told to do it the cause of my action? Or is it the reason for my action? Or is it both? The answer to this question is not, according to Anscombe, entirely clear.

Suppose I react to a command such as "Take off your hat" by obeying it. Anscombe asks how this would be different from reacting to someone hollering 'Boo!" causing me to jump. Part of what we consider in giving an answer is how quickly we react. If we react quickly, she is inclined to say that the sound is a cause. Suppose that I wiggle my fingers around my temples. I'm asked why I did this. I reply "Because *he* did it." In such as case, Anscombe would claim that there is little that differs, here, from reacting to a command by obeying it. A decision is in this case required for imitative behavior; just as in the case of following an order. This, at least, is the appearance. But if I imitated the other fellow, immediately, and without deliberation, then whether I was caused to act or acted for a reason may, as Anscombe suggests, be unclear. Let's venture a proposal based on developments in the theory of meaning subsequent to publication of *Intention*.

There have been persuasive arguments that "meanings are not in the head." (Putnam [1982] pp. 215-272) One consequence drawn is that meanings are not mental entities in the mind of the language speaker. Even so, this does not, of course, entail that meanings are somewhere in the "external world," i.e. in space-time; any more than is, say, the Second Law of Thermodynamics. What is important, however, is that commands possess meaning, and if they have causal efficacy, they are not mental causes in the sense that mental entities have, sometimes, been described as causes of action. There is a proposal one might make in addressing Anscombe reluctance to, sharply, distinguish commands as providing reasons rather than causes.

When I react to someone's doing something like moving their fingers around their temples, there may be nothing like an intention that is constitutive or presupposed by such behavior. In fact, such imitation may be, merely, habitual behavior. But a command is different in that on some accounts of meaning understanding its meaning introduces intentions on the part of the one issuing the command. H. P. Grice offered such a theory. (Grice [1989] pp. 8-118) He began with an idea which carries a great deal of intuitive appeal, but as counterexamples surfaced the theory became increasingly complex. Whether all the difficulties were, ever, worked out is a question beyond the scope of our inquiry, but his original insight is worth considering in light of the question as to where we draw the line between causes and reasons. Grice argued that when someone issues a meaningful utterance he intends to produce a response; he intends the hearer to recognize this as his intention; he intends that his hearer respond on the basis of his recognition that this action is the result the utterer intends to bring about. This is a considerable oversimplification of Grice's theory, but it serves to bring out that if we think of meaning a certain way, then there may be a way of distinguishing imitation of the sort we described from following a command, one that sheds some light on reasons and causes.

Suppose I shout a command so loudly that it results in an avalanche. Here the effect is owing to the loudness of the issuance of the command; something like the effect of the loudness of "Boo!" uttered behind the back of some poor fellow working hard at the library. However, if I obey the very same command, I do so in part because I understand the intentions of the speaker. I need not be reacting to an acoustic property of the command as a phonetic reality but, rather, to my recognition of the speaker's intent and the circumstances allowing my compliance. Knowing the speaker's intent provides an answer to the why-question: "I put on my hat because it was his intention to get me to do so, and I recognize his authority," etc. It may turn out that intentions in some sense caused me to act, but, where we react to the intentions of others, doing so carries reasons in addition to causes; and in this instance the reason is linked to the intentions of others, and not the causal efficacy of some material property such as loudness, etc. We might generalize this, saying that whenever we act in recognition of the intentions of others we act on reasons. That there is something that is, also, a cause is irrelevant; "everything has a cause."

# PART 3:
# Acting Without Reason

**SECTIONS 16-17:** *"I DON'T KNOW WHY I DID IT"*

After reviewing her discussion of those occasions where the why-question does not carry the sense associated with intentionality, Anscombe pursues another possible answer to the question that makes sense, but brings us to a high water mark of ordinary language. There are occasions when someone is asked why he did something, and he replies with something like "I don't know why I did it; I just did it, that's all." At first there appears to be something almost paradoxical in such a reply. Or consider the occasion when I answer the why-question saying "For no particular reason." In such a case the denial that there was a reason for my action does not nullify the applicability of the why-question. (Anscombe [1957] p. 25) But if this is so, then I can act intentionally for no particular reason.

Suppose I hold my thumb up in the air as high as I can. Someone asks "Why did you do that?" I reply, "I don't know." What is not being excluded is that there is *some* reason, only I don't know what it is. Another case: suppose, without knowing that I was responsible, I go to the pantry and find a bottle of milk upside down behind the canned goods. I wonder "Why would anybody do such a thing?" Or suppose, yet, another case. I am playing chess. I make a move; maybe it is a silly move. Someone asks "Why did you do that?!"

I reply "I don't know." In this last case, it is clear that I intended to move the piece; it is clear that the why-question is appropriate in the sense which carries the imputation of intentionality. But my answer implies that it was done for no reason. Even so, it makes sense to *ask*; and, because it makes sense to ask, the why-question has application. The lesson is that the extension of those cases where the why-question is appropriate is greater than the extension of the availability of reasons. Anscombe will address this matter in some detail.

It might come as some surprise that the question "Why?" in the sense appropriate to intentionality does not exclude there being no reason for my action. Imagine that I am driving and I accelerate to 120 mph. in eight seconds. The person sitting next to me asks why I did it; I reply, "I don't know." Perhaps, my action was impulsive. Anscombe would allege that I might very well have done it for no reason, even if there is a psychoanalytic account; still, there is no reason that can be given as an answer to the why-question taken in the appropriate sense of entailing intention; again, even though what I did I may have done intentionally. There are intermediate cases pertaining to subtle differences between being intentional and being voluntary. To these we shall return later in our discussion of Section 25.

## SECTION 18: *WHEN THE ANSWER TO THE QUESTION 'WHY?' MAKES NO SENSE*

If I answer the why-question, saying "For no particular reason," then what I say *may* be unintelligible, but not necessarily. Just because a straight-out reply to a question may be unintelligible does not mean the question is unintelligible. In fact, it doesn't necessarily follow that the question has not been answered, even if the answer is unintelligible; at least, it has not been argued persuasively by anyone that an answer *must* be an intelligible answer. If I ask a man if he is sane, then in certain circumstances his reply may provide a suitable answer, especially if it is unintelligible, where unintelligibility is not construed as subjective. By "unintelligible" we mean only that we cannot figure out what he means, not that his speech is garbled etc.

Take one interesting example Anscombe discusses: A man digs through all his books; takes out the green ones; climbs to the top of the house and nails them to the roof. I ask the man "Why?" and he answers: "For no particular reasons." If we maintain that only intelligible answers are answers, then this response is no answer. But it does appear to be an answer of some sort. Recall that Wittgenstein had once remarked that if a question can be asked an answer is possible. (Wittgenstein [1921] 6.5) Later he says that a question exists only if an answer exists. (Wittgenstein [1921] 6.51) Anscombe is careful to point out a distinction between a reply, say, which is senseless, insofar as its "sense" is excluded from language, and a reply which is senseless because we can't figure out what is meant in making it. The first sort of senselessness obtains when there is confusion of one "language game" with another.

Suppose someone were to say "Maybe congenitally blind people can see visual images in their mind's eye." Put this way it is senseless in one sense of 'sense'. Asked to explain "visual image," his only recourse might be to say "Something like *this*," where "*this*" refers to something private. His reply is subject to criticism based on Wittgenstein's private language argument. Moreover, he is playing a language game with 'see' that is parasitic on a different, public, language game, but with rules that either don't exist or don't apply to any possible language game. However one may interpret the application of Wittgenstein's idea of language games, the point is that the sentence "Maybe congenitally blind people can see visual images in their mind's eye" is excluded as lacking sense. It is ruled out of the language used by the speaker. It is interesting that if Anscombe's discussion of Wittgenstein correctly describes his position, then many seemingly legitimate questions may be excluded, such as "Do we dream in color?" It is easy to consider this a scientific question out of reach of *a priori* arguments based on language games. Wittgensteinian senselessness, as grounds for excluding from the language certain questions and answers, appears unwarranted. *However*, as Anscombe notes, this sort of senselessness or justified exclusion from language is something different from the unintelligibility of saying "No particular reason" as a reply to the why-question.

In this case, what we mean by "unintelligible" is that figuring out what the speaker means is impossible. We do not mean that his reply is not part of our language. What Anscombe concludes from this is of paramount importance for understanding the nature of why-questions. We circumscribe the domain of intentional actions by saying that the class of intentional actions consists in those actions for which we *expect* an answer to the why-question that falls within the range of reasons, *not* that the answer must in fact supply a reason for the action. Again, the range of why-questions is wider than the range of reasons.

## SECTION 19: *WHAT MAKES AN ACTION INTENTIONAL?*

In virtue of what, if anything, is an action intentional? Is there some property that makes it so? We have touched on this in our discussion of intentional actions as constituting a natural kind. We have meant by "natural kind," all along, a kind that corresponds to an intrinsic property. We shall leave it at that. But, now, do we want to say that there is an action and, then, there is a feature (or intrinsic property), and that this feature provides what makes the action intentional? We have seen that the same action may be regarded as non-intentional under certain descriptions but not others, and since the *same* action can be viewed either as intentional or non-intentional, it would stand to reason that there is no property of the action, *per se*, that makes it intentional. However, it would be an oversimplification to say that the action, itself, is intentional; rather, it is, according to Anscombe, what is actually *done* that is either intentional or not, not the event, itself. The relevant question, then, becomes one of whether there is a property which, when taken together with what is done, makes the action of doing it intentional.

Little attention has been paid to Anscombe's negative argument in addressing this question. However, understanding this argument is, absolutely, fundamental to understanding Anscombe larger view. We shall state the argument and, after examining it, indicate its weaknesses as well as what can be learned from it. We have it, then, that Anscombe formulates an argument against the belief that the intentionality of our actions is owing to some feature—call it "*I*." The argument she applies is of the form *reductio ad absurdum*: she assumes that there is such a property, *I*, and then argues that this assumption leads us to unavoidable confusion. We will overlook that fact that in the same paragraphs she refers to "'*I*'" as both a feature and a description, although one can easily imagine that in some discussions this might prove to be, quite, important.

She begins by considering an action that is required *for* an intentional action but not, itself, intentional: the contraction of muscles required in order that an agent might move a limb in the usual way (no pulleys etc), that is, what we have called a "basic action." She calls such an action as contracting one's muscles "pre-intentional." In a sense, this loads the argument just a bit. It is as if to say that the action pre-exists the intention. Consider the argument.

Anscombe begins by noting that on the theory she opposes the claim would be that the action of contracting the muscles, taken together with the feature *I*, is sufficient to render the ensuing action intentional. We have a pre-intentional action, the muscle contraction; we have the action that follows the muscle contraction; and we have *I*. As Anscombe sees it, the problem is this: there is no connection ascertainable by the agent (or anyone else) between the pre-intentional action and *I*. The muscle contraction and, therefore, the action that follows has nothing to do with *I*. Nor can the agent direct *I* to the pre-intentional action, since he may have no knowledge of muscle contraction etc. Any connection between the pre-intentional action and *I* can only be what she describes as a "happy accident." (Anscombe [1957] p. 28). Therefore, to suppose some feature, *I*, is what makes the action intentional is absurd and must be rejected. What are we to think of the argument? There are several weaknesses. Let us consider a few.

In the first place, there is some question as to what the theory she opposes would take to be the feature *I*. As Anscombe describes the situation whatever *I* is must be, or include, the pre-intentional action of muscle contraction. She tells us that what is done is what is intentional, but we are uncertain whether what is done is the muscle contraction, the movement of the limbs or what follows the basic action, such as flipping the light switch. I may be aware of flipping the switch, but I may not be aware, as I perform this action, of what I am doing with my fingers etc. This is related to the issues encountered in our, above, discussion of shoe-tying. There is reason to believe a far more plausible case can be made for the view she criticizes, particularly if we can justify regarding *I* as something other than some "extra feature."

The classical psychologists of the Jamesian vintage would, perhaps, argue the case for *I* in the following way: Contrary to what Anscombe suggests, the feature *I* is not to be thought of as a feature, or property. Anscombe describes it as a feature, allegedly, attributed to an action, one she characterizes as a monadic predicate, like 'happy' or 'heavy'. But advocates of something like *I* might argue that it is in fact a relational property, one that relates the action to a state of mind, not so much a feature in the usual sense. Her objection that this cannot be the case, since there is nothing intrinsic to the situation making it intentional, now encounters a reply she did not consider: You, Anscombe, are assuming that the description is monadic; you are assuming that falling under a description involves an object (i.e. an action) falling under a description that does not include any essential relation to any object other than the action itself; thus it is no surprise that there is nothing in the action, itself, that distinguishes it from the action under a different description. But there is another alternative. The intentional feature, *I*, may, actually, be relational; that is, what it describes is a relation between the idea of what the agent *wants* to do and what the agent *does* when he is successful. If I describe my "idea" (intention) as 'flipping the switch' then *I* is the relation between this mental state's description (of wanting to 'flip the switch') and the ultimate outcome—in case it is successful—of flipping the switch. *I* is not, merely, the relation of identity of description but the connection between the idea and the action. What *I* is not is a monadic feature of the action, as she appears to suggest. Construed along these lines *I* is a "nexus" and not a "thing" (quality). In addition to this possible reply to her argument there remains some uncertainty as to what her position is.

She speaks of *I* as belonging, on the views she attacks, to an action. Sometimes it accompanies pre-intentional actions and sometimes it is said to accompany whatever it is that is, actually, done. This latter is ambiguous as between the basic action and the change in the world evoked by the action. In addition, she will speak of *I* as having an "effect," but then she will suggest that it is *constitutive* of the action, this after stating the argument in term of an "extra feature." Take the notion of being "pre-intentional." Suppose contraction of the muscles is pre-intentional, as she says; but, now, how about what precedes contraction of the muscles? Suppose, further, that we trace events all the way back to the brain. Are these brain events pre-intentional? Presumably, they are if we take the action, itself, to be the only thing that is intentional. As she says, whether this is intentional will be dependent on the description under which it is described. What we have argued can be put another way. We can say that *I* is the relation between the action and those pre-intentional states which depend on a state of the brain (or mind). Keep in mind *I* is not the intention but a feature, a relation between action and state of the mind (or brain). The *relation* between action and brain state may be intentional only under some description, but what any such description would be remains a bit mysterious.

It is in fact, precisely, this relation that determines whether this description, and not some other, is such that the action *can* be described as Intentional. Anscombe begins the section by postponing having to answer in her own case what it is that she takes to be what accounts for the why-question being applicable to some events but not others. There are other areas of interest she did not examine. She cannot be blamed for not discussing them inasmuch as another book the size of *Intention* would probably be required to address them. However, let's consider a couple. First, recall her skepticism over *I* as an "extra" feature. What makes it extra is that it does not belong to the properties constitutive of the action, itself; or, at least, this is the clear impression conveyed. But there are certainly other "features" of a similar logical nature that would be legitimate on the position she defends. Take 'real' for example. Attend to an object which is such that you have no doubt that it is real and ask yourself in virtue of what feature it is it real. We cannot conclude that it is not real because we can't identify that feature. Nor do we say that it is real under one description and not another. There are differences between the two cases, however. For example, it is clear that under some descriptions, but not others, an action is intentional, but it is not clear whether an object is real under some descriptions, and not others. While the analogy is not perfect, we can say this much: one might suppose that being "real" is a matter of a relation between facts; suppose we call this relation "coherence," whereas being intentional is a matter of some action's being *I*-related to an agent or his neurological state. The advocate of *I* places his bets is on *I*'s being a relational, rather than a monadic predicate under which an action is described.

## SECTION 20: *NON-FORWARD LOOKING INTENTIONAL ACTIONS*

Are there intentional actions which do not point towards the future? In order to test this possibility Anscombe begins with two suppositions: (a) that 'intentional' applies, only, to intentional actions, and (b) that the only answer to the why-question is "I just am, that's all." In the case of (b) it is given that the why-question is applicable, as it was in earlier cases where the answer was "No particular reason." Anscombe will argue that on the supposition of non-forward looking intentions this answer would, however, cancel the applicability of the why-question and, therefore, intention. She proceeds to discuss the supposition of there being non-forward looking intentions by first considering it under (a) and then (b). Let us begin, then, with (a).

Under supposition (a) a non-forward looking action is like a facial expression. If asked why I'm making it, I may say "No reason"; and if it is an angry face, I might be asked what I'm angry about, saying in reply "Nothing." Answering this way may mean I am not angry or that I am angry at nothing in particular. Anscombe says that if intention is like a facial expression in this regard then it is a "style characteristic" which is a publicly observable feature of the action. In this case, if my action possesses it, then I cannot be said to be unaware of doing it intentionally, since I know what it is I'm doing, and it is an observable property. But intention cannot be such a "style characteristic," for an intention is such that something possessing it, an action, may have it under one description but not another, whereas I cannot have a smile under one description of my face and not have a smile under another. We leave it an unanswered question whether this means that the class of smiles is a "natural class."

If we suppose intentional actions are not forward looking, such as when I say "I am intentionally fluting the columns," and if intention were a "style characteristic," or property, of the proceedings associated with fluting the columns, then I could not say that what I was doing I was not doing intentionally, if I knew that I was fluting the columns. However, for an action to be intentional it must be possible that I may know what I'm doing under one description but not under some other. Thus intentionality is not a property belonging to action which is such that, if I know I'm performing that action, I know that what I am doing, whatever that is, I am doing it.

In supposing that our action is non-forward looking, while we suppose that we are not acting *with* the intention of doing something else in addition, we may *in* doing something be doing some other thing. To take Anscombe's example, *in* performing the non-forward intentional action of holding a glass to my lips I may be doing so *with* the intention of drinking, as long as I'm drinking as I hold the glass to my lips.

We are to conclude that if we make the assumption, (a), we have been making, then, a non-forward looking action is not intentional *if* the answer to the why-question is "No particular reason." But, since the why-question is applicable if the action is intentional, we must look to other possibilities that may render it intentional such as that it was done from a backward looking motive or some "sentimental characterization." Motive devoid of any implication of future behavior is insufficient. One reason is that the *point* of criticizing an action based on such and such motives is lost, when the action is not forward looking. As for "sentimental characterization," Anscombe is not explicit as to what she is driving at; however, it would appear that what she is saying is that if no further action is suggested the action is a matter of sentiment and not intention. Her reply is provocative and not, entirely, convincing. If we consider an artist working with clay, each movement may be forward looking with respect to the final product. But this may not be the case; the artist may improvise without taking heed of future possibilities within his artistic medium. In such a case, there is no forward looking intention and, yet, the action of the artist is intentional. The same might be said of any action performed for its own sake. This may be a weakness in her position. No attempt will be made in what follows to resolve this issue. Instead, let us consider her second supposition, (b); cases where the only answer to the why-question is "I just am, that's all."

The difficulty with this option is that if the only answer to the why-question applied to an action is "I just am, that's all," then the why-question in the sense Anscombe has singled out loses its *point*. Anscombe's position is stronger than the argument she provides suggests. If I knew that a person was doing something for no particular reason, unless there were special circumstances it would be pointless to ask the why-question; but, if I knew that a person did something for a particular reason, there might be a point to asking it. If I am interrogating that person, as I would a witness in a court of law, doing so may establish some connection between two of his actions, perhaps causally related actions. But asking the why-question about some action having the answer "I just did, that's all" suggests no other action and can only serve to distance the witness from some other action. This case is not beyond dispute, but there are other cases as well. "Why did you give change amounting to two nickels rather than one dime?" The answer may be "I just did that's all." Note, however, that the force of the why-question, however, is not lost. Unlike the cases Anscombe alludes to, the question retains its special sense. Her strongest point is that in cases where this answer is fitting there can be no distinction made on its basis between a gasp and a voluntary action. One important consequence of not being able to make this distinction, or others like it, is that we know our intentional actions independently of observation; if my only answer to the question "Why?" is "I just am, that's all," then it cannot be an action I know independently of observation. The difference between the first and third person perspective drops out of consideration. How, then, might we distinguish gasps and voluntary actions on the relevant suppositions? No matter how we answer this question we will find ourselves concluding that there must be some answer to the why-question other than "I just am, that's all," if the answer is to answer the why-question. We can't say that a gasp and a voluntary action differ in that only one is predictable. Both may be predictable but on different bases. Only a voluntary action can be predicted on the basis of reasons. It is worthwhile considering an analogy, one Asncombe does not discuss.

Somehow asks "How do you know?" and I reply "I just do, that's all." Wouldn't this be sufficient reason for denying that the person really does know? If we believe from the very beginning that such an answer would be an acceptable one, in such a case the how-question ("How do you know") would be senseless. Something similar is going on in the case of "Why?" applied to actions that we "Just do, that's all." But Anscombe takes another turn in discussing the matter. She considers whether there might be a way of distinguishing such things as gasps and voluntary actions. In particular she considers the fact that gasps are not commanded but voluntary actions are. One problem is that, insofar as we are attempting to understand the relation of intention, if any, to non-forward looking actions, we dispense with the concept of purpose, and this is certainly nothing we can dispute when our action is done for no reason at all, or for its own sake. Although there is an attenuated sense of 'purpose' that may apply. If we take this route, however, the question "Why?" is not the why-question but, rather, has the force of "Commanded or not?" It is difficult to assess the efficacy of Anscombe's arguments with respect to distinguishing gasps and voluntary actions on the assumptions she adopts for the purpose of discussing non-forward looking actions, but she does make a compelling case that actions "I just do, that's all" are difficult to capture in the net cast by the why-question, purportedly, definitive of intentional behavior.

## SECTION 21: *CHAINS CONSISTING OF ACTION*

Anscombe has made the point that, if there were no answers to the why-question besides "I just did it, that's all," then the *concept* of a voluntary action would not apply. This is not to say that on no occasion does it make sense to say that you did something "For no reason." The situation is somewhat like the one described for promising we find in Kant. We can break a promise, but if promises were, always, broken, then the institution of a promising would, soon, no longer exist. The fact that we can act for no particular reason belies what we find in Aristotle, viz. that there is always some end for which we act. Anscombe notes that Aristotle's suggestion that we must act towards some one end is vulnerable to the charge of fallacy, one related to the scope of the quantifier 'some'. Contrast "There is some reason such that actions are performed for that reason," and "For any action there is some reason for its being performed." Kenny once remarked that Aristotle's view that we always act to realize the good, resembles the claim that since all roads leads somewhere they all lead to Rome. (Kenny [1965-66} p. 87) Of course this comparison is made with tongue in cheek, but the general point is made: not only may we on occasion act for no reason, there is no particular end to which all our actions are directed. A number of years, following publication of *Intention*, while commenting on Von Wright's theory of practical inference, Anscombe would clarify her objectives in Section 21.

In this later discussion she would point out that on her position the "drive towards the end" of action does not, properly, belong to reasoning manifest in acting upon a practical syllogism. She maintains that, where wants provide such "drive," they do not belong to *reasoning* as to what ought to be done. Reasons will reveal what good is to be accomplished by the act, something wanting alone will not provide. Later in our discussion of Section 35 we shall discuss the place of wanting in practical reasoning.

# PART 4:
# Series of Intentional Actions

## SECTION 22: *ACTING "WITH THE INTENTION THAT"*

Answering the why-question in the relevant sense of 'why' often introduces "the intention with which" the action is performed. "Why did you knock on the wall with your shoe?" Answer: "I did it *with the intention* of causing the neighbors to quiet down." The intention with which we act is forward-looking towards some effect the action might have. Since causes precede effects, intentions with which we act, understood as what we are attempting to bring into being, are not causes. The issue of final causes will be broached later in our discussion. But we are not free, as yet, of the concept of a cause. When we answer the why-question by making reference to a future state, and this is sufficient, then this reference to the future is sufficient to guarantee that the action intentional.

If someone walks into the room and sees me lying on the couch and asks "What are you doing?" if I were to say "Lying on the couch," that might be taken as a joke; but if I say, I'm resting, where lying on the couch results in resting, then my lying on the couch has resting as the reason given for my action—I am lying on the couch "with the intention" of resting. It need not be the case that if I do something with the intention, $x$, that my intention is to *cause* $x$; I may, e.g., set up my camera with the intention of snapping a picture of Noam Chomsky as he walks to his Thursday lecture. He has not arrived as yet. I do not set up the camera with the intention of causing him to walk by, or with the intention of having him walk by. If someone asks, "Why are you setting up the camera?" I may answer this why-question by saying "Because Noam is going to be coming by." I do not mean that I am setting up the camera with the intended consequence of Chomsky walking by. However, there are occasions where my answer to the why-question does have as a result the intention with which I act, such as when asked "Why are you crossing the street?" I answer by saying: "To get a gander at what's in that interesting looking shop." Anscombe explores the differences between cases of these two sorts.

In the picture-taking case, the person who asked me the question "Why are you setting up the camera?" can think of no reason why I might believe that setting up the camera will cause Chomsky to walk by; but in the street crossing case, he just might figure that my intention was to look at the same interesting looking shop that he sees. Let's examine one of Anscombe's examples, one that will, probably, evoke some confusion on the part of the first time reader.

If I ask someone "Why are you crossing the road?" and he replies "Because there is going to be an eclipse next July," we can see no reason for this being a suitable answer to our why-question. But from the perspective of the agent things may be different. The agent may think that by being there he can cause an eclipse in July! Now suppose Dean Swift believes that he has the power to cause eclipses. He orders people out into the street to view it. The crowd is in the street with the intention of viewing the eclipse. The causal connection, alleged, is spurious; but the reason the crowd is in the street, much like in the case of the picture-taking example, is sufficient to warrant describing it as intentional behavior. Dean Swift may "cancel" the eclipse, but the intention of the believing crowd is clear enough. *Belief* in causal efficacy, rather than causal efficacy, itself, is sufficient—once understood by the questioner—to make the answer appropriate to the why-question. Anscombe is quick to lay out arguments against the belief that the agent must have the notion of a cause in mind in order to engage in intentional behavior.

If I say that I'm going up stairs to get my camera, I am not saying that going upstairs will have the result that I will have my camera, only that going upstairs will result in my being in a position to cause the camera to come into my possession. There will be cases where my answer may be puzzling, such as those occasions where everyone knows my camera is in the basement, but in such cases there may be things I know that they don't, such as that I have a pulley with which I shall raise the camera from the basement. My answer ("To fetch my camera") becomes unintelligible, however, if I let it be known that I have no way of causing the camera to be in my possession by going upstairs. The point she is making is this: In order to understand my action as intentional, I must have some idea that my going upstairs will result in a future state being made possible by the action. That is, it must be understood that there is some plausible connection between what I do and the intention with which I do it. But what if no, alleged, connection *is* plausible? This is where Anscombe remarks that a person lacks "absolute authority" over his intentions, and, here, Anscombe appears to mean that if, for example, event Q will take place regardless of what I do, then, if when I answer the why-question as to why I'm doing P, by saying, "So that Q," I have not in fact answered in such a way that the suitability requirement of the why-question is satisfied; in other words, I cannot do P *with* the intention Q.

## SECTION 23: *WHETHER AN INTENTIONAL ACTION HAS A UNIQUE DESCRIPTION AS SUCH*

Does an intentional action have a description which is its description *qua* intentional action? This is the question. Anscombe's answer is an unambiguous "No." It follows from an action's being intentional only under some description. But is there a unique description under which an action is intentional? The answer, again, is "No." The way we arrive at the answer, however, we cannot make equally explicit. We shall attempt an explanation of the answer that maximizes consistency. In addressing the question, Anscombe sets forth a paradigm to which she returns throughout *Intention*.

The paradigm centers on a man pumping water into a cistern, one that supplies water to a house occupied by a group of party leaders devoted to killing Jews, and planning world war. Another man has contaminated the water source with a poison that is, relatively, slow acting but for which there is no antidote. This other man has informed the one doing the pumping—call him as "the pumper"— of his having poisoned the water and why he did it. Moreover, he has informed the pumper that, if he succeeds, and the water supply of the party chiefs gets poisoned, there will follow a new and benevolent regime, one leading perhaps to the Kingdom of Heaven. Much goes on in the pumper: muscles of which he may know nothing are moving and physiological changes are taking place, as well, none of which he is aware. But other things are happening as well.

Along with these physiological occurrences there are other events which the pumper does in fact notice; and it will be important in what follows that he does in fact notice them. The pumper's arm, as it moves up and down, causes a shadow on a pile of rocks in the garden, and there is a clicking sound having a noticeable rhythm. But describing these events does not exhaust the descriptions applicable to his action. In addition to pumping water, he may be earning his wages, wearing out his gloves, and creating a disturbance in the surrounding air. If he succeeds in his labor, he may, also, be described as having helped bring about the Kingdom of Heaven. The range of descriptions, however, that applies to his *intentional* actions is limited to those for which there is an answer to the why-question. Thus the physiological changes accompanying his action do not count as intentions, assuming that what he may know about them is what he must *infer* from his knowledge of physiology. What is most important is that he doesn't notice these changes. We can ask him a number of why-questions.

We might ask "Why are you pumping?" and his answer might be "I'm pumping in order to get a supply of water into the house." But he can, also, be asked why he is performing actions that have no bearing on poisoning the inhabitants but which are consequences of doing so. E.g. he may be asked "Why are you producing that strange rhythmic sound?" and he might reply "Oh, I do it for fun." But there is another direction the questioning can take, and describing it, while crucial to explaining Anscombe's position, is not an easy thing to do. She speaks of a "break" in the series of answers we might give to successive why-questions. Because she will return to this notion of a "break," let's examine it more closely.

If the pumper is asked why he is moving his arm up and down, he may reply "In order to operate the pump." If he is asked "Why are you operating the pump?" he may reply "To replenish the water supply"; and, if he is asked why he is doing this, he may reply that he's doing it in order to poison the inhabitants of the building. Note that they are in fact being poisoned; the water supply is being replenished and the pump *is* being operated. All *these* actions follow from his basic action of moving his arm up and down. But what about saving the Jews and bringing in the Kingdom of Heaven? It is not clear that *these* events are following as a consequence of his action of moving his arm, as are the events of water moving through the pipes, or the water's being received into the cistern. In other words there is a "break" in the sequence. It helps in trying to understand this use of "break" that there may be a question as to whether we have four actions or just one, the arm movement; but it doesn't appear as if saving the Jews, and introducing the Kingdom of Heaven, stands in relation to the arm movement as the poisoning to the pumping or the pumping to the arm movement.

Suppose a man is seen carrying laundry. There is a laundry mat across the street. He approaches the street; takes three steps into the street towards the laundry mat; he stops and is hit by a car and killed. The police arrive. Their report reads "Mr. X died while crossing the street…" The description may fit, even though Mr. X never, really, crosses the street. The same might be said of a falling ladder; that is, we can say that the ladder is falling down even though it may never fall down, since someone may catch it in mid-fall. But how can I describe a man as crossing the street if he never does any such thing? The semantical issues involved have attracted the interest of linguists and logicians, alike (Dowty [1979] pp. 132-192).

From the similarity of these two sorts of situation Anscombe draws a startling conclusion: we would not appeal to intentions in attempting to justify saying "He was crossing the street." But let's suppose there are facts to be added to our example of the man crossing the street. Suppose his intention was not to cross the street but to look for a bus to bring him to work. Wouldn't such a fact render the police description inaccurate? Wouldn't they be justified only in saying that it *appeared* that the decedent was crossing the street? And, if so, wouldn't the man's intentions figure into the, actual, truthfulness of their report? Anscombe seems to think not, but this seems doubtful. There is a "break" that Anscombe is attempting to make explicit, one related to this, particular, issue having to do with intentions.

Accompanying a larger separation between what I am doing, and my objective, is an increased likelihood of a break of the sort Anscombe describes. So if I'm on a bus, and someone asks what I'm doing, if I reply "I'm going to kill Mr. X in the Loop," that may make sense, particularly, to a Chicagoan; but, if I say "I am killing Mr. X," then one can see that there is a gap or "break" between what is described by the progressive construction and the simple present construction. We see, then, that there is a certain "distance" resulting in a break between "I am $X$ing" and "I'm going to $X$." In the case of the pumper the situation is clear. There is not much of a "break" between "I'm $X$ing" and "I'm going to $X$." But, if we go one step further, the "break" seems clear; for I cannot reply, when asked why I'm poisoning these people "I am saving the Jews and bringing into being the Kingdom of Heaven," because it is unclear whether I am succeeding at *this*, whereas there is little question that I am replenishing the water supply as I pump. I can say "I am *going* to save the Jews etc." The reason is because at the time of the question the Jews are not saved but the poisoning is taking place, just as the pedestrian was, at the time he died, *going* to cross the street. What is important is that we can now say that there is no unique description associated with the basic action of the pumper's moving his arm under which it is intentional. The question, now, becomes, according to Anscombe: Given that we have a number of descriptions including moving arms, operating the pump, replenishing the water, poisoning the inhabitants, do we have four *separate* actions?

## SECTION 24: *INDIVIDUATING ACTIONS*

Before we can answer the question whether there is an action for each description, we need to realize there are other problems with actions that bear on intentions to act. We say that the pumper's action is poisoning the inhabitants of the building. But what about the fellow who planted the poison in the first place? Isn't the act of poisoning distributable over more than one person? Probably, but individuating actions remains a problem.

There is, e.g., a question related to time. Is the pumper poisoning people when he is at home waiting for the inhabitants to drink what remains in the cistern? Further, couldn't the pumper have been doing, exactly, what he was doing even if the water had not been poisoned? Isn't his *action* what is relevant? But what is that? We see, then, that there are a number of questions about action that must be answered before we can get at the root of what intentions are.

## SECTION 25: *IDENTIFYING INTENTIONAL ACTIONS*

So far, we've assumed that the pumper's actions are intentional. Davidson has argued that an action's being intentional is relative to the description we use to describe it. Anscombe holds much the same view, evidenced by her contention that what we have been calling "basic actions" are the only real actions. But now we have something of a dilemma. Suppose we ask the pumper why he is replenishing the water supply with poison; but, instead of saying something like "In order to kill the building's inhabitants," he says, "I don't care two figs about killing anyone, or whether there is poison in the water; I'm just doing my job, that's all." In such a case we cannot, according to Anscombe, in keeping with the proffered criterion of intentional action, deem it intentional. What, then, makes his action intentional? If his action is intentional, that is, his act of poisoning the building's inhabitants, it would appear difficult to locate its point of difference with the case where it is not intentional. What he *does* is the same in either case; and here we are referring to his basic actions.

If we were to say that an action is intentional under *some* description, then, we would be compelled to say that the pumper's act of poisoning the inhabitants was intentional. But we've just said that in one circumstance, where his claim is that of just doing his job, his action is not intentional. Do we wish to say that there are two actions at issue, depending on the description? The answer to this will be "No." It is circumstances such as this that make the idea of forming an intention, as an "inner movement," compelling. Anscombe in what is, clearly, a deliberate effort to discredit the idea of intentions as relying on inner mental actions, skillfully, crafts a straw man argument. She says that what is compelling, according to advocates of such an idea, is that forming an intention is what distinguishes intentional and non-intentional action. But, inasmuch as forming the intention is an action, it must be an act of will. If so, then it is within the agent's power to form an intention, or for that matter abstain from doing so. According to Anscombe, this amounts to not much else than making a little speech, inwardly, and as such it is absurd. Still, the problem remains: what *makes* an action under one description intentional and the same action not intentional under another description? Davidson's answer will be that under one description, but not another, say, a belief and desire come into play in a "suitable" way. But at this stage of Anscombe's own discussion the alternative would be to say that more than one action is at issue. The problem can be framed this way: we need to know what makes one answer to this question truthful and, therefore, the action unintentional, and some other answer untruthful, rendering his action, quite possibly, intentional.

Part of the basis for the truthfulness of the pumper's claim just to be doing his job, and, therefore, not having any intention to poison the inhabitants, is that he isn't doing anything to assist the poisoning other than doing his job. If he had assisted in any way, it would belie his claim. This is not to say he is not innocent of a crime, only that when he acted he did not act with the intention of poisoning the inhabitants. Anscombe admits to some difficulty in justifying the claim that there is a difference between the pumper's being indifferent on the one hand and complicit on the other, where that justification relies only on what the pumper says. But saying appears to be the only alternative to admitting the plausibility of "inner movements," something, apparently, to be avoided in order to escape an incipient Cartesian privacy. The pumper may, merely, grunt; and, here issuing the grunt would be a vehicle of thought—not to be confused with the forming of an intention, inwardly. The reader should take note of this expression, "vehicle of thought." Oughtn't we think of language as an instrument of communication rather than a vehicle of thought? Philosophers of a more recent vintage have discussed the matter with inconclusive results. Michael Dummett, e.g. provides a lucid discussion of the relevant issues. (Dummett [1989] pp. 192-212) Mention must, also, be made of the views of Anthony Kenny, a philosopher who is among the most vociferous critics of inner actions, but who while aligning himself with much of what Anscombe says about the verbal testimony of the agent, nevertheless reintroduces a notion *close* to what he seems to dread most, inner states.

In addressing the question of which conditions are necessary for attributing intentions, based on what the agent says, Kenny tells us that we must introduce the idea that what the agent says must be a "saying in the heart." (Kenny [1963] p. 218). Needless to say, this "saying in one's heart" is a strange peg upon which to hang a theory of intention (or volitions), especially after steadfastly rejecting "inner movements," etc. However this may be resolved, a theological component to this appeal cannot be, perfunctorily, dismissed. St. Peter enters Anscombe's discussion twice in *Intention* in a way we can relate to Kenny's reliance on "saying in one's heart." In each case, however, the point she is attempting to make is difficult to understand, and one cannot help but think that St. Peter's "saying in his heart" that he would not denounce Jesus and, then, denouncing Jesus in fulfillment of a Divine prophesy is "saying" in a sense that, strongly, resembles the sense of "inner thought" advocated by those whom Wittgenstein, Kenny, and Anscombe so resolutely oppose. Why would one feel compelled to accept, uncritically, this idea of "saying in one's heart," especially if it seems clear that the issue is not one of subvocal utterance? The inconsistency may be, merely, apparent but nothing has been said, explicitly, to exclude it.

Anscombe, to this point, has not resolved the main questions raised in this section; i.e. what it is that accounts for the difference between the pumper who is just doing his job and the pumper who is complicit in his actions? However, she does address the question of why we distinguish the action and the intention, where the action *is* intentional. She does this by, basically, restating a point Wittgenstein makes when he remarks that the reason a person may describe his intention, as well as his action, is that he wants the hearer to know something about the person who acts, and having an intention is something we may know about a person. (Wittgenstein [1953] 659)

## SECTION 26: *HOW MANY ACTIONS ARE THERE?!*

In the case of the pumper who acts intentionally, we are concerned with four descriptions.

A. Moving his arm up and down.
B. Operating the pump
C. Replenishing the water supply
D. Poisoning the inhabitants.

But how many actions do we have? Is it one action for each description? Clearly, D is causally dependent on C, and C on B, etc. We cannot, however, verify that B is happening by verifying the occurrence of A. The situation is this: B, *qua* action, doesn't just depend on A. B is A with certain circumstances entering into the basis of making the description, such as that there is a pump to which the hand is attached which is, itself, attached to the arm is. Also this: that C is just A with the added circumstances that accompany B and C, etc. In other words, the only real action is A; the rest follow as causal consequences under certain circumstances. The matter of how these descriptions, A-B, bear on the intention(s) related to action must be considered.

We can think of the four descriptions either as corresponding to four intentions, or as related in a special way to one intention, viz. D. The pumper does A *with the intention* of doing B, and B *with the intention* of doing C, etc. This is not to say that the intention, D, is only an indirect intention. In fact, it is where performing an action *with the intention that* stops. It is, so to speak, the last stop and, therefore, occupies a special position. Part of being this special position is that, at each stage of the doing *with the intention that,* the previous doing *with the intention* is said to "swallow up" the preceding intention, ultimately "swallowing up" all but the last intention associated with the intention, D. In other words, if asked of the pumper "Why did you do A?" he can answer "In order to perform the action D." We may think of D as the intended end of action and the intervening behavior, B-C, as means to this end, that is, the "how" of doing D by doing A. But there are some descriptions that may fall outside the series A-D but which are descriptive of events causally dependent on one or more elements of the series.

The pumper is described as producing a song, "God Save the King," as he pumps. He does it for fun, say. But doing so depends on events described by A and B, not on C. Still, we would not say that D "swallows up" the intention to produce the tune; producing the tune is not a *means* to D. One might add that the pumper does not B with the intention of producing the tune. However, there is something Anscombe doesn't mention. The *way* in which I perform B is with the intention of producing the tune, and the action, that is, the means, of performing D is in part determined by wanting to produce the tune. The pumper does not B with the intention of producing the tune, but the *way* he does B depends on this further intention. If the pumper is asked, "Why did you A in just the *way* you did?" he might reply "Oh, in order to produce the tune as I went along."

In this case we have disparate intentions, producing a tune and poisoning the inhabitants of the building. But the only real action is

A. Insofar as A is the only real action taking place, one must get clear as to how D and producing the tune differ; certainly not in the way C and D differ. It is difficult to accept Anscombe's most likely point of view on this matter, which would be that 'playing God Save the King' is, merely, a description of the one and only action, A, really taking place; just as D is such a description. While it is true that we, frequently, do one thing in order to accomplish two or more ends, the intentionality of our real action in this instance is now overdetermined. The satisfaction of one intention, not to mention its formation, assuming this takes place, differs from that of the other. In this sense, two "intentional events" have taken place. Can we, then, deny that two actions have taken place? Anscombe's most likely answer would be "No."

## SECTION 27: *ACTS OF INTENTING AND EFFICACY*

Are there occasions where there is in addition to an intentional act an act of intending? Suppose the pumper who professes indifference, while pumping, says to himself: "I am only doing my job, that's all." Does this exercise absolve him? Is there a purging of his responsibility by means of deliberately composing some assertion of his "real" intention in acting? But if his inner speech act is to possess the desired efficacy mustn't it be spontaneous? Wouldn't it be absurd to suppose that we could rehearse the action of forming such an intention by means of such an inner gesture? Formulated this way, it seems clear that, at the very least, the inner speech act would have to be spontaneous. Further, it seems doubtful that we can reasonably acknowledge that intending is something we can *do*, a sort of act independently performed having some affect on the culpability of actions overtly performed.

There would be evidence of culpability, even following such an inner speech act, had the pumper been told that there was an enormous reward for success at poisoning the inhabitants and he, the pumper, then went on to distract someone who, otherwise, might discover what he was up to. But if there is no outward sign of his authentic indifference to the action, attribution of this indifference is difficult to warrant. Earlier we spoke of Kenny's appeal to what the agent feels "in his heart," i.e., possible conditions under which he may have *meant* to do what he did. Anscombe presaged this gambit, remarking that, while intention is not a mental action, what an agent means, perhaps as Kenny says, "in his heart" does make a difference to the character of his actions. While Anscombe will employ the example of an insincere embrace, there are more illuminating examples that raise a host of related issues, and, while we cannot pursue them in detail, they do merit the reader's attention. Let's take a related example, somewhat, more complex that than an insincere embrace.

## *Intentional Acts of Creation*

In his book *Mahler*, (Schoken 1974 [1957]), Bruno Walter describes an incident that took place on a bridge on Mahler's estate. Walter looked over the bridge, viewing its splendor, saying nothing. Unexpectedly, perhaps, Mahler remarked something to this effect: "Don't think about it; I've already composed it." The composition in question is never identified; but, just suppose it is the Adagio of the 5th Symphony. Return, now, to the pumper. The pumper knows what he was doing (poisoning the inhabitants); and, he knows that what he was doing was done with that intention. But this story from Walter about Mahler introduces a new class of intentional actions, actions which are such that how we go about satisfying the intention cannot be a function of what it is that we want to end up doing. The one who laid the plot for poisoning the inhabitants contrived actions that would be decided upon by circumstances and, in particular, the objective. He may have reasoned that in order to get poison into the building it was best to poison the water supply, and to do this there would have to be access to the pump, as well as the cistern etc. But the Mahler example is different.

The means by which Mahler satisfied his intention of composing his view from the bridge was not determined by the intention, taken together with circumstances, as in the case of the one who plotted the poisoning. At each step in the planning, the plotter in the poisoning example reasoned that one thing would lead to another if such and such action were performed. But this was not the case with Mahler. In the Mahler case, it would make no sense for an observer to say, following the performance of the 5th Symphony: "No! Mahler has failed in his objective; this is not a composition of the view from the bridge; it is a composition of the view from the veranda!" There is observational knowledge whether the plotter succeeds in his intentions but no such knowledge of whether Mahler succeeded in his intention to compose the view from the bridge. This illustrates the following important fact: acts of creation, acts introducing novelty, constitute a different sort of intentional action. Just as Mahler attempted to compose a vision *he* had from the bridge, a thinker may attempt to compose a sentence expressing a thought *he* has on a particular occasion.

Recognizing the difference between these two sorts of cases requires not, merely, an observation that concerns some special circumstances relating to artistic intentions. It goes much deeper, for as we now realize, the creative aspect can extend to linguistic intentions. This is at the heart of Chomsky's view that the language faculty is a mental faculty insofar as it has creative employment, one manifest in the possibility of producing novel sentences. (Chomsky [1966]) Perhaps, the most important lesson to be learned from such an example, as the one Walter's book provides, is that in dealing with creative actions, tests of "truthfulness" are not possible in they way they are in the case of an insincere embrace, for example.

## SECTION 27: INTENTION AS AN INTERIOR ACT

Anscombe raises the question whether there is ever a need to introduce intentions in the form of interior acts of mind. (Anscombe [1957] p. 47). She has us reconsider the pumper who, when asked why he pumps, replies "I was only doing my usual job." But this time we are to suppose that he utters this inwardly to himself. The complication is that this inner utterance is an action in its own right and, so, we can ask why he performed *this* action, and his reply might be "So I don't have to consider whose side I'm on". It makes a difference whether when the pumper said "I was only doing my job" he did so deliberately or spontaneously. There is added sincerity in his saying this spontaneously. But, even so, we can inquire into the truthfulness of his assertion. What we cannot say, according to Anscombe, is that "In the end only you can *know* whether this is your intention or not." Instead, what we can say is "In the end only you *can say* whether this is your intention or not." Why should this be the case? The only answer given is that using 'know' instead of 'can say' is allowable only if we can imagine it being the case that the pumper might be wrong; that is, that he might at some point find himself in a position where he wants to say that he only *thought* that such and such was his intention. This is a more complex "argument" than at first meets the eye.

It may be the case that an interior action such as uttering to oneself "I'm only doing my job," will change the character of the action performed. An embrace, where there is the same inner utterance (both spontaneous and intentional), may introduce new considerations in assessing the outward action, such as whether the embrace was sincere.

## SECTION 28: *OBSERVATIONAL KNOWLEDGE OF INTENTIONS, AGAIN*

In the case of the "exterior senses," I can misjudge what I see. However, my knowledge of the position of my own limbs is not a matter of drawing some inference from an inner appearance. The lack of any role of appearances in the determination of the position of my limbs is what distinguishes what belongs to my inner sense from what belongs to observation. Observation, Anscombe is suggesting, is an occasion where appearances have a distinctive role to play. Anscombe proceeds to entertain an objection to her general thesis that we do not know our intentional actions, as such, by observation.

All along, she has been comparing our knowledge of intention to our knowledge of the position of our own limbs. The objector contends that, if the analogy to knowledge of the position of our limbs is to be sustained, then we must have knowledge-without-observation of all our intentional actions. Thus, if someone intentionally paints a wall yellow, one may wonder whether Anscombe is denying that the agent can know he is painting the wall yellow without observation. Obviously, this runs contrary to fact, since the agent can only know he is succeeding if he observes the wall, etc. Anscombe's rejoinder is that this is not the sort of knowledge that is being denied, such as when you are asked "Why did you ring that bell?" and you reply "I didn't know I was doing that!" What is, somewhat, puzzling is Anscombe's worry over this question. She remarks that her position is "difficult" to argue for (Anscombe [1957] p. 51). She introduces an additional illustration.

Suppose someone hears me moving about and asks: "What are you doing?" I reply, "I'm opening the window." If we suppose this to be an intentional action, I would not say that I know I am performing this action by observing my body going through the motions and watching the window going up, etc., as I make those motions. Consider an example Anscombe does not discuss, but which might shed some intuitive light on the situation. The contrast between deliberately rolling one's self down a hill and rolling down the hill, without the intention of doing so, recapitulates the difference between being an "agent" and being a mere "theme" of motion. A rock can role down a hill, but it cannot roll *itself* down the hill. Observationally, my rolling myself, down the hill, and my being rolled down the hill by forces outside my control, such as when I roll down the hill after tripping, are indistinguishable. Under ordinary circumstances a man rolling himself down a hill doesn't have to look in order to answer the question "What are you doing?" What the agent knows is an *intentional* action, and he knows it, as such, without observation.

## SECTION 29: *I DO WHAT HAPPENS!*

Anscombe's claim has been that there are two "knowledges": there is the knowledge of what is going on when I raise the window, that is, what can be seen by any observer, and knowledge of what I am doing, *qua* intentional act. Knowledge of what is happening and what I am doing is *not* knowledge of the same thing taken under two descriptions, rather, what we have are two ways of knowing, where *what* is known is the same thing. Knowledge is knowledge, so to speak; that is, knowledge by visual perception, or touch, may give knowledge of the same thing. Here the modes of knowing differ but knowledge of *what* is the same in both modes. So what makes knowledge of intentional actions and knowledge of what happens different? Herein lies the difficulty. However, there are questions, particularly, in regard to whether what is known *is* the same, as Anscombe maintains. Let's examine one such question, albeit, briefly before proceeding to examine the substance of her remarks.

I may know the window is being raised as I watch the window go up; but how do I know, as I watch, what I am doing that *I* am doing it? Further, seeing my body move, raise the window, etc., I may know in some sense that this is what I'm doing, but isn't what I know when I know *I* am raising the window different from what I know when I know the window is going up? In a way, the question is similar to Wittgenstein's question, "What is the difference between my raising my arm and my arm going up?" Only here the question becomes "What is the difference between "I raise the window" and "the window goes up" (in this particular case)? In the one case, what I know is that there is this body, moving in a certain way having certain consequences; the window is going up etc. But there is, also, knowledge that the body is mine and that what it does is perform an action for which I am responsible in some sense. In the second case, knowledge is of my action as intentional, knowledge "in intention," and I need not be *informed* that the body doing the action is *my* body. In fact it is logically possible that I use another body in performing the basic action as long as it is me that "guides" the action of that other body. Whatever may be the case in this regard, the point is that what I must know, *in addition* to what happens, is that this bodily movement is my moving my body. Thus what is known, it may be argued, differs in each case. This is of little concern to Anscombe, most likely, because for her 'I' is not a referring term, at all, and so knowledge of it as a *logical subject* of any attribution of intention does not enter the picture; but for one who does not take this view, there may be more reason to believe that what is known in the case of these two "knowledges" are not identical.

Some philosophers will maintain that the result of bodily movement, which is known by observation, is what is willed in the intention. The idea of being "willed in the intention" remains obscure, and the possibility of misunderstanding is increased by Anscombe's allowing for only the most limited sense of 'willing'. On the account she rejects, what we know when we know our intentional actions can be separated into two components; first, knowing our intention, without observation; and, second, our observational knowledge of what is accomplished by the intended action. She describes this account as "mad," saying that belief in the causal power of the Will, makes no sense. The only sense to the word 'willing' on such a view, she says, would be one where I might stare at a matchbox and will that it move; but when I raise my arm, for example, I don't stare at my arm and issue the command "Arm move!" To the extent that I may say that my arm moves as an act of will, I can likewise say of the matchbox that it can be moved, should I in this sense "will" it to move. There is a subtle distinction I believe Anscombe may have overlooked.

I can move my arm willingly without believing that the willing is a *cause* of the movement. But, now, relying on our distinction between an act of will and a willful act, I can say that I moved my arm as an *act of will*, and here there is the imputation of causation. Suppose, following surgery, I am asked to attempt to move my arm. I stare at my arm. I try to move my arm, and it moves. This is different from willingly moving my arm as I reach for the light switch with the idea in mind of turning on the light. This deserves emphasis because in the case following surgery what I do is, somewhat, like what I do when I attempt to move the matchbox by an act of will. Articulating the similarities is no easy matter, but upon reflection the similarity is, one would think, undeniable. Moreover, in both the surgery case and the case of reaching for the light switch I know my intentional action independently of observation, again raising the question as to whether there are "knowledges." For now, let's suppose that only two "knowledges" are under discussion. It is relevant, at this point, to recall, once more, that Davidson has given examples of things I may do intentionally in the absence of knowledge of what I'm doing. It is an interesting fact that I cannot intentionally perform a basic action, such as making a fist, without knowledge of what I am doing. It is only when I do something *with the intention that* (something else) that the possibility Davidson suggests of driving a wedge between knowledge and intention arises.

There are some, Ansombe says, who contend that there is a sense in which what we know of our intentional actions, as such, is confined to something that takes place in the agent, alone. What *happens* being something else, altogether; that is, if I intend to move my arm, say, without its moving, then although the arm does not move there is a sense in which I move my arm in intention. If this is the case, however, then there is, first off, the problem of understanding the relation between the inner goings on and what happens in the world outside my intention. There is no logical connection between the two. The connection between what goes on in me and what happens appears to become, as Wittgenstein said, "a favor granted by fate." (Wittgenstein [1961] 6.374). It is remarkable that no one has made much fuss over, or even as much as commented on, the fact that well before Wittgenstein expressed this view, remarkably, similar language was used by G. F. Stout in connection with the same issue when he said that the relation of idea to bodily movement was "a benevolent disposition of Providence." (Stout [1896])

The views of Stout and Wittgenstein suggest that in addition to one event following another, viz. a volition, there is no other agency at work, anymore than there is some special conative feature attached to event-event causation. Russell would, strongly, suggest a similar view in a paper that heavily influenced Anscombe's position on the nature of causation, although it appears to have moved her in an opposite direction, as we shall see. Indeed, Anscombe and Russell are close in their, general, approach to the problems presented by favors "granted by fate."

Russell in his famous rejection of the notion of a cause (Russell [1912-13]) alleged that it had become "a fruitful source of fallacies" mainly because it had been thought of as analogous to volition. (Russell [1912-13] p.182) Without giving a precise definition of 'volition', Russell does attempt an account, of sorts, of what it means to say a volition "operates." He says that a volition operates when "what it wills takes place.' The objection can be raised, he observes, to the effect that a volition "only operates when it 'causes' what it wills," not when it, merely, happens to be followed by what it wills. Underlying this conception is the felt difference between doings and happenings. However, to distinguish "operating" and, merely having something happen, following the event (cause), requires reintroducing the very notion of cause to be explained, a futile endeavor. Anscombe will agree insofar as she will reject the efficacy of what has been, traditionally, conceived of as volition, but for different reason.

Anscombe appears to reject Wittgenstein view and, presumably, Stout's as well. She, also, rejects (as we have seen) special inner episodes that cause actions, but in so doing we remain unclear as to how what follows from an intentional action is anything more than a favor "granted by fate." There may be a theological side to her positive views, but for now we concentrate on her rejection of the causal efficacy of acts of willing. Her reason for doing so is illuminating and cuts to the core of issues extending more widely into the philosophy of mind.

No act of willing, alone, according to Anscombe has efficacy. The problem with raising the possibility that there is an inner action, such as moving my arm in-intention, is that there is no plausible account of the relation of intention to effective action. This is not only true in the case of actions, such as opening the window, but true, also, in the case of basic actions, such as moving one's toe. (Anscombe [1957] p. 52) Certainly, part of the problem is in arriving at a conception of intention as something that happens. Where would one go to find such a happening? What, she asks, is the "vehicle" for such intentions? Are the words that formulate my intention the intention, itself? This cannot be, since for the utterance of words, inwardly or otherwise, to come about there must be a further action, and how can it be guaranteed that these words codify my intention any more than an intention may guarantee a happening in the world? The lack of a "vehicle" disposes her to reject such a conception of intention as a "bombination in a vacuum." The idea of a "vehicle" is one way of raising a question we have, yet, to ask: "In what sense, if any, does an intention exist 'in' an agent?" Anscombe would, most likely, reject the question by challenging the sense of "in." But can we accept this; that is, can we accept the idea that in no sense do intentions reside "in" the agent? The conjecture that the intention belongs to the action raises problems, among them being that there is no property of an action that makes the action intentional, there is just a happening. It may turn out, however, that we ought not to be thinking of intentions as properties exemplified by either actions or persons. We have, already, suggested as a possible alternative that intention is, fundamentally, relational and not a monadic property (or conceivably a peculiar semantic "operator") as, appears, to be the working hypothesis. There may be, yet, another alternative.

One point of view might be that an intention exists "in" an agent, somewhat, as a surface may exist "in" an object. Anscombe and Geach would, shortly after publication of *Intention,* contrast predication with existing "in" a substance in their discussion of Aristotle's *Metaphysics*. (Anscombe [1961] p. 9) I shall not explore this option except to mention that the idea of intentions being "in" a subject seems a plausible alternative to being predicated *of* some subject with the result that we would, then, be strapped with the problem of finding "vehicles" for those intentions. We are faced with a conundrum: how can we avoid regarding intention as a "bombination in a vacuum" without collapsing to identity what I *do* and what *happens*. This is a problem Anscombe acknowledges and addresses.

Anscombe's strong denial that we are to think of an intention as some *thing* or some, independent, *event* is motivated not only by a desire to avoid private entities and events, thereby denying the "abstractionism" of empiricists who rely on "direct awareness" to afford an understanding of the concept intention, but, also, because, if she allows intention as an event, she, then, invites a causal account of intentional action requiring no appeal to reasons, reasons that once given confirm the admissibility of the relevant why-question. She retains this resistance to independent intentional events throughout her writings. This is, especially, evident in her, later, discussion of the, alleged, causal efficacy of intentions. (Anscombe [1983] pp. 95-96) There Anscombe reports that people were uncomfortable with her stated view that "I *do* what *happens.*" They were dissatisfied because it seemed that while I know what happens by observation I know otherwise than by observation what I do. Her first reaction is to say that observations may guide me in my action without providing knowledge of my action. This relates to what Davidson, later argued for in his example of acting intentionally without knowing what I am doing. The difference between Davidson and Anscombe would appear to be that for Anscombe there is knowledge of what I do, even if knowledge of what is *being done* is absent. Still, Anscombe remains, at this point, faced with the problem that, if we have two "knowledges," it may be, contrary to her views, that what *is* known are two things and not one.

## SECTION 30: *AGAINST THE IDEA OF INTENTIONS AS INITIATING CAUSES OF ACTION*

Anscombe voices her opposition to one model of action that is, more or less, standard among advocates of the idea that intentions are initiating causes of action. That model would have us trace back our actions to intentions, such as when I trace back the originating causes of a boat's going out into the water as the predicted result of actions that I am performing with that intention, actions such as *pushing*. On this model what I am aware of is the pushing, what is predicted is the intended result. I push *with the intention* that the boat go out to sea. There are examples that do not conform to this paradigm. The example Anscombe offers, and which we shall discuss, is one where the intention is not the cause of the action but, rather, the predicted consequence of actions which are remote from the bodily movements I make in satisfying the intention. Her counterexample is marked by the fact that what I am immediately aware of is by no means the cause of the intended result, but rather the other way around. We need to explore this further. Let's begin by stating the counter example to the paradigm. A physiologist wants to determine whether, if I lower my arm, intentionally, at the speed with which it would fall, this will make a difference to the physiology of the nerve fibers. To this end, he has me operate a handle which will maintain some, otherwise, free-floating object at a certain level. If I lower my arm at the speed it would fall, this is indicated by fact that the object maintains its level, as I manipulate the handle. So I watch the object as I manipulate the handle, confident that as long as I keep the object level my arm is being lowered at the prescribed rate. It is important to keep in mind in attempting to understand this, seemingly, simple example that maintaining the floating object's level is not an action in and of itself.

Recall that the only real actions are actions we have been calling "basic actions," and the only real action in this sense is my arm movement, downward. Of this action I have little, if any, awareness. It is, also, critically important for understanding the point she makes to attend, carefully, to the differences between this case and the boat-pushing case. In the boat-pushing case, what I am immediately aware of is my pushing; what I am not, or need not be, aware of is the boat's going where I want it to go. I put it this way because the boat is going out, as I push it, but my intention is that the boat go out, not that it go out only as long as I push it. In the boat-pushing case, my intention may be erroneously believed to be the, ultimate, cause of the boat's going out; but in this new case the effect of my action (moving my arm at the speed it would fall) results from my intentionally keeping the floating object level, and, yet, this is the causal consequence of performing an action of which I am barely aware. Nothing, similarly, obtains in the example of pushing the boat.

The boat's going out is the intended consequence of an action with which I am immediately aware, the pushing. I push with the intention of getting the boat into the water. In the second case, I maintain the object at an even level with the intention of lowering my arm at the speed it would, otherwise, fall. I cannot "trace back" *from* my arm movement *to* maintaining the level of the floating object just as I cannot "trace back" to the issuance of a command to shut the door the bodily movements of shutting the door.

(cf. Anscombe [1983] p. 92) We shall have more to say about this, later. The point is that I cannot "trace back" to maintaining the object's being level in the way I might "trace back" *from* the movement of the boat *to* my pushing with that as the intended effect. The arm movement is what controls the level of the object, not the other way around. I do not move my arm with the intention of lowering it at the speed it would fall. I maintain the level of the object with this intention but this intention is not the cause of my lowering my arm at the speed at which it would, otherwise, fall. The cause is remote from the events responsible for my arm movement, whereas in the boat pushing case the cause of the boat's going out is not remote from the causes of my arm movement. There is a feature to this counterexample of Anscombe's that she does not mention, but of which she, almost, certainly was aware.

There is some question as to whether it can be said that I lowered my arm at the speed at which it would fall, intentionally. In fact, it may be argued that I didn't lower my arm intentionally, at all. The only description of what I'm doing derives from what I observe of the floating object. No description of my arm movement, itself, may be available to me. However, if this is so, then there is a question as to whether the action is intentional. In order to be intentional it cannot be the case that, if asked why I was doing it ("why" in the relevant sense), I, sincerely, were to reply "I didn't know I was doing that." But, if I didn't know under any description what I was doing with my arm, how could I be said to have been acting intentionally? However, if someone should ask, "Why did you move your arm down like that?" I might reply, "Oh, you see, I am in an experiment and I have to move it down at the speed with which it would fall."

On one account, my action is intentional; on the other, it is not intentional. Now I think there is a problem here. It has to do with the difference between a volition and an intention and the relation between the two. I have addressed it elsewhere. The main point Anscombe makes, and it would appear that she has succeeded, is that it is not, always, the case that when I trace back from an action to its causes I will find an intention at the other end. But if this is true, although we have indicated some reservation, then where is the intention to be found, if anywhere? If it is not in some train of causes leading up to the event, then where is it? Shouldn't we be tempted to deny its very existence? The source of the dilemma is in regarding an intention as an independent entity.

## SECTION 31: *KNOWLEDGE OF INTENTION IS NOT LIKE OUR KNOWLEDGE OF COMMANDS*

Belief that intentions are distinct from actions is, sometimes likened to commands as distinct from actions. (Anscombe [1983] p. 101) However, the fact that intentions may precede action is no basis for the claim that to be caused by an intention is what it means to act in satisfaction of an intention. Appearances to the contrary, such views lend credibility to the erroneous belief that intentions are like commands. Anscombe dispatches this comparison by revealing a disanalogy that goes to the heart of our knowledge of intentional actions. Compare (a) and (b) to (a') and (b'), respectively.

a) I'm replenishing the water supply
b) The water is running out of the pipe

a') Clench your teeth
b') My teeth are false

We might want to say that (a) stands to the order (a') as (b) stands to (b'). If we pursue this idea, then we can be made to see that the denial of

a) I am replenishing the water supply

is not

d) You are not replenishing the water supply, because the water is running out of a hole in the pipe.

If we were to hold steadfastly to the analogy, the denial of

a') Clench your teeth

would be

c') This man isn't going to clench his teeth, since they are false

But the contradiction of (a') is not (c'), rather it is (d')

(d')  Do not clench your teeth.

So if we pursue the analogy, the proper denial of (a) is not (b), but (d).

d)  Oh, no, you won't

uttered by someone who, then, makes a hole in the pipe.

As illuminating as the parallelism might be, says Anscombe, it fails to shed light on the problem of our knowledge of our intentional actions, since our description of our intentional actions takes the form of something we know, insofar as our actions are intentional, whereas a command is not knowledge.

## SECTION 32: *LISTS AND TWO KINDS OF ERROR: INTRODUCING PRACTICAL WISDOM*

It may appear to some that, at this stage of her discussion, Anscombe has departed, somewhat from the issue of "two knowledges" in pursuit of what appear to be other issues, such as the relation of intentions and causes, commands and intentions, and the possibility of error. But these are not, really, "other issues." There is a unity to be achieved in relating these notions to one, central, concern: the status of the difference between knowledge by observation and knowledge-in-intention. This section provides a bridge of sorts between understanding knowledge in intention and the Aristotelian notion of *practical wisdom*. For the first time in her discussion, the link between philosophical psychology and ethics is forged and never, subsequently, broken. To say there is a "bridge" created is not to say that there is a gap; the "bridge" is, merely, between psychology, and ethics, not between knowledge-in-intention and practical wisdom, for the latter two are inseparable. Her manner of creating this "bridge" is by way of an illustrative example, one that bears on later discussions, particularly, relevant to what came to be known as speech-act theory, *viz.* of "direction of fit," an expression, it is said, we owe to J. L. Austin, not Anscombe. This idea of "direction of fit" is not pursued for its own sake, but, rather, serves to introduce the notion of practical wisdom into the discussion of intention in a compelling way.

Imagine that my wife has given me shopping instructions in the form of a list. I go to the store and make my purchases. (Notice that the order of the purchases is irrelevant). With each purchase a relation is being set up between the list and a set of items. However, imagine that while I was shopping something else was going on: a store detective was taking note of the items I purchased. Now it is possible that either I, or the detective, err. We have two sorts of relations between the lists and the objects purchased, depending on whose list we are considering. In my case, that of the one doing the shopping, there is the relation created by the actual purchases, going from list to items purchased. In the case of the detective, the relation takes the opposite direction, going from purchases to list. There are two sorts of errors associated, respectively, with these two "directions of fit" between the list and the set of purchased items. Anscombe wants to deny the description "error" to cases where, e.g., I depart from the list because the item was unavailable. Her example is tackle for shark fishing. Once this is stipulated we can focus on two sorts of errors.

If there is a discrepancy between my list and the items purchased, then the mistake is mine. My mistake(s) is a performance error. But, if there is a discrepancy between what I purchased, and the detective's list, it is an error in the record, that is, in his list. It is important to suppress a certain class of errors in the case of the purchaser. For example, if I purchase a box of Wheaties and it turns out to contain Sugar Pops, then, even though the list does not match the items, I cannot be said to have acted in contradiction to the instructions. But suppose, while shopping, I say to myself "Now I buy Wheaties," and without looking I grab a box of Sugar Pops. This would be what Anscombe refers to as a "direct falsification" of "Now I buy Wheaties," a performance error. Such an error might be described by analogy, she remarks, as "obeying an order wrong." The fault is not with my utterance but, rather, in the event of my snatching up the wrong item.

It might be argued that the sort of error Anscombe identifies may be difficult to classify in certain cases. Let's entertain one example. Some people are unfamiliar with the convention that when a mechanic speaks of the right front tire he means the tire to the right of the driver as he sits at the driver's seat. Suppose someone familiar with the convention is in front of the car and instructs me to turn the wheels to the right. I, mistakenly, suppose that he means by "right" the direction to his right, rather than mine. In this case, it is not so clear that the error was in performance. The error may be one of judgment, insofar as I have misjudged the intention behind the command; that is, of getting me to turn the wheels to the "right." In the shopping case, I wasn't doing what I thought I was doing; but in the wheel-turning case I knew what I was doing; the mistake was in my understanding, not the performance. In neither case is my error an error in observation, as it would be in the case of the detective who thinks he sees me buy one thing, when in fact I've bought some other thing. This is a crucial difference that serves to shed light on the belief in two "knowledges." In the example we are now considering, the force of claiming that the driver has made a "mistake" cannot be alleged without qualification, that qualification being that the driver knew the convention. If the driver knew the convention, but got flustered, then the mistake would be in the performance. What is crucial, however, is the notion of "direct falsification" and how it relates to the problems we associate with defending "two knowledges." Anscombe has little to say on this; we turn our attention briefly to considering the matter a bit more fully.

There are two ways a shopper acting on a list can go wrong. First, he may get the wrong groceries, that is, groceries either not on the list that were purchased, or groceries that were purchased but were not on the list (although this is a more controversial case). Second, the shopper may directly falsify a statement of his own intention while executing the commands-to-buy which the list represents. Such a case arises where, e.g., he says "I now buy Wheaties" but picks out Sugar Pops. It was his intention to buy Wheaties; he had to have knowledge of his action in intention in order to know that he had falsified the statement he made to himself, "I now buy Wheaties." "Falsehood" is not a felicitous description of a performance error, as we shall discover, however. In order for the detective to falsify—and here "falsify" *is* the right word—what may be his own statement to the effect that the shopper is buying Wheaties involves only observation of the disparity between the list and what the shopper, actually, purchased, say Sugar Pops. In other words, in the shopper's case there are at issue two sorts of errors: first, not getting what his wife ordered and, second, not doing what he thought he was doing when he bought Sugar Pops. Knowledge of the first sort of error is observational knowledge, requiring only knowledge of what is on the list. In the second case, what is required in order to establish err is knowledge of what I intended to do, not just what I did do in fact. Both the detective and the shopper are dealing with the same sorts of things, items and lists, but the knowledge at issue may differ in each case. Moreover, executing an order that takes the form of a list pertains to practical knowledge, whereas the detective's knowledge of what I do is, entirely, observational. The idea of direction of fit, while it is not discussed, as such, by Anscombe, would become a topic of considerable interest among speech-act theorists, such as John Searle. Although it has been discussed in some detail by Searle, and others, "direction of fit" has, yet, to be fully absorbed into the discussion of semantics beyond the theory of human action. A concluding word on this useful notion and its relation to another concept we have, already, examined, viz. 'falling under a description' is not out of order.

Suppose we distinguish 'descripta' and 'descriptions', saying that, e.g., 'heavy' is a description, whereas an elephant might be its corresponding descriptum on some, particular occasion. The elephant may be said to "fall under" the description 'heavy'; but since a feather is not heavy, we might want to say that whether something is correctly said to be heavy depends on the descriptum: "It was heavy for a feather, but not heavy for an elephant." Here there is "direction of fit" in some sense where the direction runs from descriptum to description; the description's applicability is relative to the descriptum. But now take another case.

Davidson, as we have noted, says that an action is intentional relative to a description. There is no natural class of intentional actions; what counts as an intentional action is said to be relative to a description. The "direction" of fit is just the opposite of the first case; in *this* case the direction of fit runs from description to descriptum. Now whether "direction" of fit is the desired locution may be debated, but there is a "direction" to each of these two sorts of dependency. It seems likely, therefore, that making what counts as an intentional action relative to a description does not, fully, characterize the semantical features involved. In particular, such a characterization involves direction of fit from description to descriptum. Note that this is no mere truism in the sense that whether any description applies depends on whether that to which it is attributed has some property; for in the case of intentional action what is being denied is that there is a special property of intentionality to begin with. In this case, a description applies but only under *another* description, and this dependency in turn incorporates a "direction of fit" feature which is just the opposite of what we find in applying comparative adjectives.

Knowledge-in-intention relates to practical knowledge, and vice versa. Getting a hold on the relation of intention and practical knowledge will dominate most of what follows as Anscombe continues to pursue an understanding of intention.

# PART 5:
# Practical Wisdom

We see, then, that there are two "knowledges" pertaining to action. How we arrive at knowledge of what we ought to do, or what to do next, is frequently the *outcome* of a form of reasoning philosophers call "practical reasoning." If we think of our knowledge-in-intention, our non-observational knowledge of our actions, as such, then in such cases, where we reason to some conclusion as to what we believe to be best action, such reasoning is *practical*; and, so, understanding practical *reasoning* is an approach to understanding practical *knowledge*; similarly, we might come to understand non-observational *knowledge* in-intention through an understanding of practical *reasoning*. Anscombe fixes her attention on practical reasoning as she moves towards a greater understanding of our intentional actions. Her approach is guided by ideas first set forth in Aristotle, in particular Aristotle's conception of the *practical syllogism*.

Anscombe does not, merely, shadow Aristotle's thinking. She draws conclusions of her own, conclusions that clarify her distinction between the two "knowledges" of which we have spoken. What interests her, especially, is the matter of the difference between reasons and causes; her effort being to see that these two are kept apart. Recall that in describing his differences with the atomist, Democritus, Aristotle rejected making the movement of the body the result of movement of atoms. He insisted, against Democritus, that the origin of movement is not by way of the movement of other bodies, or atoms, but through intention and thinking. Aristotle says,

> *And, in general, we may object that it is not in this way that the soul appears to originate movement in animals—it is through intention or process of thinking.*
>
> — (Aristotle [*De Anima*] 406b23-25)

Our knowledge of our bodily movements *qua* intentional is not observational. The distinction between what is observational and what is not, and that between what is intentional and, what is not, begs the question of how the two categories, thus, distinguished are in fact related. The elucidation of this complex relation, largely, determines the direction Anscombe takes in her careful examination of Aristotle's views on these matters.

## *SECTION 33: ARISTOTLE'S PRACTICAL SYLLOGISM*

Understanding "practical reasoning" begins with understanding what Aristotle was talking about when he spoke of the "practical syllogism." A tempting metaphor in understanding the practical syllogism is that of a bridge that spans the distance between a want and a choice. A physician *wants* to cure his patient, something good; the way he goes about it will be his choice. When a physician deliberates on how to treat a patient, the desired result is a course of action determined by practical reason, i.e., reasoning which takes the form of a practical syllogism. Aristotle is emphatic in maintaining that we deliberate about *means* not ends. (Aristotle [*Nicomachean Ethic*] 1112b12-15) (Aristotle [*Eudemian Ethics*] 22-23) In the case of practical reasoning what we deliberate about must be something within our power to change. Such is not the case when our reasoning is theoretical or concerned with arriving at some true proposition. Practical reasoning, when it takes the form of the construction of practical syllogisms is part of the process of deliberation. For Aristotle deliberation and calculation are one and the same thing. (Aristotle [*Nicomachean Ethics*] 1139a12) Within the category of practical syllogisms there is an important distinction, although it is one that Aristotle, sometimes, appeared not to, strictly, observe.

This is the distinction between "technical" and non-technical syllogisms.

When a physician deliberates on what to do with a sick patient, his reasoning is unrelated to states of character viewed from the moral perspective. When the physician decides what he ought to do with a patient, this "ought" is a technical "ought," not an ethical "ought." It does not concern states of character. Nevertheless, it is given that the end, although it is not subject to deliberation, is itself something good. (Aristotle [*Eudemian Ethics*] 1227a25) The fundamental division with respect to practical syllogisms is that between the practical, and theoretical. While this is by and large accepted by Aristotle scholars, the subject is not without controversy. Anthony Kenny makes the distinction this way: he says that in the case of theoretical reasoning we move from "true to true," whereas in the case of practical reasoning we move from the good of something mentioned in the premises to a good conclusion, i.e., from "good to good." (Kenny [1979] p. 128) This may be something of an oversimplification. Even though a physician's reasoning is technical, the end towards which he works is assumed to be good from the very onset: the health of the patient. This may be regarded as something "external" to the validity of the practical syllogism, just as truth of the premises and conclusion are "external" to the validity of a theoretical or "proof" syllogism. (Anscombe [1974b] p. 146)

Earlier, when we discussed the concept "under a description," we had occasion to bring in "proof" syllogisms; that is, syllogisms that involve truth rather than action. Practical syllogisms, strictly, have actions as conclusions, rather than propositions. However, it is frequently maintained, Anscombe says, that ordinary practical reasoning requires syllogisms that lead from truths to truths, the truthful conclusions, taking the form of an imperative, such as in the following example.

*Everyone with money ought to give to a beggar who asks him.*
*This man asking me for money is a beggar*
*I have money*
*So, I ought to give this man some.*

Here we move from the truth of the premises to that of the conclusion, "I ought to give this man some." This may introduce some obscurity, by oversimplifying the nature of practical reasoning, at least insofar as Aristotle's view is concerned. In a, mildly, cynical remark on a tendency, among certain commentators on Aristotle's practical syllogism, Anscombe feigns surprise that no one has discussed the "mince pie syllogism":

> *All mince pies have suet in them*
> *This is a mince pie*
> *This mince pie has suet in it.*

The implication being that, if one is unwilling to distinguishing theoretical and practical syllogisms, he might as well declare one about pies, and regard it as no more distinct from other truth syllogisms than from those having to do with deliberating about actions having moral or ethical content. (cf. Mothersill [1962] p. 449)

If we accept the notion, as did Aristotle, that the two kinds of syllogisms, the practical and the theoretical, are of the same logical form, then we are faced with a problem, since if I fail to act on the basis of a valid practical syllogism I do not contradict myself, but if I believe the contradictory of a conclusion of a valid theoretical syllogism, then I *do* contradict myself. This asymmetry argues against regarding them as being of the same form. R. M. Hare (Hare [1952] p. 20) had maintained that it would be a "tautology" to assert that we *cannot* assent to a command but, then, add that we did not perform the action commanded. If we understand a tautology to be such that its denial is a contradiction, then there will be a problem, since there is no, logical, inconsistency in *asserting* that we assented to the command but did not perform the action commanded. The only recourse is an extended sense of 'inconsistency' or 'contradiction'.

If this should prove an unconvincing attack on Hare's position, then our case is best served by emphasizing this difference: whereas Hare says that a sentence $p$ entails $q$ if and only if a person who assents to $p$ but denies $q$ can be said to have "misunderstood" either $p$ or $q$, or both, the position, here, taken is that logical entailment will not suffice; that '$p$ entails $q$' is analytic if and only if affirming $p$, but denying $q$ is *evidence* of misunderstanding $p$ or $q$, or both. It is worth considering that the sense in which not performing the deduced action in the case of the practical syllogism, rather than the explicit command, may lead to "inconsistency" akin to the sort one encounters in the case of "Moore's Paradox" ("I believe $p$, but not $p$"). Some modern commentators, Anscombe remarks, would salvage the idea that the syllogisms are, essentially, of the same form by arguing that the practical syllogism should take imperatives, not actions, as conclusions. If the conclusion were 'Do $X$' and I didn't do $X$, then I would be guilty of 'inconsistency'. This solution, however, if Anscombe is right, leads to the problem of "insane" premises. As long as we conceive of the conclusion of a practical syllogism as an action, not an imperative, we escape having to accept the idea that practical reasoning requires observing the principle that an imperative *must* occur among the premises. (cf. Hare [1953] p. 28) This would tend to support the idea that there is no, fundamental, distinction between practical and theoretical syllogisms as long as we do not introduce imperatives.

At the time of her writing *Intention*, Anscombe regarded the theoretical, and practical syllogisms as differing significantly. In this respect, her view departed from Aristotle's. Later, however, she came to view them as very much alike. (Anscombe [1974b] p. 132) By this time, she had come to believe that the differences between them depended, merely, on the purposes they served. The belief that the two syllogistic forms are different, she claimed, has its roots in the belief that there is a psychological component, i.e. a "step" in one's reasoning that one is compelled to take in moving from premises to conclusion. Such a belief is at issue in her examination of Von Wright's position that the relation between premises and conclusion in the case of syllogistic reasoning is one of logical compulsion, rather than causation. While neither the idea that we act out of "respect" for the premises of a practical syllogism, nor that we are "logically compelled" by the premises to act in such and such a way, seems satisfying, one ought resist the temptation of treating the relation of premises to action as causal, merely as a default position, without substantial argument. What is at stake may very well turn out to be the "is/ought" distinction, itself. While there may be a sense in the case of the theoretical syllogism where belief is transmitted, by way of logic, from premises to conclusion, nothing similar is possible in the case of an alleged transmission of intentions along a path of syllogistic reasoning. (Anscombe [1974b] p. 135) As we have said the practical syllogism on the model of the commentators she criticizes in *Intention* may be thought of as leading from premises to conclusions which are imperatives and, so, neither indicative sentences nor actions immediately following from the premises. In order to appreciate this fact, let's consider Anscombe's discussion in *Intention*. We begin with a paradigm supplied by Aristotle:

> *Dry food suits any human.*
> *Such-and-such food is dry.*
> *I am human.*
> *This is a bit of such-and-such food.*
> *Therefore: This food suits me*

Anscombe compares this to something like the following:

> *Do everything conducive to not having a car crash.*
> *Such-and-such will be conducive to not having a car crash.*
> *Therefore: Do such-and-such.*

The second syllogism has an imperative, not a categorical, conclusion. Unlike the first syllogism, the second salvages the notion of a "middle term," viz. "to not having a car crash." There is no question in the second, unlike the first, whether action is to follow; action is, expressly, prescribed, although action is not, itself, the conclusion of the syllogism. In a sense, it possesses advantages over Aristotle's original formulation, although Aristotle, perhaps, would deny this. There is, nonetheless, a problem which casts a shadow over the plausibility of the second syllogism. The second syllogism would have us do *everything* conducive to not having a car crash. But this would include things like not driving at all; removing the tires from one's car and numerous other actions. This leads Anscombe to say that such premises are "insane." Aristotle, she remarks, must share part of the blame.

Notwithstanding Aristotle's belief that "proof" syllogisms and practical syllogisms are parallel in many respects, there is the difference that, according to him, demonstration (and, therefore, the syllogism) concerns what is invariant. Thus, the following construction is not a demonstration:

> *John will drive from Chartres to Paris at an average speed of 6 mph.*
> *He starts at five*
> *Paris is 60 miles from Chartres*
> *Therefore, he will arrive at about six.*

This is neither a scientific syllogism, since it concerns what may vary, e.g. John's time of arrival, nor is it a practical syllogism, insofar as it does not concern what John is to do. The syllogism contrasts with the practical syllogism, also, in that it moves from truthful premises to what *may* turn out to be a truthful conclusion—depending on whether, e.g., John decides to drive to Chartres at all. The *bona fide* practical syllogism is to be contrasted with what Anscombe refers to as the theoretical and the "idle practical syllogism." She takes, careful, note of the fact that Aristotle in his construction of practical syllogisms, which take action as the proper conclusion, shapes them, so to speak, in such a way that they resemble ordinary "proof" syllogisms. The following is one such example.

> *Vitamin X is good for all men over 60*
> *Pig tripes are full of vitamin X*
> *I am a man over 60*
> *Here are some pig tripes*

Notice that inasmuch as this purports to be a practical syllogism there is no apparent conclusion. But this is as it should be, since the conclusion is an action and not a proposition. However, Anscombe suggests that we suppose that, as the agent acts, he utters a corresponding sentence, such as "So I'll have some," that is, as he eats the tripe. The problem is that "So I'll have some" does not follow from the premises. It is possible, nevertheless, to construct other practical syllogisms where action is entailed. One such case would be where the following is taken as a premise,

> *It is necessary for all men over 60 to eat any food containing Vitamin X that they ever come across.*

But here, again, we have what Anscombe has, already, called an "insane" premise, as the man over 60 must eat any and all food containing Vitamin X, even if it contains something harmful. It is easy, enough, to see the similarity between this premise and the earlier one having us do anything and everything in order to avoid an accident, including such things as abandoning the car, etc. Notice that the universal "any food" follows an action verb, whereas in the original Aristotelian syllogism the universal ranges over men, "all men over 60." Such "insane" premises that involve us an entailment relation are not insane in cases of omission, however. In the case of

> *It is necessary for all men to avoid any food containing cyanide they ever come across.*
> *This food contains cyanide*
> *So, I'll avoid this.*

There is nothing insane about this line of reasoning. Still our deliberations, typically, concern what to do, not what not to do. The subject of "insane" premises resonated with Donald Davidson who took a closer look at this with a view to understanding the place of deduction in practical reasoning. We will benefit by examining how he approached the question. Before moving on to discuss Davidson's valuable remarks on "insane" premises, we ought to take note of an interesting consistency with respect to Anscombe's treatment of statements of causation and statements of intention.

We have seen that Anscombe considers 'Do everything conducive to not having a car crash' an "insane" premise because it would have the agent do *everything* conducive to not having a car crash. In her treatment of causality she, similarly, alleges that generalizations of the form 'Always, given an *A*, a *B* will follow' is never true, since we would have to qualify this with a statement that *everything* that would prevent its being true is absent. If this is to be non-trivial, an infinite number of exclusions would have to be cited. So in the case of "insane" premises we have insanity; and in the case of universal propositions of the sort related to causation we have, mere, falsehood. Although the cases differ, it seems clear that something similar is involved in both the causal case and the case of premises in a practical syllogism. If one thinks of the premises as causes of the conclusion construed as an effect, then the different cases begin to converge.

## *R. M. Hare and "Insane Premises"*

R. M. Hare was one of the great ethicists of the last century. He and Anscombe had the, frequent, opportunity to exchange ideas. On at least one occasion their disagreement was amusing. Prof. Aaron

Sloman, a well known researcher in the area of artificial intelligence, whose examiners for the DPhil were Anscombe and Geoffrey Warnock, recalls that Anscombe had remarked that, if you want something, you must want it for something. Hare retorted that if a person wants an orgasm he need not want it *for* something. This incident raises a, further, question: "If we try to get something, must we want it?" We know Anscombe believed that trying was the sign for wanting, but what about trying? Is it sufficient for attributing some want? This would appear to be the case. This was not the only occasion where sexual intercourse would become an object of humorous philosophical reflection. Ronnie de Sousa recalls, verbatim, something he heard from Anscombe. According to de Sousa:

> *Someone I know very well happened to fall asleep while engaged in fucking; and as he slept he dreamt that he was shoveling coal, and taking a great deal of pleasure in that activity. Then he woke up, and realized what he was really doing, and exclaimed: 'Good heavens, I was mistaken in the object of my pleasure.*

If we take our wants to be the objects of our pleasure rather than, say, their causes, then we might conclude from this that we can be mistaken about what we want, although, perhaps, we cannot be mistaken in believing that there is something we want.

While Anscombe rejects the idea of including within the premises of a practical syllogism a premise indicating the want that moves the action, she is not, as we have seen, adverse to the idea of including mention of some want that may be part of the reasoning. R. M. Hare shared Anscombe's antipathy for regarding wants as inner events, particularly, in the treatment of practical reasoning. In practical reasoning where wants are made explicit in the premises, such wants describe, not states of mind, but rather imperatives. In a sentence such as 'If you want to go to the largest grocer in Oxford, go to Grimbly Hughes' the term 'want' is to be regarded as an imperative, not the name of an inner state. In the proper formulation of a syllogism where imperatives are included among the premises, as they must be if the conclusion takes the form of a command, 'want' is the form the imperative may take. Thus, instead of 'If go to the largest grocer in Oxford, then go to Grimbly Hughes' one writes in ordinary English 'If you want to go to the largest grocer in Oxford, go to Grimbly Hughes'. In addition, the major premise can be relocated in stating an inference in such a way as to call attention to the minor premise.

Formulated in this way, irony may become instrumental in creating the desired effect of stating the syllogism. We begin with the following syllogism in order to illustrate how this effect is achieved.

> *Do whatever will conduce to breaking your springs*
> *Going on driving as you are at the moment will conduce to…*
> *Therefore, go on driving as you are at the moment.*

Suppose we wish to discourage the driver from driving as he is driving at the moment. We say 'If you want to break your springs, go on driving as you are at the moment'. In doing so we have done two things: first, we have introduced 'want' in a way that replaces 'Do'; and, second, we have moved the major premise 'Do whatever will conduce to breaking our springs' to the position of antecedent of a conditional. Emphasis on the minor premise, 'Going on driving as you are at the moment…', is achieved by calling attention to a premise which would rationalize the action, but which the driver, surely, rejects, viz. 'You want to break your springs'. (Hare [1952] p. 35] The sentence inspiring Anscombe's classification, 'insane premise', is 'Do *whatever* will conduce to breaking your springs'. It is not "insane" because no one wants to break their car springs; it is "insane" because it would have us to *everything* within our power to break those springs; e.g. having people jump up and down anytime they hit a bump etc. We will make three observations on Hare's employment of such premises.

First, although the occurrence of temporal predicates is eschewed in the formulation of scientific laws, this is not to exclude them *a priori* from contexts where the generalizations at issue occur in practical syllogisms. Suppose the premise were 'Do, *now*, whatever will conduce to breaking your springs'. If this were allowed would the premise be "insane," or as "insane" as the insanity that Anscombe believes is implicit, viz. doing *everything* at any time in order to break the springs? In addition, suppose the premise were 'Do whatever will *most* conduce to breaking your springs'. Wouldn't this mitigate the suggestion that in satisfying the command one must have a mania for breaking one's springs? Finally, since Hare's case is designed to introduce a special emphasis by way of irony, can we draw the sorts of conclusions about "insane" premises that Anscombe draws?

## Davidson and "Insane" Premises

One of the "insane" premises Anscombe, and Davidson, discuss is one Aristotle made use of in his exposition of the practical syllogism. From the premise 'Everything sweet ought to be tasted' and 'This is sweet' the action of tasting was said to follow. (Aristotle [*Nicomachean Ethics*] 1147a27-36) Aristotle was well aware that there could be conflicting opinions of a general nature leading to contrary actions. But in the case he discusses—the one having to do with eating sweet things—the incontinence of our action is owing to appetite, not faulty reasoning. The premises that say 'Don't eat anything harmful to health' and 'Eat everything sweet' are not, logically, contradictory. The poisoned thing is not, as a matter of logic, a sweet thing or vice versa. What conflicts with the one premise is the appetite that renders one "active." The rational course is, from the standpoint of the agent, rendered unintelligible "as a drunken man may mutter the verses of Empedocles." Davidson, however, proposes a different way of looking at this complex and controversial set of problems. Our sketch, the reader should note, is just that, only a sketch, and simplifies issues of incontinence, "weakness of the will," for purposes of getting at the core issues Anscombe and Davidson raise.

What Davidson notices is this: where the "desirability characterization" is assumed—from the condition that *whatever action is to be undertaken must be believed to have some desirable characteristic*, and the premise referring to the relevant particular (e.g. this is sweet)—the conclusion, that the action (of tasting this sweet stuff) is desirable, would follow, but only in a respect. The problem is that, given that there are other evaluative principles (such as 'It is never good to eat anything poison'), one and the same action may be both desirable and undesirable (since this stuff may be both sweet and poisonous). What Davidson proposes in order to avoid this inconsistency is that we reject the idea of evaluative principles—statements of the desirability condition—as universal generalizations, unqualified. Instead, we incorporate into the principle relativity to a certain respect, saying that actions are desirable insofar as they have a certain attribute but may be undesirable with respect to another. All that we can conclude is that an action is desirable in a certain respect; we cannot conclude from the "insane" premise ('Eat everything sweet') that insane actions—such as eating sweet poison—follow logically from practical reasoning. The judgment that something is desirable, relative to a given property, is a *prima facie* judgment. But it is not enough to justify an action.

We cannot by virtue of a deductive relation between premises, one stating the desirability condition, and another stating that a *particular* action is desirable, deduce an action (or imperative). The action may be desirable *only* in one respect and undesirable, perhaps, in many. What is required is a further judgment, one Davidson calls an "all out or unconditional judgment." (Davidson [1978] p. 98) Satisfaction of a single desirability condition, by Davidson's lights, is insufficient to judge an action to be desirable. We can, under the conditions set by the original formulation of the practical syllogism, conclude that this action, say, is desirable insofar as it is the ingestion of something sweet; but we cannot deduce, logically, that this action is desirable, *simpliciter*. An agent, typically, does not deduce his action from satisfaction of a single desirability condition made explicit by the premise of a practical syllogism. Instead, there is a weighing process involving numerous attributes, both desirable and undesirable, one that eventuates in some final resolve. This is not to say that a single syllogism will not suffice in order to deduce an action in every case. If the desirability characterization is sweeping, that is, if it unconditional and "all-out," there is no, real, difficulty with this. A pure intention, simply enough, just *is* an "all-out" judgment! (Davidson [1978] p. 99). Arriving at the "all-out" judgment by weighing all the available desirability characterizations is part of *forming* that intention.

When I act on an intention, the intention can be made explicit only by dispensing with all the conditions that must be *assumed*. That I can't make the intention explicit by citing all possible qualifications can be made clear by example. Suppose I say "I will be there if I don't get stopped for a traffic violation." Well, this is still incomplete, because in order to make the intention, completely, explicit, I must add other conditions; e.g. 'I will be there if I don't get stopped for a traffic violation or unless the car doesn't start or…" The point is that the most accurate statement of my intention in fact does not introduce causes for doubt that are not included in my beliefs about the immediate future, or about the future that includes my intended action. In other words, it is not required in order to avoid "insane" premises that I add an infinite number of conditions ruling out an action's being both desirable and undesirable. Pure intentions for Davidson will turn out to be all-out judgments of a sort (Davidson [1978] p. 102); Anscombe will use 'intention' where Aristotle will use 'choice'. At first, one is impressed by the differences among these three philosophers. The fact is, however, that they are drawn together by a common interest in practical reasoning as affording some basis for arriving at some understanding of the nature of intention. Let's conclude our discussion of this Section with a couple of historical remarks.

Kant identified practical reasoning with the Will. (Kant [1967] p. 76] While wants (and beliefs) may determine the practical syllogism explaining why we do what we do, wants can be technical or non-technical. Those which are not technical, if Kant is right, are introduced, not necessarily by mere empirical technical considerations, but moral principal. What is the role of morality in the determination of the will as opposed to technical interests? Anscombe maintained that "there is no such thing as a 'choice' which is *only* technical." (Anscombe [1965a] p. 68)] Later, the moral content of all practical reasoning comes, increasingly, to the forefront.

## SECTION 34: *WANTS AND PRACTICAL REASONING*

Recall our earlier mention of theoretical or "proof" syllogisms. One standard example is

> *All men are mortal*
> *Socrates is a man*
> *Therefore, Socrates is mortal*

Anscombe pointed out that Aristotle in his discussion of practical syllogisms tried to retain as much of the proof syllogism as possible in stating the logic of the practical syllogism. Notwithstanding this fact, she introduces syllogistic reasoning that appears, significantly, different from the practical syllogisms she has so far been discussing, although as we have, already, noted she, later, came to modify her view of Aristotle on this very point. Nevertheless, consider the following syllogism.

> *I want a Jersey cow*
> *There are good ones at Hereford Market,*
> *So, I'll go there.*

In this case, instead of beginning with something that we ought to do, or what we believe is good for us, such as 'Vitamin X is good for all men over 60', the actual starting point is something wanted. Aristotle requires that all practical reasoning begin with a desire. Anscombe, however, introduces an intriguing example. We are to consider a teacher engaged in teaching some theorem in geometry, say, about the properties of an isosceles triangle. For pedagogical reasons she makes, temporary, but deliberate use of faulty proofs. Her reason for doing this may be that she does not care to enter into a discussion of such things as the axiom of parallels, non-Euclidean geometry etc. So what is it that the teacher wants, exactly? Surely, it is not to impart a faulty knowledge of geometry. But, if not, then what? Imagine that the teacher is forthright, claiming that her desire is, simply enough, to earn her pay. Insofar as what she aims at is that "with a view to which she" teaches this faulty information, to this extent, it is beyond any "break" similar to the one that interrupted us back in Section 23. Since it is her wish (or want) to earn her salary, that goal is not attained in the sense that her want persists; that is, it goes unsatiated or unsatisfied. The comparison with the "break" in Section 23 is this: just as while it was the case, there, that in moving one's arm the pumper pumped, and in pumping he poisoned, it was not the case that he succeeded in bringing into being the Kingdom of Heaven by moving his arm up and down. Similarly the teacher did not satisfy her desire for pay in teaching students faulty proofs. It has been noted that Aristotle believed that all practical reasoning begins with something wanted, but, clearly, there are practical syllogisms that do not include premises making such wants *explicit*. What are we to make of this? To this question Anscombe turns next.

## SECTION 35: *WANTING AS THE STARTING POINT OF A PRACTICAL SYLLOGISM*

The distinction between a theoretical syllogism and a practical syllogism, at first, does not seem difficult to make. The mark of a practical syllogism, as we have seen, is that it is about action. There is a more subtle distinction one might attempt to make, however, between practical syllogisms which concern ethical conduct, and others which concern desired ends lacking moral content. There is no way of drawing this distinction based on the content of a syllogism's universal premise. Anscombe lists the universal premises of the four forms of the practical syllogism provided by Aristotle. Consider examples of major premises for each of these forms.

a) Dry food suits any man
b) [I] should taste everything sweet
c) Anything sweet is pleasant
d) Such a one should do such a thing

We shall follow Anscombe's lead in concentrating on formulation (d). Let's begin by citing the passage from Aristotle she has in mind.

> *The faculty of knowing is never moved but remains at rest. Since the one premise or judgment is universal and the other deals with the particular (for the first tell us that such and such a kind of man **should** do such and such a kind of act, and the second that this is an act of the kind meant, and I a person of the type intended), it is the latter opinion that really originates movement, not the universal; or rather it is both, but the one does so while it remains in a state more like rest, while the other partakes in movement.*
>
> — (Aristotle [*De Anima*] 434a15-23)

What is important is that in this schematized account of the practical syllogism Aristotle is not using 'should' in a way prescribed by ethical discourse; that is, it carries no ethical content as such. Anscombe is critical of Aristotle for offering a "futile mechanistic theory," presumably since the conclusion follows automatically in the form of an action. In introducing Aristotle we made clear his differences with Democritus. We remarked that the agent's thoughts and intentions were the source of action, not atomistic causes. With this in mind the reader cannot be blamed for feeling some uncertainty over Anscombe's use of "mechanical." She is attributing a sort of causation between the agent's thoughts and the agent's action in the context of a practical syllogism. It would appear that "mechanical" is a deliberate alternative to "causal," precisely because she is aware of Aristotle's view regarding the atomists' theory of causation. But what, then, is she getting at? Or is it so obvious that we ought not to make a fuss? The question goes much deeper than some may suspect. We shall address these matters briefly. Figuring out what Anscombe's view is will require at least briefly examining some ideas set forth by von Wright. Von Wright urged that the relation between premises and conclusion, insofar as that conclusion is an action, is a relation of logical compulsion, not causation. (Von Wright [1972] pp. 39-53)

As we have, already, mentioned, Anscombe insists that practical reasoning begins with something that is wanted. She will proceed to discuss why, then, what is wanted is not explicitly mentioned in the premises of all practical syllogisms. Practical reasoning may originate with a desire or something wanted. We have spoken of the satiation of a want. Ordinarily, we know what we want before we act. This much seems clear. What is not so clear is at what point we cease to want. As the action results in changes that "make" the world conform to the desire that motivates it, there is a point beyond which such a desire will not carry us. We may want to raise employee wages, but there is a point beyond which we might not care to go. If we set in motion mechanisms that raise wages there is a point beyond which the consequences of our actions may go further than our intention, such as when wage levels affect effect unemployment levels, adversely, etc. As Aquinas once said,

> *But in the action of every agent, a point can be reached beyond which the agent does not desire to go...*
>
> — (Aquinas [Summa Theologica] p. 430)

But can it be said that if we don't know that "point" *before* we act, then we don't know *what* we want? And isn't it one thing to go "beyond" what we want and, yet, another to do something without that want figuring into the picture? Anscombe makes no note of the fact that there are different mechanisms that come into play in reasoning about our actions when these deliberations concern particular consequences, immediate and otherwise, of such actions. Before continuing our discussion of what for Anscombe was the place of wanting in describing practical reasoning we shall, briefly, digress in order to discuss an issue she doesn't raise, viz. the idea of action as a process rather than an event.

## *Actions as Processes*

Adjusting our future actions to accommodate the consequences of an immediately preceding action involves discretion as an aspect of one's process of deliberation. The more complex the action—compare raising one's arm and Anscombe's example of poisoning the people in the building—the more typically it can be said to "progress" towards the objective set by the intention. This progressive action is, frequently, a function of cognitive awareness of the observed outcome of the immediately preceding action. In other words, when our actions are a response to the result of previous action in pursuit of satisfaction of a single want, what we want with respect to the immediate future as part of fulfilling our original intention develops. Such "wants" are associated with the performance of the action required to satisfy the motivating desire rather than that motivating desire itself. What I want at a particular stage of the completion of an action, one that can be viewed as a process, and what I intend to do are in *one* sense not syllogistically related: there is a dynamic component to action involving consideration of immediately preceding events related to achieving what is wanted.

This dynamic component compels the integration of volitional and cognitive elements. The point, and it is one that *neither* Anscombe nor Aristotle take note of, is that wants may guide actions but, where actions are related in a "dynamic" process, what we "want" in the sense relevant to basic actions is not determined by practical reasoning; that is, there is a relation among wants associated with basic actions, actions which are willfully produced in the performance of a non-basic action and which are of the nature of a process. Although these "wants" connected to basic actions are not part of the discussion of the practical syllogism, and may be likened, but not identified with what have been called "volitions, they figure in the satisfaction of our intentions, even when these intentions are the upshot to deliberation taking the form of a practical syllogism. Although Anscombe does not acknowledge, or discuss, them, their inclusion in a complete theory of action is unavoidable. For now, let's return to the point where we said that for Anscombe there is nothing essentially ethical about the practical syllogism.

## *Wants Not Included in a Practical Syllogism*

It is typical of an Aristotelian practical syllogism that, while the first premise, e.g., 'Dry food suits any man' mentions something desired or desirable, e.g., dry food, and may occur as a premise of a practical syllogism, the fact that it is wanted is not mentioned in the syllogism at all. The first premise, merely, informs us as to *what* it is that is wanted. The assumption behind the syllogism is that what is wanted, and what is intended in getting it, will, somehow, benefit the agent. (Anscombe [1974b] p. 116) But, suppose, that the person whose practical reasoning the syllogism represents is not the person whose want is to be satisfied. Suppose, e.g., that someone consigns himself voluntarily, or otherwise, to the status of a servant or slave. In such a case, it is reasonable to ask whose wants are subject of the syllogism, and how such wants relate to the agent who wills the action. These are difficult questions. We shall, briefly, discuss some attempts at answering them, as well as some remarks on the subject by Sir Anthony Kenny. It will be Anscombe's position that, if we include wanting in the first premise of the practical syllogism, we obscure the fact that the premises show *what* good would follow upon performance of the action inferred. (Anscombe [1974] p. 144) Wanting no more belongs to practical *reasoning* than the goodness of the sought after end. Just as truth of the premises is "external" to the validity of our reasoning so, too, the goodness of the end we seek is "external" to practical reasoning, when it takes the form of a practical syllogism. (Anscombe [1974] p. 146) Now if wanting is independent of practical reasoning, as such, then there is, as we have noted in the case of one who makes himself subservient to another, the possibility that the want may belong to one person, whereas the reasoning and, subsequent, action belongs to another, viz. the "slave." Before discussing the slave-case, one seeming difference between theoretical and practical syllogisms persists in those cases where the conclusion is an action. In the case of theoretical syllogisms, I can, always, take the conclusion of one syllogism and add it to the premises of another. But where in the case of the practical syllogism we take as our conclusion some action, we cannot create a chain of premises derived from conclusions of other syllogisms, since the conclusions are actions. Whether this difficulty, if it is one, can be obviated by taking imperatives as fundamental is something to be considered, notwithstanding whatever we may take as being "internal" or "external" to the syllogism itself.

Since the want reflected in the action of the slave is not the slave's own, it stands to reason that the want that drives the action does not belong to the reasoning of the slave, and, if this is the case, the wanting does not belong to the slave's practical reasoning. The conclusion, however, that wanting does not belong to reasoning leading to action lacks clarity. The slave, himself, may be acting on a different want, viz. the want that says "I want to avoid trouble with the master." Indeed, the slave may be operating with premises he does not, himself, believe but which are, he thinks, believed by the master. So it would appear that there is wanting here, despite the want not belonging to the agent. Does this present a problem? Almost certainly not. In either the case, where the want driving the action is the master's or the slave's, still, the want is not stated in the premises of the practical syllogism. Without disagreeing with Anscombe on these matters, Kenny issues some positive proposals.

For Kenny, just as when we reason we attempt to move from the truth of premises to the truth of a conclusion so, too, we attempt to move from good to good in practical reasoning. The slave may neither believe the premises upon which he operates, nor share the wants of the master; but, where this is the case, the proper characterization, according to Kenny, is one describing the situation as moving from *hypothetical* truths to hypothetical truths or from *hypothetical* good to hypothetical good. (Kenny [1979] p. 128). He adds to Anscombe's claim that, were proofs not to occur in some *believing* mind, there would be no point to reasoning; similarly, in the absence of a *desiring* mind reasoning would, also, lack a point.

One is tempted to paraphrase Kant, and say that in the context of practical reasoning desires without beliefs are empty, and beliefs without desires are blind. There are, of course, other permutations. We must take care not to forget that neither wanting, nor believing in any combination can be identified with choice, and that it is choice that is most, immediately, related to intention.

An animal may want something without deliberating, but a choice insofar as it is, or reflects, an intention is something upon which we deliberate. This deliberation, this calculation, is not something we want. Wanting and choosing are two different things. What we choose is what we think we "should" do, as a means of getting what we want. It might be said, then, that in a sense volition (the wanting) and intention (the choice) are two things. Volition concerns ends; intention, insofar as it involves choice, concerns means. The history of the theory of action is replete with confusion, and lack of coherence, largely linguistic, regarding how the two are related, but the question as to how they are related is fundamental. What is, specifically, to be addressed is the place of our wants in the context of our deliberative reasoning, where this reasoning is practical and syllogistic.

Although there is nothing ethical entailed, or implied, by Aristotle's use of 'should' in characterizing the practical syllogism, the practical syllogism is said to begin with something wanted; we have been calling it "a want" for short. But if all syllogistic reasoning of the practical sort involves a want, why is it that practical syllogisms lack a single premise containing *reference* to this want? Recall the syllogism discussed in Section 34, the one beginning with the premise 'I want a Jersey cow'. What is wrong, then, with including such a premise? The problem, as Anscombe sees it, with explicit want-statements as premises in a practical syllogism, is that they are misleading. If we take the example of the Jersey cow, we must take care that we not regard the move from 'I want a Jersey cow' to 'I will go to the market' as requiring some form of reasoning.

With this in mind, Anscombe takes up a different example in making her, next, point. Were I to say 'He killed my father *so* I shall kill him' there would be no *reasoning* applied in moving from his killing my father to my stated intention to kill the man who killed my father. In this sentence, "so" operates as a conjunction, and nothing more. In particular, "so" is in this instance a coordinating conjunction, as in 'My health is good, so I could settle down' just as 'and' is, similarly, a coordinating conjunction in 'My health is excellent and I could settle down'. (Curme [1931] p. 291). Although no calculation is explicit, there are cases where such a coordinating conjunction can take a use that implies calculation: "I would go to heaven I were your son, so you could love me, Hubert' (Shakespeare *King John*, IV, 1, 23). Here "so" indicates a clause of "modal result." (Curme, [1931] p. 288). But when is 'so' indicative of calculation? It is important to keep this in mind as we consider a requirement insisted upon by Anscombe.

Anscombe insists that whether there is calculation depends on the object of the want, and that depends on the description under which it is aimed at. Let's consider her example: "He was pleasant, so I shall pay him a visit." One is inclined to say that my paying him a visit is a return for his pleasantry. When I say, therefore, "He was pleasant…how shall I make a return…I will pay him a visit," in this case we have calculation. But why say *this*? Everything depends on the description under which 'return' is the object of my wish. In this example, where the description might be 'a fitting response to hospitality' "so" does not imply a calculation, whereas in case the description is something like 'a pleasant experience'—that is, the description under which the wish for a "return" is an object of my want—then what we have *is* a calculation. We see, then, that making explicit reference to a want may obscure whether what is involved is practical reasoning, or merely a polite gesture. At this point, we return to the case of the slave who acts on the want of his master, for this is a fertile area of inquiry, one that with important consequences for ethics and well as general philosophy.

## *Incontinence and the Division of Responsibility*

Hume believed that reason was the slave of the passions. Plato held the opposite view. (Plato [Protagoras] 352d) The conflict between reason and passion is brought to the forefront of ethical discussion in the debate over the best way to account for "weakness of the will" (*akrasia*). In the simplest case, this is where a man forsakes the dictates of his rational deliberation in favor of satisfying his appetite. (Aristotle [Nicomachean Ethics] 1145b10-15) Socrates held that perceptual knowledge is not *real* knowledge and that the incontinent man errs in thinking that he possesses perceptual knowledge when he does not. Even if the man possesses knowledge, he does not act on his knowledge. (Aristotle [Nicomachean Ethics] 1135b30-35). Aristotle does not, actually, contradict Socrates. The story, and the analysis that goes with it, is detailed and ongoing. We must, radically, abbreviate our account.

The, fundamental, question is how an agent can deliberate and arrive at a conclusion based on reasoning, syllogistically, and then go on to do the wrong thing, i.e., contrary to what is dictated by the conclusion of a valid argument. One approach is to say the incontinent man is carried away by his passion; one might, also, argue that he is like a drunk man who mutters, senselessly, say, the second premise of the practical syllogism, affected as he is by his passions. (Aristotle [*Nicomachean Ethics*] 1147b10-15) Although the account I have given must fall short of providing all that is needed for any final resolution of the difference, if any, between these approaches, it is adequate to our present purpose. It is introduced because few, if any, have noticed that the puzzle associated with the slave, the puzzle we discussed above, is related to this very issue.

We had been discussing Anscombe's rejection of the idea that the want that moves us in drawing the syllogistic conclusion is included among the premises. In the case of the slave this seemed to be certified by the fact that the want did not belong to the reasoning agent but to the slave. The wanting, therefore, appeared to be something "external" to the syllogism's premises. But suppose we consider the problem of incontinence (*akrasia*) as one where the agent as slave, and as master, are not discrete; that is, not entirely discernible. That is, suppose we imagine that *qua* appetitive creature the agent thinks one way, while *qua* rational agent reasons another way. In a sense, the agent becomes a slave unto himself, and it is this fact that provides the basis for any account of his incontinence. Sometimes the problem of incontinence is couched in terms of competing wants or competing syllogisms. This would be to suggest that there might be, say, two competing wants, both "external" to the syllogism(s). But how could inconsistent wants belong to the same person at the same time? The problem, at first, appears intractable. There is, however, another option: we might bifurcate not the desires, wants, or syllogisms; rather, we may take the tact of dividing the self. This possibility is explored and defended by Davidson.

If we accept the idea that wants are "external" to the syllogism, then we may be hard put to relate the master's wants and the slave's wants in any rational way. We may be compelled to accept the idea that the master *causes* the slave to adopt certain premises, induced by the demands of the master. Davidson argues (Davidson [1982] p. 303) that only by "partitioning the mind" can we overcome the inconsistency of certain "paradoxes of irrationality," incontinence we include among these. Only by doing so can we relate mental states involved in reasoning that leads to irrational action causally, noting, all the while that they are not related by way of reasons. Anscombe does not have this option available, if for no other reason than that she does not acknowledge the existence of a self to be divided in the first place, at least insofar as it is the referent of 'I'. (Anscombe [1974c]) We cannot resolve, or even describe in appreciable detail, the issues at stake, or how Anscombe might address the possibility under discussion. The point to be raised is that the matter of the relation of slave to master and that of reason and passions, affords us the opportunity to grasp, more firmly, the issue of the relation of reason and causes originating in Anscombe.

## *The Difference Between Theoretical and Practical Syllogisms*

Throughout *Intention*, Anscombe resists Aristotle's tendency to regard theoretical, and practical, syllogisms as one and the same. However, later, while addressing von Wright's views on practical inference, she takes a radical step away from this position. She admits that, previously, she had considered practical and theoretical reasoning as "completely different." (Anscombe [1974b] p.132) But, at this, later, stage in her development, the difference is seen to be, merely, one of the order in which the premises occur, and mood. The practical syllogism takes the form:

> Let it come about that $p$
> If $q$, then $p$
> If $r$, then $q$
> Decision $r$! ("Let it come about that $r$")

On the theoretical side, we have the correlative syllogism

Suppose *r*
If *r* then *q*
If *q* then *p*
Therefore, *p*

What leads people astray in thinking these two forms to be, fundamentally, different is that they conceive of there being a difference between a "step" in logic and a "step" in practical reasoning. This, however, is a mythical difference. Notice that in the first example, that of practical reasoning, the relation established by logic is one between "fiats," viz. "*Let it* come about that *p*" and "*Let it* come about that *r*." In the second case, the relation is one between indicative statements. The "reasoning," setting aside order and mood, is one and the same.

## SECTION 36: *WANTING AND ITS PLACE IN REASONING*

Wanting differs from wishing, says Anscombe, at least insofar as wanting is restricted to present or future objects, or states of affairs. It makes no sense to say 'I want President Hoover to help repeal the Smoot-Hawley Tariff'. The reason is that President Hoover no longer exists, and the Smoot-Hawley Tariff is not longer law. I can, however, *wish* that President Hoover had vetoed the Smoot-Hawley Tariff. While the "primitive expression" of a wish is 'Ah, if only...!" that of a want is *trying to get*. Much of what Anscombe says about wants or 'want' pertains to a more general discussion of what have been called 'propositional attitudes' and, in particular, the interaction of such "attitudes" and the scope of "particles" of language such as 'exists'. This topic is expansive, encompassing the conceptual distance between natural language syntax and the formalization of structures found in natural language syntax. A well known paradigm of such a formalization can be found in Russell's Theory of Descriptions, a theory that Anscombe will consider in analyzing statements about wants. (Russell [1905]) The idea of *trying to get* as the primitive expression of wanting is anticipated by Kant, a philosopher for whom Anscombe has little use. Thus, in the *Critique of Practical Reason* while discussing the basis of one's choices, Kant remarks that "the faculty of desire is determined to seek its realization." (Kant [1956] p. 19)

We have just seen that 'wish' is less restricted, tense-wise, than 'want', for 'wish' can apply to present, past, and future (cf. 'I wish you would stop glowering at my watch-dog'), while 'want' is restricted to present and future. There is the sense of 'want', says Anscombe, which describes, merely, a "prick of desire." Let's consider an example of the sort of thing Anscombe, probably, had in mind. Suppose I see a gold Cadillac driving down the street. I think to myself 'Gee, I'd like to have one of those'. Now, while I may "want" one, it is doubtful that I will go out and try to acquire one, given that I can, barely, afford a Schwinn bicycle. If I were, however, very wealthy and wanted to impress my poor relations, I might say, aloud, "I hope I get one of those things by Christmas!" In this case, increased likelihood has made 'hope' suitable, whereas before it was not. If it should be the case that when I say "I hope I get…" I mean that I hope to buy one of those things, that's one thing, but if I mean "I hope I get one of those things for Christmas" that is, yet, another. In the former case, I must act, but in the latter case my hope implies no action on my part. Anscombe is explicit: her interest is in wanting, not wishing or hoping nor, even, in the "prick of desire."

*Trying to get*, as we have seen, is the primitive expression, according to Anscombe of wanting, wanting in the sense she contrasts with 'wish' and 'hope'. It is attributable only to beings capable of having sensations, and, if she is right, it can be said, more generally that describing knowledge depends on describing volition. By 'volition' she means a voluntary action, what is known without observation in-intention. She goes, even, further, saying that the "ascription" of knowledge goes together with that of volition. This connection between sensation and volition is given concrete expression. Inspired by the story of the pharaoh Psammetichus, she invites the reader to consider color terms as we learn and, eventually, apply them. Psammaetichus, it may be recalled, isolated a child from language users to see what language would emerge in the absence of normal exposure to language use. Based on the similarities of certain sounds, and existing languages, Psammetichus inferred the innateness of language. Anscombe draws from this, by analogy, and proposes to consider a variation of the experiment in which adults use language in the presence of the child but not in interacting with the child. The outcome, she suggests, would be this: the child will use color terms to identify objects, not colors; in particular, the child will use color terms in picking out colored objects based on color. This "picking out" is volitional; the attribution of sensations of red, say, depend on attributions of "picking out." Anscombe's view is close to Peter Geach's position on the matter.

Peter Geach, who wrote *Mental Acts* at about the same time Anscombe wrote *Intention,* alleged that sensory *concepts* are not primary, and that, epistemologically, they are more fundamental than sensory *terms.* (Geach [1957] pp. 41-42). This coheres with Anscombe's rejection of inner ostentions of sensory qualities and her belief in the force of Wittgenstein's argument against private languages. It is interesting that, whereas Kant's philosophy delved deeply into the relation of thought and sensibility, Anscombe probed the relation of sensibility and action. The relation of sensation to action in contexts of *trying to get* is manifest in the simple example of the dog whose sense of smell "tells him" that there is a piece of meat on the other side of the door. He scratches at the door; there is movement towards the thing he wants and a belief, informed by sensation, that there is something on the other side that he desires. The example is, admittedly, primitive but note how sensation and action are united in *trying to get.* Anscombe will take a leap forward in relating action and wanting when she moves to the human case. She looks at sentences like 'I want a Jersey cow' and asks questions about how we are to describe such wants in connection with action. More precisely, she will address a difficulty in determining the logical status of expressions such as 'a Jersey cow' in terms of Russell's Theory of Description; then, then she will draw back from Russell's theory, somewhat, introducing the important idea of a sentence "becoming true." Thus, a link is forged between *trying to get* and "becoming true."

The logical difficulty with referring terms such as 'a Jersey cow' in "I want a Jersey cow', resides in what logicians call 'scope', a notion Russell exploits and which has been the source of much excitement in philosophy of logic. The expression 'a Jersey cow' is an *indefinite* description, whereas 'the Jersey cow' is a *definite* description. All we are concerned with, here, is indefinite descriptions. Before proceeding, a terminological note is in order: Anscombe will follow Russell in his early work by using 'it is not always false' for 'sometimes it is true'. Logicians have contended that 'some' and 'not all are not' are, extensionally, equivalent. We will simplify our discussion by speaking in terms of 'some'. Now let us return to what the "difficulty" alleged in the case of terms such as 'a Jersey cow'.

Consider the sentence 'I want a cow in the garden'. Occurring in this sentence is the expression 'I want a cow'. But, as long as we understand the sentence as not referring to a particular cow, we must contend with how it is to be interpreted, logically. There is a problem that arises owing to an ambiguity, a syntactical ambiguity. We may mean by the sentence either that there is some, particular, cow I want, or that I want a cow, where in this latter case I don't mean some, particular, cow. What is, absolutely, fundamental to understanding Anscombe's point in engaging the following logical exercise is that there may be no cow *in* the garden at the time of utterance.

We do not say there is some cow I want, but it does not exist. Just as there may be no cow in the garden, and yet I want one, so too, I may have an intention to produce a fact in the world that does not, yet, exist. As Davidson would latter observe, an intention may remain pure, that is, it may exist only in intention, just as the cow I want to get may exist only in intention without being any *particular* cow. We cannot, Anscombe says, rely on a Russellian introduction of belief where the indefinite description takes "wide scope." If we did, then we would have it that a sentence such as 'A believes there is a cow in the garden' means 'There is some x such that x is a cow and A believes x is in the garden'. It would be as if to say that from 'John wants a wife' we can, logically, infer that there is some wife that John wants. Suppose a cat is poised in front of a mouse hole. We might say "The cat is waiting for a mouse." What we *need not* mean is that there is some mouse which is, perhaps, an old acquaintance of the cat and for whom the cat is waiting. However, without pretending to know what goes on in the mind of a cat, Anscombe's position remains, somewhat, unconvincing. After all, in the case of the cat, as we have said, the cat may, indeed, be waiting for a particular mouse. There is no, ostensible, reason for thinking this is impossible. Still, her case is on reasonably firm ground in other instances. Return now the fellow who wants a wife. Without saying how she arrives at her position, Anscombe maintains that what we must say is: 'He wants 'someone is my wife' to *become* true'. This notion of becoming true ties in with what she says latter about *making true*. I want a cow; my desire may be satisfied by any cow (as long, perhaps, as it is a Jersey cow). But when by the agent's actions he bring into being some fact that makes the sentence 'I have a wife' true is it the case that the intention is satisfied?

At first it seems obvious that it must, but if John wants a wife, even though he has no wife in mind, is his want satisfied by taking *any* wife in the way I *may* be satisfied by having any (healthy) cow in the garden? Does the desire get satisfied along with the intention of finding "a wife"? Wants are not intentions, but does fulfilling the intention satisfy the desire? This and other questions are not discussed. What is important is this: When we are talking about a future state in the present—in intention—we are talking about an "idea." We seem to be moving in the direction of the "idea-idea" we encountered in James. While Anscombe tells us much else, she never discusses what, *exactly* she means *by* "idea." The Cartesian waters run deep, even in the work of those who prefer "desert landscapes" (Quine).

## SECTION 37: *DESIRABILITY CHARACTERIZATIONS*

One restriction on the admissibility of premises of a practical syllogism is that the premise containing reference to what the agent wants must in some way describe what is wanted as desirable, the "desirability condition." To see what it is return to an earlier argument:

I want a Jersey cow
There are good ones at Hereford Market,
So, I'll go there.

The first line has no place in a practical syllogism. The role of wanting is not to validate the rationality of a syllogism but, rather, to supply a motive for action following valid inference where the conclusion is an action. This much we learned in Section 35 (Anscombe [1957] p. 66). The role of wanting in the argument is not satisfied by some reference to it occurring in the premises of a practical syllogism. What is required of the premises is that one, at least, answer the question "Why do you want X," where in this example "a Jersey cow" substitutes for "X." In other words, the thing wanted must be desirable and this must show in the premises. Let's reconstruct the above syllogism to specifications. Begin with answering the question why the agent wants a Jersey cow.

> *Any farmer with a farm like mine could do with a cow of such-and-such qualities.*

*A Jersey is such a cow*
*Therefore, any farmer with a farm like mine could do with a Jersey cow.*

We now have it that the reason the agent wants a Jersey cow is that any farmer with a farm like his *could do* with a Jersey cow. The questioning goes no further. We do not ask 'What do you want "what you could do with" for?' The argument, now, might be read this way:

*Any farmer with a farm like mine could do with a Jersey cow.*
*There are good ones at Hereford Market,*
*So, I'll go there.*

We leave it at this for purposes of making clear how we have moved from including the want-statement as premise to a sentence that satisfies what we're calling the "desirability condition." But now a further question arises: Is it not the case that for any want we can construct a, satisfactory, desirability condition can be stated? An example will clarify the issue.

Anscombe considers an amusing case. Imagine that someone says he wants a saucer of mud. Suppose we ask him, "*Why* do you want a saucer of mud?" and imagine that the reply goes something like this: "Oh, I don't want it for anything; I just want to possess a saucer of mud." This, she says, is nonsense. We have been supposing all along that *trying to get* is the primitive sign of wanting. Can I try to get anything it is possible to get? Can't I want anything? Must I, always, want something *for* a reason? Anscombe is skeptical concerning the possibility of wanting anything for no reason at all. So we *give* the man a saucer of mud. We watch him. If he does nothing with it at all, we are puzzled. "Did he really want it?" we wonder. The word 'want' seems to have lost its sense. If Anscombe is right, it has.

It should not escape our attention that the desirability condition is satisfied only where a want is assumed. I may judge that avoiding smoke filled rooms is desirable; however, if I like the smell of smoke, then even though an otherwise valid syllogism may come to mind, such as,

> *Avoiding smoke filled rooms is healthy*
> *This is a smoke filled room*
> *It is healthy to avoid this room*
> *I will avoid this room*

I may act in such a way as to not avoid this room, even though practical reason tells me I ought to. This leads, once again, to problems related to *akrasia*, weakness of the will, and how we can knowingly do the wrong thing. I will not pursue these issues, further; but the reader might benefit by realizing the importance of the connection.

The point Anscombe has been trying to make all along is this: In the case of the practical syllogism there is, always, one premise that satisfies the desirability condition. All of Aristotle's syllogisms introduce premises to this end, and which ones they are can be determined by the presence of expressions such as 'suits', 'should', 'ought', 'desire', etc.

## SECTION 38: *HOW WE ARRIVE AT DESIRABILITY CHARACTERIZATIONS*

The first premise of a practical syllogism, as we have seen, introduces something wanted. Any moral issue as to the ethical status of the want can be set aside in determining the construction of a valid practical syllogism. Indeed, such issues only cloud our perception of what a good practical syllogism is. While the first premise, then, must describe what is wanted in some way, the other premises address, successively, the question 'What do you want that for?' Anscombe focuses her attention on a single example.

Imagine that you are a Nazi surrounded by Allied forces. You are in your final hour. You begin to set up a mortar site. I ask, "What do you want that for?" you reply, "This site has the advantages that will allow me to do the job of killing as many of those Jewish children as possible." "But what do you want to do that for?" I ask. You reply, "It befits a Nazi in his final hour to kill as many Jews as possible; I am a Nazi; this is my final hour." Now it may be imagined that I could ask, "Why be a Nazi." But this is not right. Raising this question may address the want, but it does not address any premise of the syllogism, itself. We have reached the end of meaningfully asking the question "What do we want that for?" Thus, we have arrived at the desirability characterization: "It befits a Nazi…" That we have, so, arrived at this desirability characterization is not to imply that the major premise cannot be denied or challenged. Anscombe recites a number of possible challenges. As she points out, one might deny that killing Jews in one's final moments does, indeed, befit a Nazi. There may be Nazi rituals reserved for just such an occasion; rituals that preclude the killing; that is, it may be argued that it is false that this killing befits a Nazi, just as a matter of Nazi ideology. But this would in fact be an error, as there is no such qualification. Anscombe illustrates how a desirability condition enters to subdue further "What for?" questions.

Again, imagine, a group of Nazis on the verge of being killed. Again, their fate is sealed. They believe that Jewish children are in a certain building close by. One Nazi begins to set up a mortar pointed in the direction of the children. The question arises "Why ("what for") are you setting up the mortar at this place?" Answer: "Because it satisfies conditions optimal for striking the children." Question: "Why set up the mortar?" Answer: "Because, then, we can kill the Jews." Question: "Why are you going to kill the Jews?" Answer: "Because it befits a Nazi, if he is to die, to spend his last hour killing Jews." In this last answer we have satisfaction of the desirability condition and no subsequent question, such as "Why does it befit a Nazi to do this," is required for the appropriate syllogism to eventuate in action, arising from a want. The syllogism runs:

*It befits a Nazi in his last hour to kill Jews*
*I am a Nazi*
*These are Jews*
*This is my last hour.*

The conclusion in the form of action, will, then follow. Every *rational* action arrived at by way of a practical syllogism must be grounded, at some point, in a premise serving to supply a desirability characterization. It is important not to gloss over the use, here, of 'rational'. What is meant is action arrived at by way of "calculation" in some sense. In this way, the notion of "rational action" becomes linked to acting "with the intention that such and such." Indeed, Aquinas introduced the notion of an intentional act over and above a simple act of will as necessarily tied to such rational, or calculative actions. (*vide* Donagan [1999] p. 72). Anscombe appears to be following

Aquinas in this respect, making the crucial move relating forming an intention and practical reasoning one which brings intention together with the notion of choice.

## SECTION 39: *THE NON-NECESSITY OF ANY PARTICULAR DESIRABILITY CHARACTERIZATION IN RELATION TO WANTING*

It is necessary in order that action follow some want or desire that a desirability characterization apply to the main premise. This is the core thesis under discussion. Operant, here, is the idea that there be *some* such, applicable characterization; which is not a matter of necessity. Return to the Nazi example of the last section.

In this case, clearly, one might challenge the desirability characterization, "it befits a Nazi...etc," on ethical grounds. One might say that it never befits a *man* to act in such a way. But taking this approach assumes the issue *is* ethical. Anscombe argues that it is not an ethical matter. The most reasonable challenge to the proposed characterization would be to say that there are other things that befit a Nazi to do and the best of the lot is "..." However, the issue is not ethical, and what is "best" is irrelevant. To see that it is irrelevant consider that we might suppose that when the question "What's the good of it?" arises in connection with determining the desirability characterization one might reply, "The good of it is that it is bad." The "good" might be my refusal to submit to the dictates of morality and, thereby, assert my freedom. Similarly, if I am a collector of three inch sticks, she says, then the desirability condition can be probed by asking the question "What's the good of it?" with no expectation of an answer based on some ethical notion. However, the same question will not apply when the objective is health or happiness. In these cases the question "What is the good of health?" makes little, or no, sense. It must be emphasized that in these latter cases this is not to say that there is a logical compulsion to act in respect of these characterizations. When she speaks of the course of action one "logically" must take, she means not only taken within an acceptable range (of desirability characterizations), she, also, means that *if* I act otherwise I face shame. But such a view depends on construing the practical syllogism as ethical; and yet, as we have just seen, the logic of the practical syllogism is not constrained by answers to, purely, ethical questions. Her important conclusion is that while *some* desirability characterization is necessary, there is no such characterization in particular which is necessary.

## SECTION 40: *THE SIMILARITY OF THE RELATIONS OF WANTING TO GOOD AND JUDGMENT TO TRUTH*

There are similarities as well as important differences between these two relations. Not everything wanted may be good; nor is everything judged to be the case, actually, the case. There is this similarity; but, there is, at least, one important difference. The truth of a proposition, so judged, consists in a relation between the proposition and *what* is known, if in fact the proposition were known to *be* true. Suppose we call this "what" a fact, although Anscombe is careful not to do so. To embrace facts in addition to judgments is, implicitly, to accept some form of the correspondence theory of truth, the idea that a belief or proposition is true because of some relation of beliefs (or propositions) to facts which makes it true. For exegetical purposes, only, we shall speak of facts. Truth, not a fact, is the "object" of judgment, just as good is the "object" of a want. 'Truth' is not an attribute of facts (or "things"). Anscombe is careful in making explicit one of her central claims: the situation with respect to wanting is just the opposite.

Whereas 'true' is attributed to judgments, or propositions, and not things, 'good' is attributed to things and not the want which is the wanting *of* those things. What we want is something good, such as a "good kettle." The want, itself, is not what we say is "good"; it is good only, derivatively, as the wanting of something *good*. What is 'true' by contrast is not the fact but the proposition or judgment. What we want are good kettles; what we, actually, have may be a true idea of what a good kettle is. Since we are talking about practical reasoning, we are not concerned with whether what we want is in fact good, but, rather, what the agent *takes* to be good. One might think of it this way: for purposes of considering action, what is good is what the agent takes to be good, but in speaking of knowledge what is true does not depend on what goes on in the mind of the knower. Anscombe remarks that, although much has been made of problems relating to matters of propositions and truth, little has been done to address similar problems regarding wanting and the good. These problems can be traced back to the epistemological views of Locke and Hume.

Allegedly, the main culprit responsible for these problems is the idea of an "internal impression." Figuring prominently among such notions, particularly in the domain of action, is pleasure. Anscombe, who is, usually, reluctant to depart from Aristotle, becomes, strongly, critical of Aristotle. She says that he was reduced to "babble" in his pronouncements on pleasure insofar as he at once identified and distinguished pleasure and the activity from which pleasure may be derived. Let's look at this with some care. As every student of the history of Ethics recalls, Aristotle said,

> …*human good turns out to be activity of soul in accordance with virtue, and if there are more that one virtue, in accordance with the best and most complete.*
>
> — (Aristotle [*Nicomachean Ethics*] 1098a16-18)

Indeed, the good life is "the most pleasant thing in the world" (1099a24-25). Since this 'human good' is 'happiness', happiness is this highest pleasure for man. To this day, controversy surrounds the precise meaning of Aristotle's view. For the purpose at hand, what is important is that happiness as something pleasant is identified as an "activity of soul." This is most likely what Anscombe had in mind when she spoke of him identifying pleasure and activity. However, not all pleasure seems to be of this sort. Take touch and taste, for example. The pleasure we associate with touch, say, is not to be identified *with* the touching but with what is consequential upon the touching. We delight in the taste, not the tasting—to take another example. It seems, therefore, that there is a problem with Aristotle's identifying pleasure with action and, at the same time, not identifying it with action. Whether he "babbled" is another matter; perhaps it is best to say that as long as there is room for uncertainty as to whether we understand Aristotle, then it is, probably, we who are confused. For the time being we let stand Anscombe's judgment. Her opposition to utilitarianism is, partly, motivated by Wittgenstein's arguments against the possibility of private languages, the idea that the sense of words is (or may be) determined by attending to private sensations or ideas.

Utilitarianism persists as one of the most influential ethical theories ever devised. Its basis is the "greatest happiness-principle." The core conception was succinctly formulated by J. S. Mill:

> The creed which accepts as the foundation of morals Utility or the Greatest happiness-principle holds that actions are right in proportion as they tend to promote happiness; wrong as they tend to produce the reverse of happiness. By happiness is intended pleasure and the absence of pain; by unhappiness, pain and the privation of pleasure.
>
> — (Mill [1861] p. 281)

Anscombe remarks that the usual refutation of utilitarianism is based on the "naturalistic fallacy." It was G. E. Moore who, first, proposed this criticism. Essentially, the problem is that, if we identify goodness with a property, say $X$, we can always raise the question whether $X$ is good. Because the question can be raised, this shows that goodness cannot be *identified* with the property $X$. The argument has a long and distinguished history. Moore's criticism depends on a somewhat peculiar notion of a "natural" property, whence the "naturalistic fallacy." Because Anscombe's objection to utilitarianism is not *based* on Moore's argument, we will simply state Moore's central claim.

> It may be true that all things which are good are also something else, just as it is true that all things which are yellow produce a certain kind of vibration in the light. And it is a fact, that Ethics aims at discovering what are those other properties belonging to all things which are good. But far too many philosophers have thought that when they named those other properties they were actually defining good; that these properties, in fact, were simply not 'other,' but absolutely and entirely the same with goodness. This view I propose to call the 'naturalistic fallacy' ...
>
> — (Moore [1903] p. 10)

Anscombe's objection to utilitarianism is that pleasure is an obscure concept. She cites Ryle whom she credits with bringing to the attention of philosophers the fact that pleasure is a far more complex concept than the defenders of utilitarianism had, previously, believed. Let's examine Ryle's position in order to understand what Anscombe liked about it.

## *Ryle on Pleasure*

For Aristotle pleasure is a sensory accompaniment of emotions (Aristotle [*Eudemian Ethics*] 1220b4). Now we ask, "Is pleasure in the experience of action the same sort of thing?" In addition, "Is pleasure accompanying actions, rightly, to be regarded as a "sensory accompaniment"? Consider the following pair (the asterisk indicates a "degraded" sentence, or expression, in the sense intended by linguists, although here the issue is not grammaticality, *per se*).

*I took pleasure in walking—I enjoyed walking*
*\*I took pleasure in feeling anger—I enjoyed feeling anger*

How do we account for this contrast in acceptability? Walking is an action; feeling anger is an experience. I can no more take pleasure in feeling anger than I can take (non-pathological) pleasure in pain. However, I can take pleasure in an action such as walking. Although it might be suggested that for the demagogue taking pleasure in anger (in one's own case) is possible—say, while delivering a fanatic diatribe—this pleasure would not take the form of a pleasant sensation. He might take pleasure in the diatribe, as an action, but he would not be taking pleasure in the *feeling* of anger. This is not to say that I cannot take pleasure in a sensation. However, I may take pleasure in taking a walk, but do I experience a *sensation* of pleasure which makes it a pleasant walk? In the case of feelings, no pleasure in sensation is possible; in the case of actions pleasure in sensation is possible, e.g. pleasure in relieving an itch by scratching, or sexual intercourse. But are sensations essential to any pleasure we may take in action? Indeed, while a sensation may be pleasant, the experience of pleasure is not a further sensation. Action insofar as it is a requirement of pleasure suggests that pleasure is not, merely, a sensation. Other philosophers besides Ryle, however, have been skeptical of the Aristotelian idea of pleasure as requiring only a feeling. Samuel Alexander, for example, identified it with an "element" *of* a sensation.

> *Pleasure in the proper sense, however, means not a pleasant feeling, but its pleasantness: as such it is only an element in sensation...*
>
> — (Samuel Alexander in *Moral Order and Progress* Thoemmes 2000 (1889) p. 203).

Alexander is a, somewhat, exceptional case insofar as before Ryle, pleasure was, commonly, thought of as a sensation. Ryle challenges this idea. In fact, Aristotle's other views sometimes suggest there are limits to the idea of pleasure as being a sensation. He asserts, e.g., that human happiness is the most pleasant thing there is, but since one would be hard put to identify a happy life with a persistent sensation there may be more to pleasure than sensations on Aristotle's view. Ryle, however, is the one who set forth cogent objections to the traditional idea. The paper Anscombe cites begins by having us imagine taking a walk. We enjoy the walk; we take pleasure in the walk. (Ryle [1954] pp. 194-205) But what sensation might we pick out that corresponds to *this* sensation of pleasure, even if we manage to find it? Clearly, if there is some such thing, it is not a bodily sensation.

Supposing our walk had been unpleasant, it would be pointless to anaesthetize our limbs in order to prevent similar unpleasant experiences in the future. Again, what is unpleasant in this case is not a sensation; but, if not, what is it that is unpleasant? We can't say that there is a feeling of pain, or pleasure, in the way there might be an unpleasant tingle in my arm; for, then, we would have to account for what the pleasure, or pain, is that we associate with *this* feeling, leading us, perhaps, to a regress. Nor do we suppose that the pleasure of our walk can be compared in its timing to a sensation of pain that might accompany an electric shock. A walk may be of measurable duration, but the enjoyment, as such, is not. Consider a point Ryle does not raise: suppose that the duration of the enjoyment of the walk coincided with the duration of the walk, itself. Then, had I stopped walking, would there have been something in my experience corresponding to the pleasure or the pleasure, itself, which stopped at the same time? A pain may be experienced as simultaneous with a sound, but can I say that there is a sensation or feeling of pleasure that is, similarly, simultaneous with some other experience? This seems doubtful. Ryle, however, has some positive proposals.

If I hum while sawing a board I am doing two things, but if I hum a song while attending, deliberately, to making sure that the song I hum is just as I think it should go, I am not doing *two* things, viz. humming and paying attention. For Ryle, enjoyment is a species of attention that stands to what I enjoy as the humming does to the heed I pay to it. The attention I give to my walk is a *way* of being interested in it; it is this which constitutes my enjoyment, or displeasure, at what I do.

> *Important as is the influence of pleasures and pain, they are far from being our only stimuli...Who smiles for the pleasure of the smiling, or frowns for the pleasure of the frown.*
>
> — (Ryle [1954] p. 550)

We have already discussed the important distinction Anscombe makes use of between cause and object. The cause of fear may be a loud sound, whereas the object of fear may be the object which caused it. This distinction recurs in her discussion of 'wanting' where she discusses an analogical relation between it and 'judging'. There is, however, an element of equivocation in her account which, once understood, reveals, further, the significance of the relation.

It is, perhaps, worth recalling that Hume makes considerable use of this distinction between cause and object in his own discussion of the passions, remarking that:

> *We must, therefore, make a distinction betwixt the cause and the object of these passions; betwixt that idea, which excites them, and that to which they direct their view, when excited.*
>
> — (Hume [1739] p. 162)

The analogical relation which captures Anscombe's attention is that "truth is the object of judgment, and good is the object of wanting" (Anscombe [1957] p. 76). Goodness is said to accrue to the object of wanting, whereas truth belongs to the judgment itself. While, at first, this appears to make a great deal of sense, questions can be raised, questions whose answers suggest that there may be more than one sense of 'object' at issue. One such question is this: if truth is attributed to the "act," that is, the judging, what does it mean to say that it is the "object" of judgment? Likewise, goodness while attributed to objects of wanting, rather than to the "act," is the "object" of wanting. At least superficially, it would appear that there are two senses of 'object' in play: there is the sense in which it is the object of the "act,' but also, a sense in which it is the *point* of the "act." There is a second question one might raise: Is there a property corresponding to 'goodness' in the case of other "acts" such as fear? That is, is there, in the case of fear, e.g., a property belonging to it, as 'goodness' belongs to wanting or 'truth' to judgment? Instead of pursuing this unlikely prospect, let's look a bit more closely at her view of pleasure.

Anscombe's view of utilitarianism is rich and complex, consisting, as we have seen, first and foremost in her rejection of the primacy of "internal impressions," such as pleasure, providing the basis for ethics. After having credited Ryle with calling attention to difficulties in taking this approach, she dismisses the usual criticism of utilitarianism based on its alleged violation of what we have described in our discussion of Moore as the "naturalistic fallacy."

For Anscombe it is not violation of this fallacy that provides the proper justification for abandoning utilitarianism. Rather, it is the faulty epistemology on which it is grounded, relying as it does on internal sensations, that renders it unacceptable. Paraphrasing Wittgenstein, who made a similar remark about internal impressions in connection with meaning, she says "Pleasure cannot be an impression; for no impression could have the consequences of pleasure." The idea of pleasure and pain as central to ethics goes back even further than Aristotle, whom we have, already, noted she has described as having been "reduced...to babble" in suggesting that pleasure is both an activity and something that accompanies an activity. While she backs off from a more complete examination of 'pleasure', she mentions parenthetically one important tie to Aristotle in this connection. She notes that her concept of 'intention' shares with Aristotle's notion of 'choice' a close tie to this obscure conception. In the context of her discussion of intention, the most important fact about pleasure is that 'It is pleasant' serves to bring to a conclusion the chain of why-questions essential to practical reasoning.

## *Choice, Volition, and Intention*

In Section 40 of *Intention*, Anscombe uses "artificial" in describing Aristotle's concept of choice. Later, she remarks that she used to think Aristotle's idea of choice was "spurious." (Anscombe [1965a] p. 71)

Whether "artificial" in *Intention* is to be read as "spurious" is impossible to say for certain, but it does appear to be a, likely, possibility. That it is is suggested by the fact that just as in *Intention* she linked her use of 'intention' with Aristotle's use of 'choice' in this later essay, while she no longer believes that Aristotle's notion of choice is spurious, she continues to forge a connection between his idea of choice and her own use of 'intention'. Her discussion in this regard is obscure and difficult to follow. She introduces the possibility that the incontinent man may have "further intentions" in doing what he does. What does she mean? She may be this: while the uncontrolled, that is, the incontinent man, may lack the will to do what he does, he may have intentions that go beyond satisfying some bodily desire. In this case, desire that is not to be identified with the Aristotlelian idea of the will, since it is devoid of moral content (good or evil), but there is, also, some further intention that may have such a grounding in the will. If so 'intention' in Anscombe's sense is required. Such a view tends to link her idea of intention with Aristotle's notion of the will. Further treatment of this "tendency" would, however, require and inordinately extended examination of Aristotle.

Anscombe doesn't use the term 'volition' with any deliberate meaning until sometime after writing *Intention*. One can, only, infer from certain passages (e. g. Anscombe [1965a] p. 68) that she associates a volition with each step in the fulfillment of some intentional action. Even so, there are occasions (Anscombe [1965a] p. 69) where she appears uncertain as to whether it is volition or intention of which she speaks. That there is a difference between volition and intention seems clear from the fact that whereas in Section 40 she informs the reader that Aristotle's use of an "artificial" concept of choice coincides with her use of 'intention' one would be hard put to identify Aristotle's concept of choice with volition; more likely he identifies it with wanting; but, even so, problems would remain. One reason for believing this is that in speaking of the differences between the incontinent man and the licentious man she observes that, while the reasoning is the same, it is only the latter who exercises control or "choice" in his action, although the steps that each of these two sorts of men undertake may be one and the same. Thus, given that volition is associated with these common steps, volition and choice are not to be regarded as the same. This represents an advance in Anscombe's thinking, at least within the corpus of her published work. It is of considerable interest that for Anscombe the licentious man is such that volitions associated with the steps he takes in seducing his neighbor's wife are choices, as well; but, in the case of the incontinent man such volitions are not choices. That the licentious man is acting consistently with his moral character, whereas the incontinent man is not so "controlled," appears to supply the basis for making this distinction. The relation of volition to the will is of fundamental importance, although it has, always, been a gray area. Anscombe does not address the issue in any significant way, but it is crucial to understanding the difference between her view and some her predecessors on this and related matters.

We have seen that there are steps related to action corresponding to the stages of argument in a practical syllogism. In Section 35 where she introduces several examples of practical syllogisms in Aristotle, there are two she doesn't mention. The ones we are interested in come from the *Movement of Animals*. We restrict our comments to one in particular:

*I need a covering*
*A cloak is a covering*
*I need a cloak*
*I must make a cloak*

Anscombe does discuss this syllogism in "Thought and Action in Aristotle" (Anscombe [1965a] p. 73). But, she notes that, while the conclusion, "I must make a cloak," expresses a *choice*, action concerns *making* a cloak. This requires a number of different steps. Once we work our way down to what to do first, presumably by way of the "technical" syllogism (as the doctor reasons, practically, to an initial procedure in treating the sick), we have, finally, arrived at an action. Each step involves an action, whereas the practical syllogism, understood as reasoning to what is good for the agent in this instance incorporates action, merely, as a conclusion. The point is that there are numerous steps; each step when executed suggests a volitional element not explicitly adapted to the want or desire that "moves" the action. What is willed is the cloak; what is done is, say, beginning to sew fabric by moving one's hands in such and such a way. It can be argued, based on Aristotlelian principles that volition and the will are, fundamentally, different.

In his remarkably lucid discussion of Aristotle, Anthony Kenny, recapitulates the details of Aristotle's argument in the *Eudemian Ethics* against defining voluntariness in terms of desire. There is a distinction to be made between the will and desire. Without digressing to discuss this important detail, however, it should be noted that, if we allow for a distinction between voluntariness and the willfulness, and identify volition with action *qua* voluntary, then we can show that for Aristotle, at least, volition and the will cannot be one and the same. This follows from the fact that incontinent man acts voluntarily but not willfully. In other words, the very existence of the incontinent man is sufficient to dismiss requiring assimilating volition and the will. If correct, this is a, highly, significant conclusion insofar as intention, arguably, belongs to the will and only derivatively, at best, to volition.

## *Speculative Remarks on Volition and Intention*

It would not be far-fetched to analyze all actions into volitions and intentions (i.e. 'choice' taken in a particular sense). Volitions, unlike intentions, cannot be "pure" (in Davidson's sense). Volitions follow from intentions, as voluntary actions follow from "ideas" in James' psychology. This is not to say that volitions are "blind" in the way that intuitions without concepts are "blind" in Kant's metaphysics. Rather they constitute the "actuality" of an action; something like pulling the trigger in an act of firing a gun. Anscombe does not say this, nor is it to be supposed that she would be, very, sympathetic. Such analogies, however, are no substitute for clear understanding. Yet Anscombe's vague remarks insofar as they can be understood as relating volition and intention invite this sort of speculation. This distinction between volitions and intentions, or between volitions and intentional action is, perhaps, a recapitulation of an idea present throughout the history of discussions relating ideas and actions. Von Mises generalizes a, closely, related dichotomy when he says:

> *Every action has two aspects. It is on the one hand a partial action in the framework of a further-stretching action, the performance of a fraction of the aims set by a more far-reaching action. It is on the other hand itself a whole with*

*regard to the actions aimed at by the performance of its own parts.*

— (*Human Action: A Treatise on Economics*, The Foundation for Economic Education, Inc. New York, 1996, p. 45)

What relates volition and intention will relate to how we analyze the notion, above, of a "further-stretching action." We turn to Aristotle in search of illumination. If volition and intention, as we have described them, were unrelated, something difficult to conceive, then it would appear that volition is, merely, movement and not action. In the absence of an intention, what we have been calling a "volition" would be little more than a muscle spasm.

Suppose in a dream I reach for a doorknob and my body moves, accordingly, even though I am not awake. Volition is associated with the bodily movement in such a way that it bears some undisclosed relation to our intention. Intention in a dream is intention, nonetheless; a bodily movement guided by the intention lends "reality" to an action that, otherwise, might exist only in a dream. Nature (in Davidson's sense) does nothing in fulfillment of the desired outcome. If I move in my sleep to grasp a glass in my dream, the movement and the action I intend are distinct. Aristotle suggested that action and movement are to be distinguished: "that movement in which the end is present is an action." (Aristotle [*Metaphysics*] 1048b22-23) Aristotle, further, distinguishes action and actuality. The "end" he tells us is not the actuality, rather the actuality is the action. No less cryptically we might suggest that intention relates to potency, volition to actuality. It is likely that philosophers such as Bradley had this in mind in speaking of volition as the realization *of* the idea with which the agent becomes "identified." (Bradley [1902] p. 476] Elsewhere, I have discussed these notions in considerable detail.

We have drawn the distinction between the steps taken in fulfillment of a single intention, each step being expressed by some proposition in a practical syllogism. But at the level of basic actions "steps" are not at issue, at least insofar as the basic actions are continuous when viewed mechanically. We can say that "he raised his arm" is a basic action, but the actual raising is continuous and not discrete; that is, it is not undertaken stepwise. Whether "He is raising his arm" differs from "He raised his arm" in respect of volitions is something we shall not elaborate upon, since Anscombe doesn't address the question. But it is interesting to note that just as we tend to use 'try', mainly, in retrospective descriptions (*post factum*), similarly, we tend to speak of volitions when they are related to actions described in a tense other than the progressive. It may turn out that volitions are not, as Moore and others at one time suggested, "explosions," but more like combustion. If so volitions may be conceptually relevant to describing continuous voluntary bodily actions. We can say at least this much: volitions are typically associated with voluntary bodily actions, regardless of whether they are "guided" by some intention; that is, whether or not they are performed with or without some reason behind them.

## SECTION 41: *ETHICS AND PHILOSOPHICAL PSYCHOLOGY*

Anscombe has been discussing Aristotle's practical syllogism in an effort to elucidate practical reasoning. Practical reasoning for Aristotle involved what is good for man (Aristotle [*Nicomachean Ethics*] 1143b22-23). But the practical syllogism ranges in application from technical syllogisms, such as those the doctor employs in arriving at a course of action, to actions with moral content. What all applications have in common is their relevance to action and not, just, bodily motion. Anscombe has, so far, engaged the practical syllogism in its detachment from moral theory.

In her first explicit reference to "philosophical psychology" in *Intention*, Anscombe again emphasizes the difference between treating practical wisdom as concerned with choice, choice which may not involve deliberations on matters of moral substance, and practical wisdom with ethical content. Her claim is that, *if* the practical syllogism is to be brought within the purview of ethics, a "correct" philosophical psychology must, at the very least, be proposed. In *Intention* she does not elaborate on what all would be required. However, in her highly influential essay "Modern Moral Philosophy" she sheds some much needed light on the subject. In this essay, she is more adamant, than ever, that philosophical psychology be made distinct from ethics, recommending the "banishing of ethics totally." (Anscombe [1958] p. 38). That she retained this view to the end of her life is unlikely, given certain facts. E.g. later in a 1982 address to the American Catholic Philosophical Association, she would commit herself to arguing that "All human action is moral action." (Anscombe [1982] p. 209) It should not be considered a forgone conclusion that this is an inconsistency in her views, but owing to the fact that the practical syllogism concerns action, questions can be, understandably, raised as to the independence of these notions. In connection with her ethical views there is another issue she raises that may cut across otherwise, seemingly, distinct interests.

## *'Ought' and the Divine Law*

The practical syllogism may tell us what we "ought" to do in a sense of "ought" devoid of ethical import. But in an important footnote (Anscombe [1957] p. 78) Anscombe remarks that the modern moral sense of "ought" carries with it a certain amount of historical baggage. In particular, she asserts that the modern sense contains the vestigial remains of a "law conception of ethics." Indeed, as she will ague in "Modern Moral Philosophy," the idea that a viable moral philosophy depends on a workable philosophical psychology has been buried beneath the weight of a conception of ethics based on such a "law conception." In "Modern Moral Philosophy," she describes the law conception as maintaining that in order to be virtuous our actions must conform to divine law. Once the "divine" is detached from "divine law," the law conception becomes unintelligible. Although she doesn't mention Kant in this context, it is Kant who championed the concept of the "moral law" in the absence of reliance on direct appeals to the divine, instead invoking the idea of the form of the law in its unconditional, i.e. categorical, formulation, a formulation deduced from synthetic *a priori* principles. In a sense, understood as Anscombe understood it, the Kantian conception supplants divine law with the synthetic a priori, although, we hasten to add that she does not entertain Kant's views beyond a perfunctory wave of the hand. However, it is not Kant whom she faults for taking the "divine" out of "divine law," thereby rendering the law conception incoherent; it is Hume with his notion of *moral sense*, along with the Protestants.

Hume's famous pronouncement that one cannot derive an "ought" from an "is" was, if Anscombe is correct, the ineluctable consequence of separating the "divine" from "divine law" and, then, preserving "ought" within the scope of moral sense or moral law. It is, somewhat, surprising—and suggestive of Anscombe's neglect of Kant's views—that remarks by Anscombe cohere, quite nicely, with comments made by Kant in regard to how imperatives are related to lawlikeness. According to Kant, were an agent incapable of acting on any moral maxim inconsistent with the moral law, that agent would have a "holy will," but insofar as man is a finite and imperfect being the possibility persists that he will act on maxims inconsistent with the moral law, as prescribed by the categorical imperative. It is because man's will in not "holy" that what is categorical with respect to the moral law becomes an "imperative." (Kant [1956] p. 32). In other words, on an Anscombian view, just as "divine" is taken out of "divine law," while retaining a law conception of morality, the idea of an imperative, or command, is necessitated by Kant's appeal to the categorical without an immediately evident divine presence. According to Anscombe, it is precisely because the divine law is "divine" that there is an implicit imperative conveyed by what it prescribes, thus signifying an interesting complementarity between her conception and Kant's.

It has been maintained, throughout, that the practical syllogism is not necessarily ethical. It is so only if at least one general premise is explicitly moral in content. Although she implies in her analytical table of contents of *Intention* that the main point raised in this section is that "the mark of practical reasoning is that the thing wanted is *at a distance* from the immediate action" (Anscombe [1957] p. 79) the most intriguing point is that, according to Anscombe, practical reasoning enters the ethical dimension only when philosophical psychology must be introduced into the "philosophical system of ethics" at issue. Nevertheless, this notion of "distance," whether in space or time, may suggest something deeper than that calculation requires a "distance" between wanting and the first action taken to satisfying it. She contrasts use of the practical syllogism in arriving at action with situations such as those where from, say "This is a nice day" we go to "So, I'll go out." We touched on this earlier. It is interesting to compare occasions where this latest example applies with such occasions where one might say "This book is green, so I'll tack it onto the roof." One arrives at some intentions by way of the practical syllogism, but not so in *either* of these cases; the relation between one's going outside and its being a nice day introduces a reason without reason*ing*. I do not reason from the niceness of the day to the conclusion that I shall go outside. I may go outside *for* a reason but my going outside *because* it is a nice day is more akin to action following a mental cause than acting which follows a train of reasoning. In the green book case, I neither reason nor have a reason. "Distance" may recapitulate salient distinctions involving mental causation vs. acting with a reason. Aside from this possibility there is another.

Anscombe may be reflecting on a distinction we find in Aristotle. Aristotle notes that not all actions which are voluntary involve choice. When I act impulsively, I may, nevertheless, be acting voluntarily. In such cases, there is no question of such an action being a matter of choice. Choice we associate with the conclusion of a practical syllogism, thus impulsive actions, or actions done on the spur of the moment, such as going out because it is a nice day, perhaps, are voluntary but not matters of choice, at least not in the sense Aristotle has in mind in speaking of choice. (Aristotle [*Nicomachean Ethics*] 1111b8-10). Whether this is the sort of thing Anscombe has in mind is difficult to tell, but this remains a distinct possibility.

## SECTION 42: *PRACTICAL REASONING AND MENTAL PROCESSES*

We noted in our discussion of Section 40 that Anscombe described Aristotle's notion of 'choice' as "artificial" and, elsewhere as "spurious." Here she admits that her own "construction" with respect to the pumper was "artificial." What she means, here, by "artificial" may be something a bit different or, at least, its application may not be the same, however, as it was used in describing Aristotle. Here she is commenting on the fact that the steps in practical reasoning may not be psychologically realized in the consciousness of the agent. She realizes that the same may be said for the characterization of his actions from the pumper's point of view. In this sense it is "artificial" to delineate the precise steps involved in rationally deliberating about the action, eventually, occurring. Practical reasoning, as such, describes a certain "ordering", but not psychological processes, that in fact take place in time.

A practical syllogism will help indicate how close the "distance" is between what is wanted and "immediate action." This "distance" need not be present to consciousness; the syllogism, merely, details the *order* of the steps to be taken prior to one's first action. These steps mirror the series of why-questions appropriate to intentional action. Indeed, they are in a sense identical with the answers to these very questions.

## SECTION 43: *THE COMPLEXITY OF 'DOING'*

Comparing questions that differ, minimally, often reveals complexities related to what one might call "logical grammar." Consider, then, two questions:

*What is the stove doing?*
*What is John doing?*

If we wanted these to be minimal pairs, strictly speaking, we might want to substitute 'What is the boss doing" for the second sentence, but for our purposes it makes no difference. Anscombe entertains the question whether there are parallel answers to these two questions. In particular, she suggests that whereas in the case of the first question a suitable answer might be "Burning well," a parallel answer to the second might be 'Resting'. Clearly, 'doing' is understood differently in each case. It is worth noting that, whereas, the first question makes most sense when the stove has operated strangely, or not at all, in the past, the second question carries no such suggestion. I don't wake up in the morning wondering what the stove is doing unless it has caused problems or some such thing. I may, however, have an interest in John based on no particular preceding events. To make the difference more vivid, consider the question "What is the stove doing, now?" Alternatively, I may ask 'What is John doing now?' without any suggestion that there may be cause for alarm. What Anscombe wants to point to, however, is the complexity of the word 'doing' in its relation to convention, or what we might call (following Popper) "institutional facts."

The importance of these facts is made evident if we consider more complex cases, such as when we describe someone handing a girl two pieces of paper as opposed to describing the "same" action in terms of paying a gas bill, say. Anscombe cites Wittgenstein's *Tractatus* on this matter. (Wittgenstein [1921] 4.002) Wittgenstein's most important point in the cited passage is that while a language may be capable of expressing every sense, the logic of that language is made elusive by the fact that the "outward form" of that language has purposes other than making its own structure apparent. What the practical syllogism provides, that is, Aristotle's practical reasoning, and what her successive why-questions provide, is a way of making explicit what language conceals; it provides an understanding of the "stretch," so to speak, between wanting and doing.

## SECTION 44: *ACTING WITH AN IDEA OF AN END*

Consider someone in the following situation. He thinks to himself: "If I do *this*, then such and such will happen; and, if I do *that*, then some other thing will happen; so, I'll do this." Anscombe considers three possibilities facing such a man. In the first case, the fellow has no end in view. Suppose he is offered two foods, one high in protein, the other high in vitamins. He is unmoved by this difference, however, and simply eats what he wants. A friend may say "This will give you vitamins and that will provide protein." The man takes the first and, when asked why, says "Oh, I thought I'd have some protein." If his indifference has the result that he yields to his friend's offer of a vitamin filled food, he may act without reasoning to an end, even though he eats what he does because he just thought he'd have some protein. Here there is no practical reasoning going on, but there is choice. There is another possibility, however, one where the man may have an end in mind, viz. that of eating healthy food and, only, healthy food. Such a man may on all occasions be offered healthy food, but only of one kind. If there is a choice to be made it is only *whether* to eat, not *what* to eat. The third possible scenario Anscombe discusses is the most common.

In this case, the man has multiple choices and he has an end in view, as well. The end he has in view is not, however, determined by the available choices before him, since any would be sufficient for the attainment of his end. Anscombe's considers another example, that of the house builder who arrives at that point in his construction where windows must be added. The options may all fit his plan. Still, there is some calculation involved, for if he chooses one sort of window it will give one visible result, and, if another, then a different noticeable result. She does not mention the fact that, while the general idea of the end in view may be clear, viz. a completed house, the house whose end in view he has will differ depending on this choice, so the choice is not vacuous. It is worth our while to entertain an example she does not discuss, one where there may be an end in view; there may be different alternatives that "fit" the end in view, but in this case the choice makes no difference to the outcome. Like the third case, there are available alternatives consistent with the end in mind, but the choice may be of little or no consequence.

In such cases, there may be no calculation but, unlike the first case Anscombe discusses, the man may have an end in view. The example I have in mind was discussed early in the twentieth century by a number of philosophers absorbed in the idea of voluntary action. Let's consider the case proposed by F. H. Bradley (Bradley [1903] p. 528). Suppose I hold up two indistinguishable pieces of candy before a child and say "Take one!" The child takes one. There is no practical reasoning in play in the child's making his decision. The hands are equidistant from the child; the child is ambidextrous; he is neither right nor left eyed, etc. One may question whether there, really, is a choice. The child takes one of the two pieces of candy; and, so, there is the inclination to say that he has made a decision and, if so, then he has made a "choice" in some sense. This case is more complex than those Anscombe considers. For if we assume that there is *no* difference in the candy or the distance from the child, or the appearance of the hand (aside from the fact that one is to the child's left and the other is right) etc. Now it would appear that there is no sufficient *reason* for preferring one piece of candy to the other. But, if there is no such reason, then the child selects one over the other without a reason and, yet, he has an end in view, that of having a piece of candy. Bradley maintained that in this instance no choice has been made, that in order for there to be a choice the child would have had to *reject* one of the pieces of candy. But for what reason? Such a case differs from Anscombe's earlier example of acting for no reason at all, the case where a fellow tacks all his green books to the roof. The child has an end in view, one arising out of a desire to satiate his appetite for sweet food; nothing similar can be said of the fellow who nails his books to the roof.

This introduces questions of great complexity, particularly, those whose answers are required in resolving the relation of appetite to the actions of the incontinent or evil man, who may perform his actions according to the dictates of a practical syllogism.

## SECTION 45: *THE PROBLEM OF PRACTICAL KNOWLEDGE*

Up to this point, Anscombe has had a great deal to say about practical reasoning and practical wisdom. This discussion is related to the question raised in Section 28 as to how we can know our intentional actions without looking. Recall the point of entertaining the possibility of "two knowledges." We might think here of the contrast, as she described it, as one between knowledge of what one intends by doing what one is doing in contrast to knowledge of what one is doing. But in this section there are problems with the latter insofar as without observation there is lack of transparency in what she might mean by *knowledge* of what one is doing. She is a bit cagey as to how she would resolve this question, but her comments, at the very least, clarify the problem. She discusses "practical knowledge" in this section by considering an unusual example.

Suppose, then, that there is a builder who is directing the building of some structure without ever seeing what is going on; he knows each step of the process, and we might consider him to be what Plato would call a "master craftsman." He settles everything that is to be done in, exactly, the order it ought to be done. He imagines each step as it would occur, assuming the orders are followed. Anscombe tells us that his knowledge of what is done is practical knowledge. Notice that for someone observing the construction what is known is known by observation and is not *practical* knowledge—it is knowledge of what happens, merely.

If the builder's orders are not followed, the question, then, becomes "In what sense can the builder have practical *knowledge*. A different, and simpler, case is considered next. I am at the blackboard writing some sentence, say, "I am a fool." But imagine that as I do this with my eyes closed that the chalk fails (it may be wet without my knowing it). Even if such a thing were to happen, Anscombe says that what I know would remain unaffected. How can this be if what I know is knowledge of what happens? But this is just the point: practical knowledge is not knowledge of "what happens." Contrast this with the case from Davidson we discussed earlier. In that case, I press down in writing something, hoping that the carbon paper will cause what I'm writing on the page before me to appear on pages beneath the page upon which I am, actually, writing. Davidson supposes, correctly, one would think, that this is an instance where my intention to act and my succeeding in what I am doing does not entail knowledge; that is, I can act intentionally without knowledge of what I am doing. The difference between this case and Anscombe's is that Davidson is saying that I can do something intentionally, and, even though what I intend to do does happen, I may not know it. This is not a case a *practical knowledge*, only a case of not knowing what has happened, although what has happened is the result of my intentional action. It is worth noting that the case of the builder is not, quite, like cases involving basic actions.

In the case of the builder, we have a complex intention, one that requires an understanding of each step of the project to be undertaken. But, now, consider the case of raising my arm. We have it that I have knowledge, without observation, of the position of my limbs; and while Anscombe doesn't explicitly discuss the matter, I also, it would seem, have similar knowledge of my having *moved* my body. If this is the case, then we can ask whether this is "practical knowledge." If this sort of knowledge is knowledge of what comes about as a result of practical reasoning or practical wisdom the answer would appear to be "No." But is this, merely, a case—say in arm-raising—of knowledge of what has happened? The answer, again, would appear to be "No," since what I know I know I know without observation. Before addressing the problem of practical knowledge, let's entertain one more likely area of difficulty for Anscombe.

Much of our intentional behavior is what one might call "adaptive." In the case of such behavior I adjust my actions in conformity with my intentions, depending on the effects of my preceding actions on the surrounding environment; that is, on the world as it becomes altered by my actions. In this case, knowledge of what happens is a determinant of my subsequent intentions; and, so, practical knowledge of the sort we encountered in the case of the builder, who knew all the steps *ab initio*, is not the same sort of knowledge. Knowledge of what is happen*ing* is an integral part of knowledge of my intention. This is not to suggest a fatal blow to Anscombe's account of the situation, but it is to suggest that the circumstance may be far more complex than she has implied. Let's return from this digression to the following question: If what happens does not affect my practical knowledge, then what is it that I know, if what happens is not what I believe is happening, as I act intentionally? It is at this point that Anscombe, again, becomes a bit cagey.

She remarks that there is the temptation to regard the object of willing, that is, what is known in the case of practical knowledge (aside from what is, actually, happening), as an *idea*. This temptation she traces back to Wm. James. However, there is a risk, here, that we obscure James's, actual, position, for in drawing our attention to James she speaks of the "object" of willing. James, however, rejected the act/object distinction owing to his commitment to "neutral monism" taken together with his radical nominalism. Russell would follow. Even though she obscures James' point, she may not be in error *if* by 'object' she means that for the sake of which one acts. (*cf.* Aristotle [*Eudemian Ethics*] 1226a7).

## SECTION 46: *INTEREST AND THE 'WHY' QUESTION*

The world we observe is in flux. How we conceptualize such a world depends on our interests. Although Anscombe cites Wittgenstein, the idea is not so recent. But seldom, if ever, has it been applied to concepts associated, specifically, with action, at least, not in the way Anscombe suggests. One important question she raises is why we conceptualize. There is a curious connection between 'interest' and why-questions. Certainly, the notion of interest is not coextensive with the domain of applicability of why-questions. We may take interest in something out of curiosity, alone, and in such circumstances the question of why we take such an interest may not apply. However, when Anscombe's why-question can be raised, and where it has an answer, in such cases there is, always, a point of interest at issue. 'Interest' is difficult to define but, since we see that its application extends beyond action, much like 'game', there may be no universal criterion that supplies a necessary and sufficient condition for its attribution. But this is true with many concepts and, so, some general reflections on the nature of interest are well within the scope of Anscombe's attempts at elucidating intentional action.

According to Anscombe we cannot describe what an action is before understanding, and being able to apply, the why-question. Suppose that she writes 'I am a fool' on the blackboard. Our "special" interest in human action is not directed towards bodily movement, or the configuration of chalk over the surface of the blackboard.

Setting causal explanations aside, when asked "Why did you write 'I am a fool' on the board?" our interest is in something besides the movement of the molecules and muscles required for writing the sentence. Anscombe entertains an interesting example, one that would appear to have an history of its own.

Writing 'I am a fool' on the blackboard requires a directed articulation of energy and movement of the finger muscles. Return, now, to our example of talking leaves. The movement of leaves on a tree can be equally subtle and, yet, among the movements of the tree there are none satisfying any description available to us corresponding to the assertion of 'I am a fool' or, for that matter, any meaningful linguistic expressions. It is instructive to consider a very similar example we find in H. H. Price. Price talks about how it is that a sound of leaves may resemble words, words that may even convey new information. (Price [1938] p. 133) In Price's example we do not notice a class of movements of leaves corresponding to a class movements of "articulatory mechanisms" of speech (Ladefoged [1975] that result in the production of audible words of some language by human beings; we, merely, hear sounds emanating from blowing leaves that resemble acoustically, certain, such spoken words. Setting aside the possibility of new information being conveyed, consider that the basis of our belief that certain meaningful words are being produced comes down to resemblance. Is this sufficient to conceptualize the sounds we hear as speech? What is our *interest* in such sounds, if we do not consider the fact that we possess concepts of language under which those sounds are subsumable? Interest here depends on conceptualization not, as she appears to suggest, the other way around. Likewise, it may be said that our interest in bodily movement is interest in human action only if we are in possession of concepts that allow that sense be made of why-questions.

It is important to keep in mind that for Anscombe visible resemblance is sufficient to identify what we see or hear as writing and, therefore as action. This can be challenged. Putnam describes the case where a bug walking on the sand may leave a pattern conveying an impression of intentional behavior. (Putnam [1981] p. 2) Are we to say that we may ask our why-question of the bug? Can we ask this question under these circumstances intelligibly? There is similarity here to an example Kripke raises in connection with our discovering a horned creature that meets *all* descriptions of a unicorn. Is it a unicorn? Whether a pattern is in fact a word, or whether an animal *is* a unicorn, may depend on factors besides visual resemblance. If asked why we categorize this pattern as a word, we may be able to supply a convincing explanation, but whether our characterization of the pattern as a *word* is correct is another question.

## SECTION 47: 'INTENTIONAL' AND THE FORM OF DESCRIPTION

We have had occasion to discuss Anscombe's original, somewhat, persuasive remarks on falling 'under a description'. She wrote at a time when "ordinary language philosophy" was gaining traction and would soon expand its influence over much of the field of analytical philosophy. Although her work was regarded by many as falling within this school of thought, this is a mischaracterization by way of oversimplification; for, even though her methodology was informed by the work of the likes of the later Wittgenstein and Ryle, she wrote extensively on metaphysics in a way neither of them could, easily, have endured. With this in mind, let us begin by considering, however, her views on description and 'intention' and how she might have taken the "linguistic turn" too sharply.

She begins with the observation that many descriptions of events depend on the *form* of description of human actions. This seems innocuous, enough: descriptions depend on form, and this dependence may relate to what these descriptions are descriptions of. There is a relation between linguistic forms and sorts of expressions. So much seems, entirely, acceptable. She elaborates by saying that even such descriptions that depend on forms related to intentional human action have application to episodes where the events are unintentional, episodes such as 'offending someone'. In this case, I may offend someone intentionally, or unintentionally. But, next, she says something that ought to, at least, arouse our skepticism.

She remarks that there would be no such thing as offending someone if the description 'offending someone' had never applied to intentional action. This would be a trivial assertion if it meant, only, that 'offending someone' in fact applies to intentional action; so that if it never did there would have been no offending someone on any occasion by uttering these sounds. The salient non-trivial reading is that, without the description's having such and such use, the events it purports to describe would not be possible. But can we say that the existence of something depends on its having a description? Institutional facts are a complex case; we will not digress into a general discussion of the issues involved, such as what is required in order that an expression *be* a description; but, we can question whether the possibility of my offending someone depends on there being a *description* of my action, as such. This seems doubtful.

Philosophers, such as Kant, have held that there are things that exist "unconditioned." In Kant's case, there are, e.g., certain *causes* that are unconditioned. (Kant [1956] p. 50) If we think of falling "under a description" as something's being conditioned in some sense, then we can ask: is there anything more to a thing, or event, than what is expressed by the descriptions under which it, may, fall? Or is it the case that things unconditioned, such as a good-will (according to Kant) nonetheless depend on there being some description under which they may fall. I suspect that, just as in her discussion of 'under a description', she would, at this point, say that here we are in "bare particular country." (Anscombe [1979] p. 209). She would contend that believing that there is something "underlying" all possible descriptions under which a thing may fall is to assume the existence of some "bare" particular, whether it is a thing or an event. However, it may be argued that, while there are no bare particulars, there are conditions (properties) of things and events which may not be expressed, or expressible, by any description of any language but which obtain in the case of the particulars being discussed, although the discussion does not involve use of descriptions referring to, or expressive of, such properties.

If this is so, then there is no *a priori* reason for believing that one cannot, possibly, offend someone without there being some description under which it can be regarded as offensive. Whatever the case may be, it is to be noted that she provides no, actual, argument favoring the view she maintains; she, simply, asserts that without such descriptions there can be no such actions. Her motivation is to reject the idea of 'intentional' as referring to a "natural class," a consideration that compelled Davidson, it will be recalled, to relativize what we call an intentional action to a description. While, owing to the nature of omissions, she will question Davidson's methods, nevertheless, it was she who supplied the motivating idea behind his proposal. Notwithstanding her possible vulnerability on this matter, her stronger claim, is central to her discussion of intention.

The stronger claim she makes is that 'intention' refers to a *form* of description of events. Notice that she is denying that 'intention' refers to *actions* of a sort, claiming, instead, that it corresponds to a form of *descriptions*. Let's examine this novel approach, without giving reasons for why one might be reasonably skeptical regarding its prospects for success. Anscombe claims that there are some descriptions that must fall under the form 'intentional actions', if they are, even, to have a sense. Here she has in mind expressions such as 'signaling', 'greeting' etc. Other descriptions may, or may not, fall under the form, terms such as 'intruding', leaving alone' etc. This approach could be expanded to include a treatment of the difference between mere vice and evil. This might be possible if we could, successfully, argue that in order for 'murder' to have meaning it must fall under the form 'evil' just as 'signaling' falls under 'intentional action'. Likewise, 'rage' no more entails falling under 'evil' than 'intruding' falls under 'intentional action'. This is not to say that she would agree with this proposal; it is, only, to argue that there may be, if one accepts her approach, as yet unexplored applications.

## *Animal Intentions*

Anscombe includes animals among beings capable of having intentions. However, this is not to say as much as one might suppose. Applying descriptions implying intention is dependent on being able to describe what an animal is doing *in* doing something, where this "something" is close to being "merely physical." Thus intentions are indirectly attributable; that is, we describe what an animal does *in* doing something else, although this is not to imply, as in the human case, that there are two actions at issue. We may say that *in* crouching a "further" thing being done is stalking. Stalking being an intentional notion; its attribution in this instance depends on something closer to being "merely physical," i.e. crouching. We might, even, prefer an "enlarged description," such as that the cat was stalking with the intention of catching…with the intention of eating, etc. Now she does not say this; that is she does not say that an animal may do something *with the intention that* some other thing be done. Given that she hugs the material bases in the case of animals, the "merely physical," she might object to this, but there is no, ostensible reason for rejecting its possibility. By confining herself to descriptions, and not recognizing natural classes of action, her position enjoys a certain advantage.

We report an animal's intentions in our own language to others in our language community. There is hearer's meaning, as others have pointed out, and speaker's meaning; but there is no animal's meaning since animals are not language users in the sense that they are capable of producing "novel" sentences, as far as we can judge. Still, there are questions. If being intentional is, as Davidson says, relative to a description, then under which descriptions is animal behavior intentional? Do we say that under the description 'crouching' the cat's behavior is intentional? If we say this, then having an intention is not a *property* of a cat or its state of "mind." It is, just, to say that certain reports containing descriptions which are intentional in the reporting language are applicable to the cat's behavior. A cat may be reported as believing that the x-ray tube is a bird, even though 'x-ray tube' is not in the conceptual repertoire of the cat. But if we say "The cat thinks the x-ray tube is a transistor," then it is difficult to determine whether this is false or absurd. The cat may, however, be familiar with transistors and x-ray tubes as toys, and confuse the two on some occasion. It is a contingent fact, or at least it would so appear, that the cat has neither the concept of 'x-ray' tube nor 'transistor'. These words, used by the one reporting the belief, belong to the language of the reporter. It should be noted that in the case of a sentence such as 'The cat thinks the bird is the x-ray tube' we may be making a truthful attribution, should the x-ray tube be correctly describe as 'the thing the cat likes most to play with'. However, in a sentence such as 'The cat thinks the bird is an x-ray tube', we have an attribution of a different character. If we are attributing bare "physical" actions we can, to use an expression Anscombe uses elsewhere, "pick any description you want." But when attributing belief, or any of the other "propositional attitudes," we are more restricted. I will not explore the conditions, further, except to say that what obtains in the case of the "attitudes" holds in the case of attributing actions.

## SECTION 48: *PRACTICAL KNOWLEDGE AND 'KNOWLEDGES'*

Anscombe tells us that a description under which what happens acquires its status as a description of a doing—that is, of an intentional action—is, often, determined by what the agent knows about what he is doing. The vagueness of this proposal is reduced by considering the following simple example. My arm is placed outside the window, as I drive; my left arm is extended outside the window and bends, at the elbow, resulting in my hand going up. This describes what is happening. Now what allows for describing what happens, here, as an action, and not just a happening in the world, is given by the fact that I know what I am doing in having my arm move in this way. I know that what I am doing *in* making my arm move in this way is signaling. The signaling is an intentional action. Saying "I signaled a left turn" describes what happens *qua* intentional act. My knowing that what I am doing is signaling is practical knowledge of my action.

What is important is that this characterization of what happens as something "done" depends on such practical knowledge. Signaling is an "executed intention," and I know it for what it is. This knowledge is practical knowledge; knowledge of what *happens*, as opposed to knowledge of the intention as executed, is *not* practical knowledge. It is "speculative" knowledge. Although Anscombe doesn't mention it, it is worth pointing out that practical knowledge does not entail completion of the act being "done."

I may have practical knowledge that I am signaling even if I haven't completed the signal as yet; just as the pumper may have practical knowledge in Anscombe's sense that he is poisoning people, even though they have not yet been poisoned, given that no one in the house has, as yet, drunk the water. In other words, I can have practical knowledge of what I am doing as well as what I have done. Speculative knowledge, strictly, is limited to knowledge of changes that have, actually, taken place in the world. I can describe someone as opening a window, if the window is not yet open, *only if* I have knowledge, or belief, with respect to the agent that his intention in behaving as he is, presently, behaving is to see to it that he opens the window. It is virtue of what we have been calling "practical knowledge" that the agent, himself, knows that what is happening is something he is doing. Anscombe's thinking in this regard may reveal a problem in earlier accounts of volition, such as we find in James.

Recall that in the case of James we have an idea of action, isolated in attention from all others, something like a Cartesian "clear and distinct" idea of an action. From this idea the action follows.

Following Bradley, one would say that the world "particularizes" the idea as the intention is satisfied. If Anscombe is right more is required than this sort of mental causation, that is, causation by an idea, if the voluntary action is to be intentional. Voluntary action and intentional action are not to be lumped together. Recall that these are different notions, since the uncontrolled man, as Aristotle says, may be said to act voluntarily but without intention. If Anscombe is correct, acting voluntarily in James's sense is not sufficient for intentional action. In other words, even if the Jamesian position on volition is accepted, this would not suffice to explain intention. James can be thought of as identifying the idea, itself, with what is intended; but Anscombe would claim that this is not enough. This is not to say that the "classical" view of volition is wrong. Bradley emended the approach by introducing the agent's "identifying" himself *with* the idea and it may be reasonably held that this will do the work of 'practical knowledge'. But the work required to make this a viable position is daunting.

In conclusion: intentional action presupposes practical knowledge. Knowledge of our intentional actions, as the case of the builder illustrates, does not require observation. We have, then, two "knowledges": first, there is the knowledge I may have of what is happening as I act; the other is knowledge of what I am doing, where "doing" presupposes practical knowledge. Knowledge *of* intentional actions may not, itself, be practical knowledge, but *what* it is I know when I know what I am doing presupposes such knowledge. Knowledge of what happens is "speculative," whereas knowledge of my intentional actions is knowledge that presupposes practical knowledge, and this can be had without observation.

## SECTION 49: *THE MEANING OF 'VOLUNTARY'*

Anscombe is concerned to distinguish the intentional and the voluntary. What we do intentionally we do voluntarily although, perhaps, with regret. However, what we do voluntarily is not, *necessarily*, voluntary. She makes four comments on the relation of being intentional and being voluntary. We just mentioned one, let's examine the others.

First, we might say that our action was voluntary, but not intentional, if when asked the why-question we say something like "I was just fiddling." This sort of situation would appear to create little need for controversy. More interesting is the second consideration in making the distinction between voluntary action and intentional action. Suppose I am doing something with my hands, like tying a knot. I may be unaware of what I am doing, but if I think about it, she says, I might be able to tell you what it is. Before going further, however, let's consider whether this is as certain as it appears to be; that is, *am* I able to supply a description of how I move my hands when I tie a knot? We have discussed this at great length in Part 2 Section 6b. What may, at first, seem easy enough to do, as we saw in our earlier discussion of shoe-tying, turns out to be difficult or even impossible. Also, what would be the criterion for successfully describing what I did with my hands? Again, what, at first, seems to be obvious may not be the case, for I may describe my actions with the result that you are able to tie a similar knot, but how do I verify the claim that I did with my hands what I say I did, even if I can articulate what it is I did? Let's set these complications aside and assume that Anscombe has no problem. The example of tying a knot is productive; we said in our earlier discussion of tying knots how productive the example could be in connection with Davidson's view. But there are other examples that are, perhaps, richer. In the cases relevant to those Anscombe discusses there is one thing they have in common: no intention is "formed" in connection with the voluntary action. I may have the intention of untying or tying a knot, but I do not "form" an intention to move my hand in such and such a way. We have, already, distinguished acts done willfully and willful actions. This distinction is operative in the discussion of this section. Davidson addresses cases where there is voluntary action but where no intention has been formed.

## *Davidson on Voluntary Action Without Intention*

Davidson observes that not all intentional actions require "forming" an intention. (Davidson [1978] p. 88) But if intentions are not entities, or states, or something over and above beliefs, or desires, what *is* an intentional action which does not follow upon the formation of an intention, and how does it differ from other intentional acts? His language, particularly, in his discussion of what goes on in writing the word 'action' suggests that the distinction he draws is little more than the distinction between "ideo-motor" actions and voluntary actions we find in James. But this is difficult to determine with any degree of confidence, just as it is difficult to determine whether an action performed without an intention being formed is an action that is voluntary but not intentional in Anscombe's sense. If James is right, however, then there is little reason to believe that writing the letter 'a' with the intention of writing the *word* 'action' is intentional or, for that matter, even voluntary.

Isn't writing 'a' with the intention of writing 'action' like taking off my coat in order to take off my shirt? Don't these two actions resemble one another insofar, at least, that I neither deliberate nor "form an intention" in pursuit of some other accomplishment such as writing a word or taking off my shirt? In such cases, according to James, my action falls short of, even, being voluntary (James [1890] p. 519); and, if it isn't voluntary, it is doubtful that it is intentional. Why would James say such a thing? I believe that what he had in mind was that the action of taking off my coat is no part of any *voluntary* action. For it to qualify as a voluntary action, attending to an idea would be required, which in this case may be entirely absent. There is an interesting difference between James's case and Davidson's. In James's case, we need to keep in mind that it is not always true that I must remove my coat to get to my shirt; but in Davidson's case I must always write 'a' if I'm going to write 'action'. So what is it that leads Davidson to believe that writing 'a' in such a case is intentional, except for the fact that it was no accident?

If we take "pure intention," as Davidson says, to be "intending that is not accompanied by an action" (Davidson [1978] p. 88) and, yet, insist that our writing 'a' was intentional, then what would rule out a pure intention to write 'a' with the further intention of writing the word 'action' which is, likewise, a pure intention? Or, for that matter, what rules out a pure intention to write 'c', although our intention to write 'action' of which writing 'c' is a part is not a pure intention, since we have, already, written 'a' with the intention of writing 'action'? Are these possibilities to be ruled out, at all? But if they are not what role can such pure intentions serve? Doesn't it make better sense to say that pure intentions are possible only when an intention has been formed? If I am interrupted, while trying to write 'a', can't I say, retrospectively, "It was my intention to write 'a' but I was stopped"? Note that 'it was my intention' may be attributable, only, *post factum* in cases where the act is a component action, just as taking off one's coat is a component of the action of taking off my shirt. But if so, aren't intentions possible without having associated with them a belief and a desire? Compare in this case the fact that we seldom use 'try' unless we fail. Elsewhere, I have discussed this class of cases, i.e., where verbs and, certain, auxillaries are applicable only *post factum*, and mention it here only in passing. What is most important is that we don't want to confuse acting *with* an intention with the intentional, since there are actions, e.g. some basic actions, where the action *does* follow upon forming an intention, but neither is it performed with the intention of doing something else, such as when the doctor instructs us to raise our arm after being treated for some injury.

## *Observation and Voluntary Movement*

We have been discussing the distinction Anscombe draws between voluntary and intentional action. We have discussed cases where the agent is unaware of his, exact, movements in undertaking some action, such as while tying his shoes; he may, however, know *that* he is acting. The action may be voluntary but, as we noted, for Anscombe there may be no intention associated, specifically, with each event making up the action in its entirety. How does such a man know these actions; does he know them by way of observation? Anscombe says no.

One reason for her answer is that the man may not have to look at his hands to know what he is doing. If the action has already been performed, he may try to familiarize himself and, maybe, others with the action by performing the same actions over again. He may rely on imagination. But this does not carry the observational "weight" that, say, an experiment ordinarily does. It is interesting to place this observation, one Anscombe actually does make, alongside Wittgenstein's remark about the results of imagined experiments in his discussion of private language. Perhaps more important is to note that whereas we discussed, earlier, how we know the position of our limbs without observation, and our knowledge of our intentional actions without observation, here we are prepared to consider that knowledge of our voluntary actions is not observational. Since all intentional actions are voluntary, and voluntary actions are known to be such without observation, mightn't it be the case that it is knowledge of voluntary actions, and not knowledge of intentional actions, as such, that is knowledge without observation? Anscombe does not, specifically, address this possibility but there doesn't appear to be anything in what she says that would rule it out. The distinction between intentional and voluntary action carries with it significant ethical implications and even though Anscombe doesn't discuss the matter in *Intention* it is important enough to discuss even if only briefly.

It was central to her criticism of Sidgwick that he had matters all wrong with respect to intention. Sidgwick, it will be recalled, averred that a man is responsible for the results of any of his voluntary actions insofar as they are intended. (Sidgwick [1907] p. 60) But this, Anscombe alleges, flies in the face of good judgment insofar as one ought not to be held responsible for all evils that may follow as a result of good actions. (Anscombe [1958] pp. 35-36). If a bad result follows from an intended action then we might ask the agent: "Why did you do that?" If it is the case that a bad result followed from a good action, then Anscombe's point would be that we cannot raise the why-question, here, at all with respect to the bad result. What the agent did was voluntary, but may not have been intentional; that is the point to be made. Significantly, the why-question applies to intentional actions but not, necessarily, voluntary actions, as such. There is a third consideration in distinguishing voluntary and intentional action.

At Anscombe's suggestion, let's imagine I am on a boat. We may add to the imagined case that the boat is hung up on a rock or some such thing. Someone on shore pushes the boat with a stick, say, and the boat is freed from the rock. In this sense from my standpoint the action is voluntary in the sense that I am pleased by what has happened. This is a strange case, however, insofar as it is something that happened to me (and the boat), not something I *did*. As the boat's occupant I might say "I let it happen voluntarily," but this is somewhat different. Anscombe, perhaps realizing the peculiarity considers another case. We will embellish it, modestly. There is someone I would like to see knocked down. I am on top of a hill. Someone pushes me. I begin to roll down the hill and, eventually, bump into the person knocking him down. Did I *do* anything voluntarily? Clearly not; so, if I'm asked why I did it, I might reject the question by saying that I was pushed. However, someone knowing the situation might have noticed that there were numerous things I could have hung onto in order to prevent the collision. This person remarks "You didn't grab hold of anything; you did not attempt to stop yourself from rolling etc." Now, even though the why-question does not apply it may turn out that the collision was from my point of view voluntary, albeit not intentional. Notice, further, that this is a case of omission. This complicates matters. I may intentionally omit, but seldom can I be said to voluntarily omit in the absence of an intention. However, we shall leave the matter as it stands.

## SECTION 50: *INTENTIONS AND PREDICTIONS*

Earlier Anscombe spoke of predictions as concerning the future as do intentions. But there is a difference between the two. Volitions, insofar as we have distinguished them from intentions, take place in the present; intentions, however, are directed towards the future, as are predictions. What, then, makes intentions and predictions distinct things? An intention, unlike a prediction, is such that the why-question applies. Hope, similarly, concerns the future; but, unlike mere predictions, it is such that the why-question may be applicable. When I say "I hope to go to the meeting," the why-question *is* applicable. In fact 'hope' may apply *to* an intention, as is suggested by 'I will be polite to him—I hope'. In addition, the basis of hope may involve reasons for wanting: 'I hope he arrives before everyone else so we can talk about the schedule'. Further, included in the bases of a hope may be a belief that what is wanted may, very well, happen: 'I hope he makes this penalty kick, because if he does we will win'. But in the case of intentions the bases are reasons for acting, not for wanting or believing.

## SECTION 51: *WANTING AND THE FUTURE*

Recall that in Section 18, Anscombe commented on the man who nailed all his green books to the roof. If when asked why, he should say "For no particular reason," then we are inclined to think this "unintelligible." Suppose, however, that we are not talking about a past action but, rather, an intention to perform some future action. In such a case I might be asked why I intend to do such and such. Should I reply "I just want to," Anscombe has no, similar, objection based on unintelligibility. The agent may have the desire to do something he has never done before. Although I may like doing what I'm doing because I've never done it before, this may presuppose a past time at which my intention was to do something because I'd never done it before.

The difference has to do with the fact that "I just want to, that's all" may convey different meanings, depending on whether the action is future or present. Uttered in regard to the present, it is frequently a way of expressing discontent with the question, meaning something like 'Leave me alone'. Even so, we might reasonably *ask* "Well, what is it about what you are doing that you find pleasant or interesting?" But if I ask, "Why are you set on going to Paris"? and your reply goes "Oh, I don't know, I just want to that's all." Here the answer is intelligible, and I may in this case, as well, ask what it is you find about going to Paris that is pleasant etc. I do not ask "What do you find pleasant about going to go to Paris." So, tense makes a difference to this sort of answer, i.e., "I just want to, that's all." Let's consider a, somewhat, different situation.

Suppose, says Anscombe, that someone is looking through a story in the newspaper and decides that as an idle diversion he will try to find all the letters of the alphabet in a single news story. If such a man were asked why he is doing this, the answer 'I just want to, that's all' will not explain what he's doing. It may be compared to the answer in the case of the man who is, presently, nailing green books to the wall: "Oh, no particular reason." But there are cases where the answer, "I just want to, that's all," may convey some information.

Anscombe entertains the following example: I see a spot on the wall. I get up and walk over to the wall. I am asked what I'm doing. I reply that I'm going to see if I can put my finger on it while standing only on my toes. I am, then, asked why. I reply "I want to, that's all." In this case, I *do* say something intelligible; I am excluding, at least, the idea that I have some other reason for acting. I just want to see if I can reach it, that's all. But, now, she considers what the situation might be if I touch the spot and continue to hold my finger on it. Now I may be doing this for a variety of reasons. I may be trying to see how long I can do it, or some such thing. In case my reply is "Oh, no reason at all, I am *not* excluding the possibility of there being some explanation, besides impulse; that is, if asked why I continue to touch the spot, I reply "I just want to, that's all," unlike future tense cases, I am not excluding the idea that I may have some other reason for acting.

In the first case we were addressing my intention to perform a future action; in the second case, present tense is at issue. Tense makes a difference, but more may be involved. There are other cases where 'I wanted to, that's all' may be an intelligible reply. Recall that in Section 18 she remarks that it's not always the case that replies such as "I just thought I would," etc. are unintelligible. This is a case where there is intelligibility, but there is a contrast, affected by tense, in what information is conveyed by replying in such a way. Let's consider a case she does not entertain.

Imagine that I a runner. I am not a competitive runner, and run by myself for reasons of health and amusement. One day, I have the idea that I just might be able to make my run a half mile longer than usual. I might succeed. If I do, someone might ask why I did it. I might reply "I just wanted to, that's all." What one may infer from this is that at some "present" time, a past present time, 'I just want to, that's all' would have provided some informative answer to the why-question addressing what was, then, my present intention. Again, tense enters the picture, significantly.

Anscombe goes so far to say that there may be a mood introduced into language where future tense expresses doing something simply because one wants to. Similarly, we might introduce a mood with the force of 'I wanted to' in the case of a "past future" tense; but, in this latter case there would be no present in this mood having this "force."

## SECTION 52: 'I AM GOING TO BUT I WON'T'

Suppose I conjoin two sentences, 'I am going for a walk' and 'I am not going for a walk', in a single utterance: "I am going for a walk and I am not going for a walk." Have I contradicted myself, even if the first conjoined sentence, 'I am going for a walk', is being used as a statement of intention, whereas the second sentence, 'I am not going for a walk', is being used as a statement of belief? Anscombe observes that, although we would not have an explicit contradiction in the usual sense, there would be a contradiction in the sense that the sentences cannot have the same truth value. The statement of intention, the first sentence, carries the implicit prediction that I will go for a walk, as long as nothing prevents me. Whence the appearance of a contradiction should the second sentence, 'I am not going for a walk', turn out true. If the first statement had not contained an implicit prediction, then, assuming that I didn't fulfill it, the question "Why didn't you go for a walk?" could be answered by "Well, I wasn't making a prediction. I was just expressing my intention." There may be the temptation to say that the first conjunct, the statement of intention, means "I am going for a walk, unless something prevents me."

The problem is that if we take this to mean "I am going for a walk unless I don't" it becomes a simple tautology; it says "I am going for a walk or I am not going for a walk." What we bring from this is that "unless something prevents me" doesn't convey the same meaning as "unless I don't." Anscombe emphasizes the similarity between this situation and cases where people say something like "If my memory serves me right, then ..." But there is nothing to prevent this being said in *every* situation, if we mean that in any particular case my memory may fail me. There are cases where doubt might warrant the use of 'If my memory serves me right...', but I can never be certain of which cases they are. Anscombe's conclusion is that when I say "I am going for a walk" I am stating a prediction which may in fact go awry. Although Anscombe does not discuss the matter, there is a more general point to be made.

The general point is that sometimes we make use of expressions in a "hedging" way. Thus, if I am very confident that I know something, I will use "believe" in a way that I would not were I to say "I believe this to be the case but..." This latter employment of 'believe' carries a hedging sense. So the question is whether all statements of intention are of this latter sort. In other words, the question becomes one of whether whenever we state an intention we are hedging a prediction. Anscombe appears to say that this is seldom, if ever, the case, although the textual evidence for this is inconclusive. This is, mainly, owing to the fact that she says that we are "mostly" not prevented from carrying out our sincerely stated intentions. Still, this does not resolve the question of whether, like 'believe' statements, statements of intention possess this dual possibility of interpretation. There may be respects, however, in which hedging belief differs from statements of intention where one believes there is the possibility that one may not fulfill the prediction. Anscombe does not discuss hedging, as such, in cases of statements of intention. She remarks that if someone is "considering" that he may not, actually, do what he says he intends to do, even where there is nothing to prevent him, in such a case it *does* make sense for him to say "I am going to do this unless I do not do it." That this is a hedging sense is the only clear way to understand the assertion, once we set aside its being intended as a mere tautology: "Either I'll do it or I won't." Consider in greater detail hedging in the case of belief.

It may be that I am firm in believing that I *believe*, where *what* I believe is something I doubt. I may, for example, know that I *believe*—however weakly—that so-and-so will win the election but have a reasonable doubt that he will in fact win. Compare this case to the man who is hanging from a cliff but believes he will lose his grip, even though he has every intention of hanging on. He may be firm in his intention to hang on, but he may have his doubts. If someone were to see him hanging and ask: "Are you going to hang on?" he might reply "I am going to hang on." If he should say "I am going to hang on unless I don't," what he is hedging is not his intention but, rather, the prediction that comes with the statement of intention. Here intention stands to belief as prediction to what is believed in our description of hedging uses of 'believe'. In this instance, with respect to intention, the one who hedges states his intention but hedges on whether the prediction contained therein will prove valid. But there is the converse case where one states that he has the intention not to do something but does.

Such was the case with St Peter who thrice denied Christ against his stated intention not to do so. He was neither prevented nor did he change his mind, according to Anscombe; and yet he did not act on the implicit prediction that he would not. In this case he might very well have said that, since Christ said he would deny him, he believed he would and, yet, he might have added without contradiction that he intended not to do this. If we are right, his first statement, that he would not deny Christ, did contain a prediction, but it was a prediction based on a stated intention involving a hedging commitment to the prediction implicit in the statement of intention, given his belief in Christ's omniscience, even though it was sincerely expressed.

We have now concluded our discussion, section by section, of Anscombe's *Intention*. What remains is to attain a greater understanding of the place of causation in human action. This cannot be accomplished without understanding her views on causation generally. It is to this that we turn next.

# PART 6:
# Singular Causation

Causation is fundamental to Anscombe's discussion of intention. Causal explanation contrasts with rational explanation. The why-question, that is "Why?" in the sense relevant to discourse about intention, is not answered, appropriately, using causal language. If asked why I killed so-and-so in this sense, I may reply "Because he killed my brother"; I would not answer *this* question by describing my neurological state, immediately, before the act. In the discussion which follows, we shall examine the issue of causation, largely, from the perspective of the time at which she wrote *Intention*, but we will not restrict ourselves, entirely, to this point of reference.

Russell enjoined the philosophical community to abandon 'cause' in favor of 'law'. Law became an essential element in so called "covering law" models of scientific explanation. Such models appear to have been proposed first by Popper, Hempel, and Oppenheim, although the history is not entirely clear. William Dray, who coined the expression, describes the "covering law" model as subsuming the *explanandum*, the event to be explained, under a law which "covers" it. (Dray [1957] p. 1) As Hempel points out, and Dray perfectly understood, the subsumption is "deductive." (Hempel [1965] p. 345) We explain events by subsuming them under laws, deducing them from such laws taken together with initial conditions that are, frequently, identified with causes. However, the covering law model is a species of the "regularity" theory of causation. Shortly, we shall attend to the details of both the regularity and "singularist" theories.

The nature of scientific law became an important issue around the time Anscombe wrote *Intention*. In particular, a challenge was lodged against Hume by some proponents of the covering law model based on the semantics of counterfactual conditionals. Counterfactual conditionals are conditionals where the antecedent is false but unlike material conditionals in logic the truth of the conditional is not, thereby, guaranteed. In addition the verb is in the subjunctive, e.g. 'If John were the coach he would throw Dribbles off the team," where John is not the coach in fact. The covering law model itself came under attack from a direction other than providing explanations in science: the philosophy of history. Dray entertained a number of valuable criticisms that were taken seriously by the original proponents of the covering law model. Although Anscombe does not address this model in particular, she spoke out against the Humean view of causation, and the "regularity" theory. Her advocacy of the opposing "singularist" position would ramify throughout her thinking on intention, but how it does is never discussed nor, explicitly, acknowledged. We shall attempt, therefore, to fill in an historical gap between her views on causation, generally, and her views regarding human agency in particular. We will, e.g., examine her criticisms of Chisholm, even though Chisholm came to view his earlier theories as inadequate, perhaps, in part owing to these criticisms.

Anscombe's position on causation is decidedly influenced by Russell; it is a rejection of a number of his central ideas, such as the role of law in supplying an adequate theory of causation. Russell's view is, frequently, cited but, rarely, examined with care. An examination of his 1914 work *Our Knowledge of the External World*, however, reveals that he anticipates much that is contained in the theory advocated by Davidson and, earlier, C. J. Ducasse, that reasons can be causes, where 'reasons' describe beliefs and desire working together resulting in human action. We shall touch upon this interesting historical fact and describe Anscombe's notion of intention against the backdrop of Russell's theory. We believe the historical facts suggest that Russell's statement on the importance of law led not only to the covering law model but, also, to the debate initiated by Nelson Goodman's ingenious proposals concerning the "new riddle of induction." The reader who is impatient with the statement of some of the details of the evolution of these issues may be encouraged by the fact that once they are absorbed, Anscombe's own, sometimes, murky views become much clearer.

## *a) Hume, Popper and Regularity*

Anscombe's discussion of causation begins, as do those of most philosophers, with the position taken by Hume that causation is not an essential relation between objects or events but, rather, a connection between impressions and ideas in the mind. Hume maintained that, with the understanding that causation is a "natural" relation, we can think of a cause as "An object precedent and contiguous to another, and where all the objects resembling the former are plac'd in like relations of precedency and contiguity to those objects that resemble the latter." (Hume [1888] p. 170) We may view cause not only from the standpoint of a "natural relation" but a philosophical relation, as well. Since this involves no difference in subject matter, let us state his final definition of 'cause' as a "natural relation."

> *An object precedent and contiguous to another, and where all the objects resembling the former are plac'd in like relations of precedency and contiguity to those objects, that resemble the latter.*
>
> — (Hume [1888] p. 170)

It is from resemblance that the very idea of necessary connection arises. (Hume [1888] p.164) Like other relations, according to Hume, causation is a relation of ideas such that, where one is present to the mind, a transition to another is "facilitated" by the imagination. (Hume [1888] p. 204) In other words, causality is a relation of ideas, not "objects" in the sense that we call tables and chairs "objects." There is reason to believe that Hume is not, always, consistent as to what he intends by "objects," but in the case of causation there would appear to be little doubt that here we are talking about a relation of ideas, or of impressions, to ideas, merely. Causal efficacy, i.e. necessity, then, is the felt determination of mind to move from idea to idea or impression to idea, not something in the essential nature of things. Nor does it arise from an impression of the senses; rather, it is an idea of reflection arising from an internal impression of repeated transition from idea to idea.

## *b) Russell and the Idea of Lawlikeness*

Hume's theory of causation is properly identified with the origin of what has come to be known as the "regularity" theory of causation. This theory has it that any, particular, occasion of a cause and effect relation instantiates a "causal law." However, Hume's notion that causal necessity is, merely, subjective leads to the further question of what a "causal law" actually is, aside from the habitual association of subjective ideas and impressions. How is it possible to maintain that causation is an objective feature of the world but depends on generalizations taking the form of causal laws? Doesn't such a dependency imply a reintroduction of causal necessity into the world itself? If not the world, then, perhaps, something like *synthetic apriori* principles may be involved. This is a position eschewed by the logical positivists and one for which Anscombe had little, or no, sympathy. What is important for us is to see is how she departed from the regularity theory in asserting what has been dubbed the "singularist" position. We will, briefly, examine the conceptual and historical circumstances leading to her dismissal of the regularity view. The regularity view is not to be *identified*, however, with the Humean view. There were those who rejected Hume, or who at least appeared to reject Hume, who embraced the idea that causation is to be understood in terms of laws. Our story begins in earnest with Bertrand Russell.

On the matter of causation Russell was a good Humean. He proposed, however, (Russell [1912-13]) that the term 'cause' be purged from the scientific and philosophical lexicon altogether, although its practical application at the level of common discourse might be preserved. It would not be, entirely, out of the question to purge 'reality" from scientific discussion for many of the same reasons, however. Nevertheless, according to Russell, instead of talking about "cause," we should be talking about laws. At one point he remarks: "... the laws which replace causality in such sciences as physics have no room for any two events between which a nexus could be sought." (Russell [1912-13] p. 183) This seems to exclude any "third thing" that might supply an ontological grounding for necessity over and above the events which instantiate such laws. But what is the status of these laws with respect to the world? It would not be long after Russell that a compelling argument against Hume, persisting to this day, would come to dominate the discussion. Let's sketch how this came about.

Counterfactual conditionals, we have seen, have a special form. But there are two sorts of counterfactuals. The contrast between the two goes to the heart of a number of issues, including the nature of scientific laws. One class of counterfactuals is exemplified by 'If this match had been scratched, it would have lighted'. In this case, the consequent 'it would have lighted' follows from the antecedent, 'this match had been scratched', only if we introduce a "connecting principle": 'Every match that is scratched, well made, dry enough, in enough oxygen, etc. lights'. (Goodman [1954] p. 18) But there is a second sort exemplified by sentences like 'If P (this coin) had been in my pocket on VE day, P would have been silver', and this sentence is very different. Even if we introduce a suitable "connecting principle," such as 'Everything in my pocket on VE day was silver', we cannot infer 'P would have been silver'. The difference between these two sorts of counterfactuals is that in the first case the "connecting principle" is a scientific law, whereas in the second case the principle is a. mere, "accidental generalization." Goodman's strikingly original remarks on the issues raised are well known, although many of the details leading up to his contribution to the subject were supplied by Carl Hempel. What this portends is a protracted discussion of lawlikeness in connection with the regularity theory, for if there are no laws, then there is little to value in the regularity theory.

It was William Kneale, writing in 1950, who brought much of this to light. Kneale would claim that in the case of one class of counterfactual conditionals the generalization required for inferring the consequent, given the initial conditions, could not be a merely "accidental generalization." (Kneale [1950]) The implication from antecedent to consequent could not be captured by material implication. Recall that this flies in the face of Russell's claim that material implication would be sufficient. This represented a remarkable turn in the discussion. Notwithstanding the evolution of Karl Popper's views on causation, it was Popper who most persuasively used these facts in challenging Hume. Popper at a critical juncture made the following claim.

> *Hume...only looked at the events A and B themselves; and he could not find any trace of a causal link or a necessary connection between the two. But we add a third thing; a universal law; and with respect to this law, we may speak of a causal link, or even a necessary connection.*
>
> — (Popper [1943] p. 363)

Although Hume is credited with originating the "regularity" theory of causation, it should be noted that, notwithstanding, his employment of the word "all," the notion of a law is not explicitly mentioned. There is for Hume no, actual, difference between accidental generalizations and lawlike generalizations. Only later would the idea of a "law" be introduced as an important concept in addressing Hume's claims with respect to causation. How this came about is not, exactly, clear. Popper, at this stage of his development, departs from Hume because Hume cannot meet the demands of a semantics for subjunctives.

Humeans, it has been alleged, cannot provide a semantics for counterfactuals because to do so requires taking into account lawlike statements. What Hume overlooked, according to the "champion" of counterfactual semantics, Nelson Goodman, was that not all regularities establish the "habits" Hume associated with the transition of mind from one idea (the cause) to another (the effect). (Goodman [1954] p. 82) For Goodman the difference between accidental generalizations and scientific laws is that only generalizations which are laws can be confirmed by what instantiates them. (Goodman [1954] p. 72) There are, however, requirements imposed on confirmation that we cannot, here, discuss. (*cf* Goodman [1954] pp. 71-72)

We have seen that lawlike statements entail support for counterfactuals. If it is a scientific law that all physical objects possess a velocity below the speed of light, then if something is introduced into the room it "must" travel below the speed of light; but, if someone enters the room, he may not be wearing shoes, even though the generalization is, presently, true that everyone in this room is wearing shoes. For "extensionalists" the logical notion of necessity requires, only, that the truth of a generalization be preserved regardless of what logically appropriate values we substitute for the variables contained therein. (Russell [1912-13] p. 200) More generally,

Hume cannot supply a semantics, or account, of subjunctives. We arrive at subjunctives by way of counterfactuals by changing the mood of a sentence while retaining the assignment "false" to the antecedent. Subjunctives, then, are essential to asserting counterfactuals. The logic of subjunctive propositions was of paramount importance in the development of philosophy of science. Because the topic introduces subject matter extraneous to understanding Anscombe's *Intention*, and because I have dealt with it, elsewhere, at some length, we shall not engage the topic, significantly. However, there are a few things that need to be said if we are to understand the importance of Anscombe's views on causation as they apply to intentions. When Popper decided to "add a third thing," he did so for a number of reasons. We can only speculate as to, exactly, what he had in mind, but certainly he realized that introducing this third thing risked departing from the extensional logic that Russell and Carnap had affirmed. The logical positivists, and logical empiricists, had tried hard to defend verificationism, or some variant thereof, a view that tied meaning and, therefore, semantics, to the need for empirical verification, or confirmation, of statements in the "language of science." Secondly, they attempted, as best they could, to retain extensional logic as sufficient for any analysis: a logic which required that the truth of a conditional depend only on the truth values of constituent propositions. Carnap reacting, in part, to criticisms of demands for complete verification had attempted an elaborate semantics based on a theory which assumed an extensional logic and expressed the meaning of theoretical terms by way of "bilateral reduction sentences," without the need for introducing unruly non-extensional elements such as subjunctives. (Carnap [1936-37] p.47) This met with limited acceptance, and when Popper introduced this "third thing" he, at once, restricted what could be accomplished within the compass of extensional logic alone, a logic which appeared insufficient to the task of accounting for the distinction between accidental and lawlike generalizations. The new element would become *modality*, and this is where we must go no further in detailing the context of the disputes that interest us; for what interests us is how all this connects to the issue of agency and voluntary action. To get a firm grasp on the big picture, we must look a bit closer at Russell, because Russell's 1912-1913 paper would exert, considerable, influence on Anscombe.

## c) Regularity vs. Singularity

Anscombe's views on causation were never stated in a unified way; she was, as we have said, a "singularist" with respect to causation as opposed to being a regularity theorist. No satisfying account has been given of the singularist position, and while we cannot provide anything like a complete account, we shall attempt to supply clarity sufficient for the discussion that follows. Russell in fact provided what is, perhaps, the most succinct statement of the singularist position in stating his opposition to it. Russell, at one point, he remarks:

> *Moreover, since the causal law is general, and capable of applying to many cases, the given particular from which we infer must allow the inference in virtue of some general characteristic, not in virtue of its being just the particular it is.*
>
> — (Russell [1914] p. 217)

At the core of Hume's account of causation is the regular succession of experiences, given similar preceding experiences, and their habitual association in the mind of the observer. This regularity is made explicit in the formulation of scientific, and other, laws. The association of causation and lawlikeness is found not only in Hume but, also, in Berkeley's *De Motu*, while the idea that all of nature proceeds according to law found a powerful formulation in Helmholtz who remarked that "The principle of causality is nothing else than the supposition that all the phenomena of nature are subject to law." (Helmholtz [1882] p. 17). The role that law plays in causal explanation would become clearer over time, eventually taking the form of "deductive nomological explanation" which we discuss under the more general rubric of "the covering law model."

The covering law model, which owes its modern formulation, mainly, to Carl Hempel and Paul Oppenheim (Hempel [1948]) was anticipated by Mill, Jevons, Popper and others. This way of looking at scientific explanation does not regard law as providing a cause, but rather makes use of law as a "bridge" between causes and effects. From a set of empirically verifiable initial conditions ($C_1...C_n$), which in Kant's philosophy amount to being intuitions, and scientific laws ($L_1...L_m$) a conclusion, $E$, which is sometimes thought of as the effect, is deduced. This deductive relation is what justifies inferring the effect from the cause. (Hempel [1948] p. 324) However, the regularity theory as traditionally formulated relies on the idea that causes are subsumed under scientific laws, laws possessing universal generality. Laws are, then, something like "universals" in that they bring together similar phenomena. But this does not entail that *all* explanation based on similarity depend on regularity.

This is evident once we consider cases where events are not subsumed under law in providing a causal explanation. This was noticed by W. S. Jevons. Although Jevons held that "the most important process of explanation consists in showing that an observed fact is one case of a general law or tendency," (Jevons [1874] p. 533), he believed that similarity entered into some explanations without subsuming events under a law. He says,

> *This similarity may be of any extent and depth; it may be a general law of nature, which harmonizes the motion of all the heavenly bodies by showing that there is a similar force which governs all those motions, or the explanation may involve nothing more than a single identity, as when we explain the appearance of shooting stars by showing that they are identical with portions of a comet.*
>
> — (Jevons (1874) p. 533, italics added)

The reader should take note of Jevon's use of "identity." Later, a prominent singularity theorist, Ducasse, would use *difference* in applying Jevon's general idea for the purpose of stating the case for singularity.

Ducasse insisted that Hume had confused constant conjunction (of similar cases etc) with causation and that this was his "epoch making blunder." (Ducasse [1924] p. 21) Causation, Ducasse maintained concerned single cases. Suppose my car, suddenly, stops running and I'm wondering what the cause might be. If Ducasse is right what I am looking for is the "single *difference*" between the conditions that obtained immediately before the car stopped and its present condition. (Ducasse [1924] p. 19) What I do *not* do is once having found this condition proceed to inquire into the laws which taken together with this difference might explain the car's having stopped. This insistence that causation is a relation between particular events absent of any need to subsume events under law is the defining characteristic of the *singularist* view of causation. Causal explanation requires, if singularism is correct, only events, not events taken together with laws.

Such a view is at odds with the covering law model of explanation, and is a repudiation of Russell's position that talk of cause can be replaced by speaking in terms of instantiating laws. It is, especially, important that the singularist position is adopted by some philosophers of history who aver that explaining historical events cannot be a matter of finding laws under which those events are to be subsumed. Anscombe will not only adopt a singularist position; her introduction of the why-question we have been discussing is very much like, if not identical to, the why-question historians raise when, e.g., they ask "Why did the French Revolution take place when it did?" Later, we shall discover that a more extended discussion pays significant dividends when we apply Anscombe's singularist view to issues related to what has come to be called "agent causation." Before discussing agency, however, let's entertain one relevant but speculative proposal.

Russell made an interesting claim, a claim which may have implications for the dispute between singularists and regularity theorists. What Russell claimed was that, if we reject, as we must, the notion that scientific laws are *a priori*, then we must accept the possibility that the validity of scientific laws is transitory. But if the validity of scientific laws is transitory, then if we assume the truth of our initial conditions, and draw our inference, indirectly, from these conditions, taken together with the law as our major premise, then our conclusion will be less probable than if we were to argue directly from particular instances to particular instances. In other words, in such cases it is better "to argue immediately from the given particular instances to the new instances, than to argue by way of a major premiss." (Russell [1912-13] p. 190) This notion of "arguing immediately from given particular instances is subject to multiple interpretations. The interpretation we shall place on it, and soon discuss, is that causation can be thought of in two ways: as a two place relation that is intransitive, such as 'parent of', or as a two place relation such as 'ancestor' which is transitive. These are two, logically, related ideas, related in such a way that we hope to be able to offer a constructive suggestion as to how Russell's regularity theory and Anscombe's singularity theory are to be reconciled. For now the Russellian devotion to 'law' over 'cause' is to be regarded as the foremost consideration in pitting regularity theory against singularism.

The singularist will argue that in all cases we should in speaking causally dispense with such laws. This is not to say that in contexts of explanation laws are eliminable, only that, where causes are at issue, laws do not enter the picture. Russell's remark on the matter of the possibly durational character of lawlikeness may appear inconsistent, given his positive disposition with respect to regularity, and his determinism etc. Perhaps he would reply to the point just raised that as a matter of fact we cannot "argue" from instance to instance without introducing at least one law. In any case, no one has singled out Russell remark for consideration, most likely owing to the uncertainty of his intent given other of his views and its relation to so-called "inductive statistical" explanation. It is to Hume that Russell is reacting. Russell was not perfectly Humean, however, with respect to causation, particularly with respect to the causal efficacy of reason in human behavior; but it is to Hume that Anscombe turns in attacking the source of the regularity theory.

### *d) Anscombe on Hume*

Anscombe criticizes Hume's argument that beginnings need not have causes and, therefore, it is false to claim that all beginnings, necessarily, have a cause. Her reasoning is based on two fundamental logical considerations. First, that in the statement of his argument Hume uses 'any' differently than one, typically, uses 'all'. Secondly, she relies on a point of modal logic that one cannot infer from a statement of the form 'for all $x$, it is possible that not...' to one of the form 'it is possible that for all $x$ it is not the case that'. We shall, first, cite Hume's argument; then, we will state Anscombe's objections, followed by our reasons for believing her criticisms are not decisive.

> *All distinct ideas are separable from each other, and as the ideas of cause and effect are evidently distinct, 'twill be easy for us to conceive any object to be non-existent this moment, and existent the next, without conjoining to it the distinct idea of a cause or productive principle. The separation, therefore, of the idea of a cause from that of*

> *a beginning of existence is plainly possible for imagination, and consequently the actual separation of these objects is so far possible, that it implies no contradiction or absurdity.*
>
> — (Hume [1888] pp. 79-80)

One way of understanding the argument is to say that cause and effect are distinct ideas. As such, they are "separable," and being separable one can be imagined in the absence of the other. What is imaginable is possible. Thus, given that I can imagine an event in the absence of its cause, which is an idea distinct from it, it is, therefore, *possible* that a beginning takes place without a cause. Anscombe will embellish this overly simplified characterization of the argument.

First she will not speak of "ideas" but, rather "objects," raising the question *which* objects it is possible to imagine without a cause. The answer she says is "a beginning of existence." (Anscombe [1974c] p. 96) She, then, gives examples: imagining a star or rabbit's beginning to exist. She notes that, for Hume, it is not possible to imagine a beginning without imagining the beginning of something in *particular*. What this implies is that when I imagine the cause of some beginning I must imagine some particular cause of that beginning. Thus Hume's argument is said to be that for any cause I can imagine of the beginning of this rabbit, say, I can imagine the beginning of the rabbit without imagining *that* cause. But is Hume's argument, then, one where from the fact that I can imagine the beginning of some object without *any* particular cause, I infer that I can imagine the beginning of some object having *no* cause? If so, Hume is faced with a problem.

The problem is that one cannot infer from a statement of the form 'for all *x*, it is possible that not...' to one of the form 'it is possible that for all *x* it is not the case that'. She maintains that, logically, the situation can be likened to one where I attempt to infer from

A. For *any* color, I can imagine that a rose is not that color

the proposition (B):

B. I can imagine that a rose has no color.

Is this argument against Hume valid? There are several reasons for thinking it may not be.

When Hume says that "all distinct ideas are separable from each other," he can, easily, be construed as meaning that all distinct ideas can be thought of in isolation; that is, *any* distinct idea can be conceived in isolation. A distinct idea for Hume is what, according to Kant, allows us to refer to an object as single, viz. an *intuition*. (Kant [1787] A320) Suppose I say the bricks making up this wall are distinct. It would be silly to suggest that this entails that they are separate from each other but that there may be other bricks from which they cannot be separated. Anscombe comes very close to considering this a possibility. I can, she says, imagine a rabbit coming into being; however, nothing follows from this she, further, maintains. The reason is that all I'm left with is a picture in my mind with the title "a rabbit coming into being," and, surely, this will not allow me to infer that it is reasonable to suppose an uncaused beginning is possible. This answer is not satisfactory for a number of reasons.

First, the suggestion seems to be that unless there is some way of linking the idea of the beginning of the rabbit with a cause then it is just a picture in the mind. Her point appears to be that unless we can connect this picture with some idea of a cause we cannot argue that it is an "effect" without a cause. However, the only basis for insisting on some linkage of the image with an image purporting to be a cause would be by requiring that we speak of 'cause' and 'effect' as relative terms, something she has already dismissed as "frivolous." Secondly her analogies are cherry picked to create an impression that may not suffice for making the more general point.

Suppose Hume had said "I can imagine any house without a garage." Now suppose someone, Anscombe perhaps, saying: "Well since you can only imagine particular houses and particular garages, you may argue that for any house you can imagine a particular garage not attached to it, but you can't argue from this that you can imagine a house with *no* garage." Hume's obvious reply is: "I can imagine a garage by itself; you are suggesting that I cannot prove, thereby, that I can imagine a particular house without *any* garage. But, since I can separate the idea of a garage and the idea of a house, I can as a matter of empirical fact argue from the imagined possibility to the possibility in actuality. You are looking for an *a priori* argument, thus demonstrating your lack of understanding of my empiricism." Moreover, in our lengthy quote from Hume, where he says "'twill be easy for us to conceive any object to be nonexistent…," he uses 'any' in a way that doesn't require specifying a particular. If I say "take any hammer from the box" that would be one thing, but if I say "take all hammers from the box" that would be another. But if I should say "any spoiled child will cry for candy" I mean "all spoiled children will cry for candy." In other words, sometimes 'any' has the logical force of 'all' and such is very easily understood to be the case in the quote from Hume.

It is not uncommon for a reader to become confused over whether Hume is talking about ideas (or impressions) or the physical objects of common sense waking life. Anscombe's criticisms of Hume on the question of whether beginnings must have causes reflect some of the problems that arise from this sort of confusion. It cannot be said that she, herself, fell victim to Hume's unintentional ambiguity, but the ambiguity does figure in what one might say in reply to her attack on Hume. (Anscombe [1974c]) Nevertheless, Hume's argument is straightforward, and its survival in one form or another is in part owing to its clarity and intuitive appeal.

The criticisms raised by Anscombe are set forth in, relative, disregard of an important distinction between events and physical objects. Sometimes she will speak of the imaginability of events without causes, such as boiling water, while elsewhere she speaks of the imaginability of objects, such as a rabbit, coming into being without a cause. (Anscombe [1974c] p. 96). An event, for our purposes, will be regarded as "substance entailing," i.e. an event is a change in *something* and that something is what has changed, not the change itself. The coming into being of a rabbit, as Anscombe understands Hume, need not be a change in something, but, rather, something that suddenly happens; the boiling of water, on the other hand, requires a change in some substance. We will not dwell on this fact, but it should be noted that to speak of the beginning of a thing's existence, without speaking of a change that results in the beginning of a thing's existence, presents some difficulties that must at some point be resolved. Anscombe's strongest criticism of Hume, however, relies on the logical difference between 'any' and 'none'. Understanding the argument requires care. Her criticism of Hume is far more difficult to understand than Hume. Even if we suppose that the above remarks critical of Anscombe's attack on Hume are insufficient, there remain other components of her argument that can be challenged.

She interprets Hume's argument as saying that from

1) For any beginning (or modification) of existence $E$ and any particular cause $C$, I can imagine $E$'s happening without $C$.

Therefore,

2) For any beginning (or modification) of existence $E$, and any particular cause, $C$, $E$ might be supposed to happen without $C$: i.e. there is no contradiction or absurdity in the supposition.

The problem, as she sees it, is that it will not follow that

3) I can imagine this: there is a beginning (or modification) of existence without any cause.

Suppose someone attempted to argue as follows: "You (Hume) observe that whenever you have had the idea of a beginning, $E$, with a cause, $C$, you have been able to imagine the former without the latter. You conclude that, since what is imaginable is possible, it is possible that a beginning may not have some cause. But all you have argued is that in the case of $E_1$ with cause $C_1$ you have been able to imagine $E_1$ without $C_1$. So far, for any $E_n$ you have been able to imagine it without its cause $C_n$, and you go on to conclude that it is possible, therefore, that $E_n$ might have existed without $C_n$. But what about some event, $E_{n+1}$, one you have not thought about? How can you be so sure that *its* beginning will be imaginable without its cause? That is, how can you be so sure that the future will resemble the past with respect to one's ability to imagine one event in the absence of another? And if you can't be so sure of this, how can you be sure that a beginning may not have a cause?" Hume's reply might go something like this. "When I use $E$, I am talking about an impression or idea. Ideas come from impressions and impressions require an attentive mind. The notion that there are ideas which, recall, originate with impressions that I have yet to examine presents its own problems, but beyond this the entire point, here, rests on the fact that, *because* I have no reason to believe that there is an idea whose cause is inseparable in imagination from it, and every reason to believe otherwise, I am justified in saying that *no* beginning *must* have a cause; that is, a beginning may be uncaused. There is no warrant for alleging a necessary connection, but neither am I offering an *a priori* argument to the contrary." Anscombe's argument is very much like the one we have described Hume as addressing. A closer look at her argument suggests as much.

With Hume's argument, as she has described it, (1)—(3), in mind she entertains what she regards as an analogous situation. She would have us consider that

4) For *any* color, I can imagine that a rose is not that color

Moreover, I might attempt to infer

5) I can imagine that a rose has no color.

She is assimilating roses and effects, on the one hand, and causes and color on the other. But this, she avers, makes clear what makes the argument invalid. It appears, however, that Hume has a way out of this apparent dilemma.

Suppose I am presented with a rose. It is clear from the passage cited (Hume [1888] pp. 79-80) that when he speaks of an "object" Hume is talking about either an idea or impression. But, if so, were we to imagine the rose of a different color it would be a different idea, or "object." Two ideas of differing color cannot be the same *idea*. In addition, there is reason to believe the example trades on the "felt" connection between the "object" and its color, a contention she would no doubt strongly reject. Notwithstanding this fact in cases where this connection is not felt to obtain, her argument doesn't appear as strong, even if we discard our present defense of Hume.

I can imagine an extended object without imagining it at some particular place. For any place where I may imagine an object being, I can imagine it being at some other place. It would be a *non-sequitur* to conclude on the basis of this line of reasoning that I can imagine this object being nowhere. However, I *can* imagine a physical object being nowhere, even though it is extended. If this is so, then, even if we were to accept Anscombe's example of the rose and its color, it would be open to argue that the causal case is like the case of the relation of an object to its place. I might distinguish the place of an object and the object, by imagining the object not being *there*, perhaps, being nowhere.

In addition, to the criticism she raises against Hume regarding an event's, or object's, beginning she tackles another of Hume's positions, this one having to do with the time at which an object can be said to exist. Anscombe considers Hume's contention that "There is nothing in any object consider'd in itself, which can afford us a reason for drawing a conclusion beyond it." (Hume (1888) p. 139) Her reasoning is unclear and the topic she, herself, admits is "obscure," and for this reason we might feel inclined to make an easy escape, but her claim that Hume's principle has been "disproved" (Anscombe [1974c] p. 95) warrants at least an attempt at understanding what she has in mind.

Hume's "principle" has it that we cannot infer anything from an "object consider'd in itself." If we think of a thing's place and time as not contained in what is to be considered in the object itself, then what fixes its time and place cannot be the object itself, given this principle. But the time and place is determined by the brute fact of the object's existing at such and such a time and place and, so, the principle is not true. On the other hand, if it is not the object, itself, that determines by some brute fact that object's place and time, then it must be something else; but, if so, then this something else allows us, contrary to Hume's "principle" to infer something from the idea of the object itself. This may be one way of reading Anscombe.

### e) Russell's Anticipation of Davidson/Ducasse

Anscombe, sharply, distinguished reasons from causes. The cause of my killing so-and-so may be described in terms of brain states and physical circumstances combined with laws governing the behavior of physical events and processes. But if someone asks "Why did you kill so-and-so?" it is one thing to make a reply in terms of brain states, etc. and another to reply with something like "Because he killed my brother." Donald Davidson, however, in an, extremely, influential paper (Davidson [1963]) took exception to the idea that reasons could not be causes.

What Davidson argued was that a reason consists in a belief, or "pro-attitude," and a desire (Davidson [1963] p. 5), and that, as such, we may say that someone performed such-and-such action *because* of such-and-such reasons. (Davidson [1963] p. 9) Later, in discussing Hempel, Davidson would note, without expressing surprise, that Hempel had made similar points in his 1961 address to the Eastern Division of the American Philosophical Association, but that he, Davidson, had overlooked this fact. He expresses some surprise that he hadn't recalled C. J. Ducasse, who had argued, similarly in a much earlier paper that beliefs combined with desire could be regarded as a cause. (Ducasse [1926] p. 543) But there is a bit more to the story than this.

In fact, Hempel and Oppenheim had made the point that beliefs and desires could be regarded as in some sense causes in a much earlier paper. (Hempel and Oppenheim [1948] p. 327) In addition, there is reason to believe that Ducasse is not the original source of the idea in its modern formulation. In a work that predates Ducasse's paper, one Davidson, almost, certainly read, Russell had argued for the same view.

> *Every act which realizes a purpose involves two causal steps in this way: C is desired, and it is believed...that B will cause C; the desire and the belief together cause B, which in turn causes C.*
>
> — (Russell [1914] p. 228)

The use to which Russell puts this idea is to allow for the subsumption of volitional acts under causal principles. Earlier he had identified treating causation on analogy with volition as "a fruitful source of fallacies." (Russell [1912-13] p. 182) Taking this new approach he could avoid volitions as special and, thus, obviate the fallacies incipient upon recognizing them as possessing non-physical properties. Very much the same thing was part of Davidson's program, to avoid introducing intentions as special entities. It is noteworthy that in 1914, after having rejected the notion of cause in his 1912-13 work, Russell speaks of "causes" a great deal. He does so because, as he says, it is "convenient." (Russell [1914] p. 223) Still he rejects causes in science. Taken together with his rejection of volitions as falling outside science what he is left with is the notion of scientific laws and what falls under them. Earlier (Pt. 1, Sec. *b*) we discussed Russell's Humean view that laws could replace causes in science. We noted that this raised problems about what a law is as opposed to an accidental generalization. This in turn led to the anti-Humean idea that laws support counterfactual conditionals whereas accidental generalizations do not. These are issues beyond our scope, but there is an interesting side to the dispute, one relevant to "mental causation."

Suppose Russell is right that beliefs and desires, together, possess causal efficacy, 'cause' here being a term of convenience. But, next, suppose that scientific laws are generalizations supporting counterfactuals. Retain the idea *cum* Anscombe that I can do something for no reason at all. If we analyze causation counterfactually, that is, if we are allowed to say that C caused E only if we can say that had C not occurred then E would not have occurred, then beliefs and desires can never be adduced with any certainty as causes for the following reason. Whenever the evidence suggests that had I not believed such-and-such and had I no desire to do such-and-such then I would not have done such-and-such, it can be said that I might have done such-and-such *for no reason at all*. The truth of the counterfactual can, always, be challenged. If we attempt to escape this problem, we obscure the difference between explaining *why* in the sense of giving a material cause and explaining *why* in the sense of giving a reason. So that if I say "No you wouldn't have done such-and-such because you were in an inappropriate brain states," then you might as well have gone with brain state explanations to begin with, reasons be damned. A different escape may be attempted by configuring "anomalous monism" a certain way. There is another aspect to this the theory we have been discussing.

Those who advocate the idea that beliefs and desires combine to cause action, typically, fail to take into account what, for want of a better word, might be called "intuition." Two sorts of situations have not been sufficiently distinguished. Suppose I want a cookie from the jar at the top of a shelf I can't reach. I want the cookie, so desire is present; I see that the shelf has a stool just beneath it. This seeing is an "intuition" in the sense we use the word. The desire combined with the intuition results in a belief: the belief that if I step on the stool I can reach the cookie and satisfy my desire; action follows. In this sort of case a belief may be thought of as a function of desire and perceptual intuition. Belief in this case is not desire's "equal" in a sense. There is, however, another sort of situation where desire and belief are connected to such intuitions. Imagine a, somewhat, different situation. In this case, I want a cookie; I believe there is a cookie in the other room; I believe, further, that if I go into the other room, I will see it (or the jar in which it is contained). I enter the other room and find myself in a situation of the first sort. In this second sort of case, a belief combines with a desire; this leads to an intuition, and this, in turn, leads to action. In this second case, having the perceptual intuition is a function of a belief and a desire, just as action is alleged to be. The point is this: in any case where belief and desire are alleged to possess causal efficacy in relation to action, action requires perceptual intuition as well. In other words, a belief plus desire analysis is, essentially, incomplete, requiring the addition of a cognitive element not just doxastic or conative elements.

## f) Anscombe on the Singularity of Causation

Anscombe's criticisms of Hume must be taken in concert with her rejection of the regularity theory of causation. If laws are not required for causation at the level of particular events, then determinism is open to challenge, for it is the law which "determines" that one event will follow another, where it is correctly regarded as the other event's cause. Once laws are not available to provide an explanation, this opens up the possibility of a world where neither do causal relations support explanation. Moreover, the role of hypotheses in scientific explanation is backed by the role of theory; where there is a diminished role for law in explanation, there is a diminished role that theory can play. This is not to exclude theory, as such, but a theory is, typically, designed to account for the empirical facts "covered" by law. Denying the regularity theory reintroduces the question of what causality is.

Anscombe comments that while we may be unsure as to what causality is we do know that parents cause children to come into being. What is fundamental, according to her, is that a causal relation is one where an effect is *derived* from some cause. (Anscombe [1971] p. 134) The idea of derivativeness has seldom been discussed but has received informed consideration by a number of philosophers. (Makin [2000] pp. 59-73). Causation understood, merely, in terms of universality, or necessity, will not tell us that a causal relation obtains in any concrete case, but concrete cases are integral to any, possible, reconciliation between singularists and regularity theorists.

It is a central to Anscombe's views on causation that we must distinguish the claim that every event has a cause from the claim that *this* event must have had *that* cause. Largely on the basis of her taking positions of this sort, she is regarded as a singularity theorist, rather than a regularity theorist. (Cartwright [2000] p. 47) Even if it were a logical truth that every beginning of existence has a cause, we could not infer from this that the fact that any *particular* cause had a *particular* effect is, itself, a logical truth. (Anscombe [1974a] p. 151). Both views are to be distinguished from McTaggart's that, while particular cause-effect relations are logically necessary, the general claim that all events are caused is false.

Part of the problem with regarding laws as essential to understanding the concept of a cause is—as we have had occasion to note—that they depend on the idea of generality. Generalizations must be hedged in the individual case; and, so, there are few, if any, occasions where determination depends on a *stated* law, as such. According to Anscombe, a preferred alternative to saying 'Always, if *B* then *A*' would be to say 'If not *A*, even though *B*, then there must be some cause'. In this case the general term 'always' does not occur and the dubiety of the generalization, owing to unstated qualifications, is avoided. The idea that events are *determined* by laws and initial conditions is, sometimes, confused with the notion of events being caused; as if to say that, because every event has a cause, every event must be determined. That this assimilation of 'determined' and 'caused' is a confusion Anscombe makes clear by pointing out that to be caused a thing must happen, but it need not happen in order to be determined. (Anscombe, [1971] p. 140) Being determined, typically, is said to entail being related to one, and only one, set of antecedent conditions. Certainly, once an event has taken place, its antecedents are "determined," ("*Post Factum*") but Anscombe is interested in "pre-determination"—not what one might call "retro-determination." Determination is a slippery notion, one which is sometimes made easier to grasp by way of analogy.

Consider a game of chess. Any, given, arrangement of pieces on the board in the course of the game might have been reached in some other way. If we single out a particular configuration of pieces on the board, then there is no one antecedent set of conditions that *determines* it; that is, it may have been arrived at as the outcome of any one of a number of preceding gambits or strategies. But, if we think of this configuration of pieces as one among, given, successive positions in a particular ("singularly concrete") game, then antecedent conditions may, in some sense, be said to "determine" the arrangement, given the tactics and psychology of the players involved, etc. Stated another way, the contrast is between the relation of a given configuration of pieces and possible antecedents as a set of available permutations, and a given configuration of pieces and a preceding set of configurations in what is, essentially, a causal process; where we make no assumptions about the relation of reasons and causes. But even in the case involving the causal process in a concrete circumstance events are not, if Anscombe is right, predetermined. No move has been made that has been required by the rules of the game, etc. But, now, suppose I find myself in check with only one move affording me an escape. By the *rules*, I must either resign or move to that space. In this case, my move is "pre-determined," by the rules. There are, then, moves that are not "pre-determined" on the basis of the, given, arrangement of pieces—which includes the result of all moves up to the point of check—and there are moves that having been made "pre-determine" an action, such as moving out of check. In this latter case, we have what is analogous to causes which necessitate. Anscombe, however, does not reject *all* necessitating causes.

There is a sense in which some regularity theorists believe that all explainable events are like the move of the chess player who "must" remove his king from check, i.e., where there is only one available square into which he *can* move in conformity with the rule (law), although, of course, he does have the option of conceding the game. These would fall under what Anscombe calls "necessitating causes." Anscombe is quite right to say that in chess, while the moves are not determined, it may be the case that no one breaks the rules. (Anscombe [1971] p. 143) Some determinists, as we have noted, are determinists who take a radical regularity view of causation, and "reduce" causation to law governed change. They allege that all moves are determined, and that if we removed ourselves to a wider perspective, such as when someone moves back to capture the entire image of a large painting, all moves would be like that of the player who must move out of check; that is, they are "necessitated." In this case, not only are there laws, but initial conditions must be determined in lawlike fashion. The chess analogy may, also, be thought of as suggesting that all states of affairs on the board are "non-necessitated," even for the player who finds himself in check who may, after all, resign. A chess player, then, may be unaffected, causally, by a preceding move, that move being "non-necessitating."

However, he may have *reasons* for moving the way he does, given his opponents move, without being *caused* to make the move he does. We see, then, a relationship between singularity, as a view on causation, and the idea of reason distinct from causes, even where there are causes involved in how reason is exercised.

## *g) Applying Kripke to Singular Causation*

In the last great masterpiece of analytical philosophy, Saul Kripke (Kripke [1972]) casts doubt on both the belief that necessary truths are *a priori* and that that all *a priori* truths are necessary. We, next, examine one attempt at relating Kripke's position to the debate over singular causation. Some will consider the next section, where we discuss the contingent *a priori*, an unnecessary digression. However, there is a common component, the theory of rigid designation, underlying both issues, and while we shall not engage this theory, specifically, we will examine a number of its applications.

In an artful display of philosophical skill, David Armstrong addresses the issue of singular causation. We cannot take up his numerous proposals and insights. Instead, we examine his claim that Anscombe views causation as "essentially" singular. In particular, we examine his claim that singular causation instantiates laws of nature. (Armstrong [1997] p. 202) Armstrong asks "Why should it not be the case that the identification of a causal sequence with the instantiation of a law" is a necessary *a posteriori* truth? Elsewhere, Armstrong and Adrian Heathcote in a brief but thought provoking essay provide reasons for believing that we *should* make this identification. (Heathcote and Armstrong [1991]) Such a belief, if correct, would amount to a compromise position between singularist and regularity theorists; but it would, also, amount to the rejection of singularism as an *alternative* to the regularity view. It is doubtful that Anscombe would have agreed with their take on the matter. We shall examine why she might have found their reasoning unconvincing. Our examination will yield the added dividend that by accepting our intentional actions as knowable independently of experience, as Anscombe did, we are afforded additional insights into the relation of the intentionality of sensations, such as pains, to action. Although Anscombe might not approve of some of the arguments to be proposed, it is quite likely she would have rejected the Heathcote/Armstrong application of Kripke's notion of the *necessary a posteriori*.

Saul Kripke in a remarkable argument based on his theory of "rigid designation" has argued that, if sentences like 'water = $H_2O$' are true, they are necessarily true, albeit *a posteriori*. (Kripke [1971] *passim*) His argument, briefly considered, is this: 'water' and '$H_2O$' are "rigid designators," meaning that they refer to the same thing in every possible world in which they designate at all. Thus, if 'water = $H_2O$' is true, it is true in all possible worlds, meaning that it is a necessary truth; and because 'water = $H_2O$' is established by observation and experiment knowledge of 'Necessarily (water = $H_2O$)' is to be regarded as *a posteriori* knowledge.

We will challenge this idea, but before we do we will address singular causation in light of Heathcote and Armstrong's contribution to the discussion of singular causation.

Elsewhere, I have argued that Kripke's argument when applied on behalf of Cartesian dualism is vulnerable to considerations having to do with diversity, rather than identity. (Bayne [1988]) Our objective in what follows will be to show that, contrary to what has been argued by Heathcote/Armstrong, Kripke's argument can be turned against the very position to which they enlist its support. According to Heathcote/Armstrong the identity of instances of singular causation with instantiations of laws is necessary *a posteriori*. The position they argue for is that "Just as investigation shows that water is $H_2O$ and can be nothing else, so investigation shows that causal sequences are essentially nomic." (Heathcote and Armstrong [1991] p. 67) What we wish to call into question is whether the identification of singular sequences with instantiations of laws is sustainable. Let us begin with a brief restatement of Kripke's original argument.

We have it that 'water = $H_2O$' is a necessary truth. Suppose, however, this is challenged by claiming that since I can imagine water's not being $H_2O$ it may not *be* $H_2O$. The one asserting the identity must explain the illusoriness of this appearance of contingency. (Kripke [1971] pp. 100-101). The "illusion of contingency" is explained by pointing out that we might be in the very same "epistemic situation" as we are in when identifying a substance as water, even though what we are presented with is not water at all. Thus I may go to Mars; come upon a substance and be in the same epistemic situation as I am on Earth when presented with water but in fact be presented with some different substance. The point is that I pick out water by means of contingent properties. As long as there is a contingent property by which I identify water, the illusion of contingency can be explained. There are cases, however, where identities are asserted but where no contingent property is present by which we identify at least one of the things asserted to be identical. The sentence 'pain = C-fibers firing' is one such instance. A consideration well worth pursuing comes from David Wiggins who contends that if a name, such as 'water', is to stand for a natural kind there must be some "nomological grounding." (Wiggins [1980] p. 80) But how much of this "grounding" is required in order to justify an identity statement, such as 'Water = $H_2O$'? If we believe, perhaps following Bohm, that this "grounding" has no natural end, that it goes on indefinitely as a consequence of there being infinitely many physical variables, then there is some question whether identity statements about kinds are ever known to be true, and possibly never are true.

One might care to consider another identity statement, 'Heat = Molecular Motion'. One potential difficulty for rigid designation is using submolecular exemplars in order to fix the reference of 'heat', say, plasma. In this case 'heat' may not refer to the same thing in all possible worlds in which there is heat. This may not be an intractable problem, if it is a problem, but it warrants attention it has not received. For now, we focus on the more immediate case at hand, the case of pain and brain states.

In such a case there is no "epistemic counterpart" of pain which is *not* pain; that is, there is no contingent property we use in identifying pain which is such that that that property is instantiated even though there is no pain, as there may be some epistemic counterpart of water which is not water. Whatever way we experience pain is, itself, pain. From this Kripke infers that pain cannot be identified with neurological states, whereas water can be identified with $H_2O$. What Heathcote and Armstrong maintain is that "singular causation is identical with the positive instantiation of a law" in the same sense that water is identical to $H_2O$. (Heathcote and Armstrong [1991] p. 71)

What first arouses our suspicion that there may be something wrong with their argument is that they supply no sentence analogous to 'water = $H_2O$'.

In other words, they provide us with no assertion of identity where something takes the place of 'water' or 'H$_2$O', only assurances that for any instantiation of a law there is some singular causal sequence with which it is identical. Is this omission evasion, unavoidable, or suggestive of a potential flaw in their argument? Let's consider the last possibility. Since they don't supply the relevant sentence, let us attempt to supply it. It must be emphasized, however, that owing to the uncertainty of what they are, actually, claiming owing to this omission the argument we discuss may not be the one they had in mind.

We represent a particular singular causal sequence as '$C_{1,2}$' and the instantiation of a scientific law this way, '$L_{a,b}$'. The sentence at issue, then, would be '$C_{1,2} = L_{a,b}$'. It is important to note that, whereas in the case of 'water = H$_2$O' we are concerned with *kinds*, in the case of '$a$' and '2', etc., we are dealing in particulars. Nevertheless, let's consider whether '$C_{1,2} = L_{a,b}$' can be regarded as a necessary *a posteriori* truth, as 'water = H$_2$O' typically is. It is an important part of Kripke's argument that 'water = H$_2$O' has the *appearance* of contingency. Whoever asserts 'water = H$_2$O' must be able to give an explanation of this appearance, for if it cannot be explained, then the possibility that the identity fails has not been ruled out; and if that cannot be ruled out, then the sentence is possibly false; and, if it is possibly false, then (contrary to hypothesis) the sentence cannot be necessary; and if it is not necessary, then the original identity sentence is false. The claim being made appears to be this: any pair of events regarded as singular and not as kinds is identical to the instantiation of *some* law. Let's take the ordered pair of events in a singular causal relation, <1, 2>, as being expressed by '$C_{1,2}$', and let's take the ordered pair which is the instantiation of a law, <a, b>, as being represented by '$L_{a,b}$'. The claim is that '$C_{1,2} = L_{a,b}$' and 'water = H$_2$O' are alike in all relevant respects. We say "relevant" because the second pertains to natural *kinds* not particulars. Still, if this is the case, then '$L_{a,b}$' must be a rigid designator. This sentence states a particular instantiation of a law, $L$. One problem with this is that, as Russell may have been the first to note (Russell [1912-13] p. 198), laws may have duration; that is, laws may not persist throughout all of time. There is nothing necessary about a scientific law beyond physical necessity. The duration of a law in one world may not be the same as in another possible world. If this is the case, then the following possibility cannot be ruled out: at some future time the identity

'$C_{1,2} = L_{a,b}$' will not be true, let alone necessary. Moreover, either it fails because '$L_{a,b}$' doesn't designate at all, although '$C_{1,2}$' does, or it will not designate an instantiation of a law. In other words, there will be at least one occasion where the identity fails, even if it succeeds at some other time. There is at least one other problem, one having to do less with matters of necessity and more with the *a posteriori* side of 'necessary *a posteriori*'. If, as Russell says, laws may not endure indefinitely, we are faced with a puzzle Russell did not discuss. This is not to say that no one realized the potential problems that might arise were it the case that scientific laws are transitory. Karl Popper claimed that if laws are transitory, then "it would be the end of scientific progress." (Popper [1957] p. 103)

Insofar as Russell is a classical determinist in the sense that from an initial world state, and differential equations, any subsequent state of the universe is said to be predictable, it is peculiar that he did not, explicitly at least, consider the possibility that not only may the laws not endure, but if they do not his Laplacian determinism must vanish of necessity. This would hold even without considering the quantum indeterminacies that would, later, make indeterminism the dominant point of view.

Since we are dealing not in kinds but singular instances, there is some question as to whether we can in fact know, even if it is true, that $C_{1,2}$ is identical to $L_{a,b}$. Suppose the scientific evidence has it that experiment has permitted the "meta-inference" (Harthcote and Armstrong [1991] p. 71) that singular causal processes are identical with instantiations of laws. What is to exclude any particular case from being evidence to the contrary? 'Singular causal processes' will in this case refer to a sort or kind, not an instance of a singular causal process. If we compare this circumstance to that where chemistry has shown that water is $H_2O$ certain important differences become, immediately, obvious. One can show that in all likelihood *this* water is $H_2O$, but can experiment show that *this* pair of events is identical to some instantiation of a law? The "meta-inference" may not suffice to enable this inference. I can take a sample of water and show that it is $H_2O$ but can I show on the basis of my knowledge of *this* singular sequence of events, *qua* causal relation, that it is *this* instantiation of a law? This seems very unlikely, if not impossible, altogether.

But, now, with respect to '$C_{1,2} = L_{a,b}$' we raise the question: "Do we pick out $C_{1,2}$ by means of a contingent property?" If so, what is that property? Heathcote and Armstrong need something like

$\langle 1, 2 \rangle = \langle a, b \rangle$. To get this we need '$1 = a$'; but how do we arrive at this? Instantiating a general law will not allow this; and existential instantiation will not either. Moreover, given that there must be such identities, then we need 'Nec ($\langle 1, 2 \rangle = \langle a, b \rangle$)'—'Nec' meaning 'necessarily'—and there is no obvious way of doing this without showing '$1 = a$', '$2 = b$'. This seems question begging. Do we want to say that since lawlikeness is what makes a causal relation necessary that since the identity obtains it follows by rigid designation that if a causal relation is identical to the instantiation of a law that is a necessary not contingent relation? Do we want to say that from '$C_{1,2} = L_{a,b}$' we can derive 'Necessarily ($C_{1,2} = L_{a,b}$)?

Because what is at issue are singular sequences, rather than *types* of singular sequences, the answer is not so clear. If '$C_{1,2}$' designated a kind, rather than an individual sequence, then we might say that we rely on contingent properties of the sort Hume might invoke in alleging a causal connection, properties that include similarity to other sequences, for example. To know that a singular sequence is causal, according to the singularist, "we need only look. The verifying situation is right before our eyes." (Black [1958] p. 41) In order to know that a sequence is an instantiation of a law it is not enough to look. It is important to note, however, that I pick out an instance of singular causation on the basis of contingent properties. It may be the case that, although what is "right before our eyes" *is* an instance of singular causation, some other event caused the effect we attribute to what we thought was the cause. Thus, there is no way of ruling out the truth of identity statements involving a singular causal sequence, $C_{1,2}$, on the basis of the fact that we cannot imagine cases where we are in an identical epistemic situation as we are when we observe $C_{1,2}$ but where the identity fails. Significantly, we do not *pick out* causal events based on the *property* of singularity.

If I report seeing a rock breaking a window, I report an instance of singular causation. But it may turn out that the window broke a fraction of a second before the rock struck the window. So I can imagine being in the same situation, epistemically, even though something else broke the window. I can, therefore, identify the rock's breaking the window with the rock's going through the window, where that identity, if true, is necessary. But what I can't imagine is that the singularity of either event is a contingent property; that is, I cannot imagine being in the same epistemic situation I am when I observe the event taking place but where *the* event is not singular.

One senses that this is important but what importance it is remains elusive. Moreover, although we have raised possible objections to arguments against the compromise solution to the conflict between singularist and regularity views, the proposed solution, Heathcote and Armstrong's, remains too obscure to say that we have disposed of it. Our point is that it is sketchy and, quite possibly wrong. However there is an important difference between observing that a rock in motion causes a window to break and knowing our own actions. Our extended remarks allow us a more precise statement of the unusual features of intentional action and our knowledge of them.

The sentence 'a = b' may be *a posteriori* and true, but even if we concede the force of what we shall call "the Barcan Principle," that from 'x = y' it follows that 'necessarily (x = y)', it does not follow from this that 'necessarily (a = b)' is *a posteriori*. For Kant *a posteriori* knowledge is knowledge we get "only…through experience." (Kant [1781] B3). It is true that, traditionally, the sole alternative to *a posteriori* is *a priori*, and that to be known *a priori* is to be known "absolutely independently of all experience." (ibid) This would suggest to some that 'necessarily (a = b)' cannot be *a priori* because it is from the identity 'a = b' that we come to know 'necessarily (a = b)' and, 'a = b" can be known only through experience, rendering 'necessarily (a = b)' *a posteriori*. But the proposition 'necessarily (a = b)' requires only the Barcan Principle applied to a proposition asserting a true identity. We ought no more consider 'necessarily (a = b)' *a posteriori* than we would consider 'The cat has two heads or the cat does not have two heads', or (and this is important) "Every change has a cause," as *a posteriori*. Both follow from logic, alone, applied to propositions, which are not propositions of logic, viz. 'a = b' and 'The cat has two heads', both of which may be *a posteriori*. Schematically the similarity can be represented, thusly,

(…or ~…) /<p>

(Nec …) /<p>

In the first case, what is represented is the form of a proposition where 'p' is substituted, whatever it may be, for '…' in '(…or ~…)';

similar remarks apply, as well, to the second. The point we take to be fundamental is this: Where it is the case that 'a = b' is an *a posteriori* truth, 'Nec(a = b)' is not an *a posteriori* truth. Why? I know the former to be true by way of experience, whereas I know the latter only by *inference*. Knowledge by way of inference is not knowledge by way of experience. *Given* that 'a = b' I know 'Nec(a = b)' independently of all experience. The skeptic will reply: "Of course if it is "given." But this riposte would be insufficient. Clearly, there are differences, as well as similarities, between 'Nec(a = b)' and 'Tom is tall or Tom is not tall'; I need to know 'a = b' by experience before I can know 'Nec(a = b)' but I do not need to know that 'Tom is tall' or 'Tom is not tall' in order to know 'Tom is tall or Tom is not tall', or that 'Nec(Tom is tall or Tom is not tall)'. What I need to know in order to know 'Nec(Tom is tall or Tom is not tall)' is that 'Tom is tall or Tom is not tall' is true in all possible worlds. I may claim to know this because I know, among other things, the truth table for 'or' and 'not'. It is a logical truth and, so, I am confident that I can infer 'Nec(Tom is tall or Tom is not tall)'. But what of 'a = b'? How do I know *it* is true in all possible worlds? I either infer it ala Barcan or I infer this from its truth *and* the fact that 'a' and 'b' are rigid designators. In either case knowledge of its truth is a matter of inference not experience.

In the case where we infer 'Nec(a = b) from the fact that 'a' and 'b' are rigid designators and 'a = b' is true, we still fall short of being able to maintain that 'Nec(a = b) is *a posteriori*. Why? Because no statement of necessity can be known to be true by way of experience; that is, I cannot know that a proposition is true in all possible worlds by way of my experiences in this world without some inference based on logic or a theory about all possible worlds and rigid designators; neither logic nor the theory of rigid designation are empirical. I may know that 'a = b' is true by experience in this world, but not 'Nec(a = b)'. "But, surely," it may be said, "if I know that 'a' rigidly designates the same thing in all worlds and I know 'b' designates the same thing in all worlds, and I know that in one of those worlds, this one, 'a = b' then I *must* know that 'Nec(a = b)'!" The interlocutor has missed the point. The point is that, even arguing from rigid designation, knowledge of 'Nec(a = b)' is inferred from *a priori* principles governing inferences based on rigid designation and logic. This is not to reject Kripke's theory of rigid designation. What we are challenging here is the notion of a "necessary *a posteriori*." At this point, we may not be able to rule out the possibility that such statements of necessity are closer to being *synthetic a priori* than to being necessary *a posteriori*.

## h) Calling into Question the Contingent a Priori

It is sometimes claimed (Aune [2008] p. 41) that Kripke argues against Kant's Idea that all knowledge of necessary truth is *a priori*. What most people don't know is that the idea of a necessary *a posteriori* had been introduced, already, by another philosopher in attacking Kant's views. Again, we have occasion to mention Reichenbach.

> *It is therefore not possible, as Kant believed, to single out in the concept of object a component that reason regards as necessary. It is experience that decides which elements are necessary (italics added—srb).*
>
> — (Reichenbach [1920] p. 88).

Reichenbach proposed an alternative to Kant's synthetic *a priori*. Because of this he could not allow the Kantian idea of the "concept of object" to be determined *a priori*. Instead, following Schlick, he introduced the notion of "principles of coordination," principles having a basis in the "successive approximation" by induction to a concept of an object in circumstances characterized by our evolving knowledge of physics. If we accept neither Reichenbach's, nor Kripke's, view of the necessary *a posteriori*, then we are most likely to be driven back to Kant's idea of the synthetic *a priori*. There may be another, possibility, however, one such that those who are quick to accept Kripke's argument, as one directed against Kant's position, fail to consider. Kant's theory, as he actually states it, reveals that his concept of the *a priori* is not limited to knowledge which lacks empirical elements. For Kant, there is a distinction to be made. Not all *a priori* knowledge is "pure." It may be argued that allegedly necessary *a posteriori* knowledge is "mixed" rather than purely *a priori*. Whether all *a priori* propositions which are not "mixed" are synthetic *a priori* is a question we shall not pursue. There is, however, *another* issue, whether there is such a thing as a contingent *a priori*.

Kripke not only argues for the "necessary *a posteriori*" he argues for the "contingent *a priori*" as well. Notwithstanding the fact that only the first has been shown to have a direct bearing on causation, we shall entertain, briefly, arguments for a contingent *a priori*. Strictly speaking, for Kant this would be a contradiction. Our discussion of whether this is a useful idea begins with Kripke's discussion of an analogy raised by Wittgenstein.

Wittgenstein in his *Philosophical Investigations* discusses, at one point, the impossibility of attributing 'being' to *elements* of one's ontology. He brings up what he thinks is an analogous impossibility:

> *There is one thing of which one can say neither that it is one metre long, nor that it is not one metre long, and that is the standard metre in Paris.—But this is, of course, not to ascribe any extraordinary property to it, but only to mark its peculiar role in the language-game of measuring with a metre-rule.*
>
> — (Wittgenstein [1953] 50)

Kripke is incredulous. Immediately, before, entering objections to Wittgenstein's view, he dismisses consideration of the concept of 'the length of' as "not important." (Kripke [1972] p. 54) We shall, soon, see that it is the very thing Wittgenstein has in mind. Kripke, then, remarks that he thinks Wittgenstein "must be wrong." (Kripke [1972] p. 54). The reason he gives for believing he's wrong is that since I can take a ruler and measure the stick in Paris, discovering that it is 39.37 inches, I *can* attribute being a meter long to the stick residing in Paris. In this case, however, it can hardly be maintained that S's being 39.37 inches is contingent *a priori*, since in this case knowing by measurement in inches that S is one meter one is known by observation. When Kripke argues that 'Stick S is one meter long at $t_0$' is *a priori* he must be thinking of S in its special employment as introducing a unit of measurement. Insofar as it can be regarded as an ordinary stick it can be measured with a ruler to confirm its being a meter long, but then we can't say its being a meter is known *a priori*. On the other hand, if we treat it as a special stick, we cannot regard the sentence as contingent. In the course of Kripke's argument there appears to be a shifting back and forth between these two ways of regarding the stick. The problem is that we can't tell what he means when he uses 'S'. Taken under one description, 'used as a standard for determining the unit *meter*' the sentence may be necessary, assuming we can overcome Wittgenstein's claim that we can't even attribute being a meter to it. In this case, using a ruler to determine its length as one meter will just beg the question by, eventually, raising another the question, viz. the question of the standard for fixing 'one inch' and how we know its length.

Consider the sentence

(Q1)  S is one meter long.

If we take 'S' to stand for 'the standard meter stick' then I know *a priori* the truth of 'S is a meter long', since

(Q2)  The standard meter stick is one meter long.

is true of any standard meter stick. In addition (Q2) is necessary with this understanding. It must be kept in mind that 'Standard meter stick' is not like 'United Nations', applied to nations that are in fact divided, or 'Holy Roman Empire', where the Church is not being described thereby as Roman or an empire. 'Standard' is being used in 'standard meter stick' as an adjective, not part of name, although one *could* give the stick this name.

Even if the stick is heated, as long as I don't specify a time it will still be a meter long, regardless of how much it expands. Or, we might treat the notion of being a meter as subject to change depending on the temperature and, therefore, the length of the stick. The reference is not fixed but the sentence Q2 is nonetheless true and *a priori*. If I stipulate a time, then Q2 retains its status as *a priori*, adjusted for time of utterance, but is no longer necessary, according to Kripke's proposal, because if heated its length changes. Q3 is warranted:

(Q3)  The standard meter stick at $t_0$ is one meter long.

In this case the sentence is neither necessary nor *a priori*. So far our alternatives are Q2, which is both necessary and *a priori*; or, Q3, which is contingent and a posteriori. So where does Kripke get the idea that the sentence Q1 is both contingent and *a priori*? (Kripke

[1980] p. 56). If we are right his proposal trades on an ambiguity, an ambiguity that is papered over by using 'S' instead of 'The standard meter stick in Paris'. Using 'S' creates the illusion that we are talking about just any stick, rather than some stick taken under the description 'standard meter stick'. If we construe 'S' as a proper name of a stick, then

(Q4)  Necessarily S is one meter long

is false. If we take 'S' as a description, 'the standard meter stick', then

(Q2)  The standard meter stick is one meter long

is necessary and *a priori*; that is, where S is taken under the description 'standard meter stick' 'S is one meter long' is both necessary and *a priori*, just as 'The number of planets is necessarily greater than 7' is *false* where 9 is taken under the description 'the number of planets' (Quine). But in case 'S' simply names a stick then 'S is one meter long' is, merely, contingent and a posteriori. What Kripke does in order to get a "contingent *a priori*" is shift back and forth from one reading to another. That is, in order to get the *a priori* reading he takes 'S' as 'the standard meter stick'; but in order to get the contingent reading he regards 'S' as just the name of a stick. This can be expressed in familiar terminology. Consider (Q5)

(Q5)  The standard meter stick is necessarily one meter long.

If we regard 'necessarily' as *de dicto*, then it is necessary and *a priori*. If we construe it as *de re*, then it is false but contingent. By surreptitiously alternating his reading of (Q5) he feels that he can assert that (Q1) is both contingent and *a priori*. It should be noted that the objection being raised depends on Dummett's suggestion that the theory of rigid designation comes down to scope. (Dummett [1973] p. 128) Nor, even, that deriving the possibility of a contingent *a priori* amounts in any way to a reductio ad absurdum argument against the theory. Only that Kripke arrives at seemingly paradoxical conclusions by equivocation. It is easy to overlook another aspect of his treatment of this situation, one that is especially important.

He says that the one, whoever it is, who fixes the reference of 'one meter' has a certain length in mind that he "wants to mark out." (Kripke [1972] p. 55) and, so, he finds a stick that has "that length." This is a peculiar thing to carry around in one's mind, that is, the idea of a particular length. What would be the "vehicle" for such an idea? Might it be something like the idea of being some fraction of the distance between the moon and Jupiter? But, then, we need some unit measure in order to begin our search for a standard meter; either that or we have very long arms. What, exactly, *do* I have *in mind*? How do I determine that the length of this stick is the length to which I want to fix the reference of 'one meter'? In any event, armed with this idea, he sets out to find some stick having this length, and behold, he finds it.

Alternatively, we may discard this notion of a pre-existing idea of a certain length. But, now, Kripke notes that in the case of S it is not the meaning of 'one meter' that is being given, even though, in some sense, he calls the procedure a "definition"; rather, what is going on is that the reference of 'one meter' is being *fixed*. This notion of giving a definition without giving the meaning, actually, goes back to Schlick's notion of coordinate definition. Suppose we say that by 'one meter' we "mean" 'the length of S' (whatever that might be). Kripke is, fully, aware that we might have chosen another stick, even though, if we were looking to fix reference to a particular length we have in mind, we would have to find a stick of the same length. A word, next, on the alleged cases of necessary *a priori* truths.

I can know *a priori* that if 'a = b' is true, then 'Nec(a = b)' is true; that is, that it is true in all worlds. But from my knowledge that *a* and *b* are identical I cannot know from this fact, alone, that they are identical in all possible worlds. So when Kripke describes the necessary truth of 'a = b' he is fine, but when he adds "*a posteriori*" he is equivocating, moving from the metalinguistic idea of the *truth* of 'a = b' to a truth about objects, not sentences. Let's be clear about something, I think, Kripke misses. From the fact that two things are identical it may follow that they are necessarily identical. But the fact that 'a = b' is true in all possible worlds in not known a posteriori. In other words, the sentence 'Necessarily (a = b') is *not* known by experience; it is known by *inference*; what we know by inference. I may know 'a = b' by experience, but I cannot know 'Necessarily (a = b)' by looking, even if I can only know 'a = b' by looking. To reflect on an earlier proposal: I may know that 'Tom is tall' or 'Tom is not tall' only by way of experience, but no experience is required in order to know the truth of 'Tom is tall or Tom is not tall'. Let's return, briefly, to Kripke's discussion of Wittgenstein and the meter stick for some concluding remarks on why Kripke misunderstood Wittgenstein.

Wittgenstein's point, as far as the meter stick is concerned, is that in its capacity as a *representation* of a unit of measurement it is a conceptual error to believe the stick can be checked to see whether it really succeeds at representing a meter. The question should be: "How can I say one way or the other whether the meter stick in Paris really *represents* a meter?" A ruler will not suffice to provide an answer to this question. Again, there is no fact of the matter to check. This is what Kripke misses. Any particular concept of length depends on what we select to measure length, not the other way around. It is possible Kripke sees this as a potential problem. However, this idea is the locus of Wittgenstein's argument. There are historical reasons for believing this to be true.

In a lecture some years ago, the philosopher of science, Rom Harre, commented on the early Wittgenstein's involvement with philosophy of science. The influence of Hertz is well known. But Harre's point struck a chord with this writer because he had been, strongly, impressed by the possibility of understanding some of the later Wittgenstein's aphorisms in terms of developments in physics. In most cases the influence is subtle, but it so happens that with respect to the discussion of the meter stick in Paris it is not so subtle. In particular, the influence of Reichenbach, whose views in connection with Wittgenstein have already been mentioned, seems nearly certain. Reichenbach makes *precisely* the same point Wittgenstein appears to be making, only many years earlier. Reichenbach addresses certain criticisms of the Theory of Relativity, distinguishing the "logical" and "technical" impossibility of measurement.

> *There is the impossibility of making measurements which is due to the limitations of our technical means. I shall call it technical impossibility. In addition, there is a logical impossibility of measuring. Even if we had a perfect experimental technique, we should be unable to avoid this logical impossibility. It is logically impossible to determine whether the standard meter stick in Paris is re-*

> *ally a meter...It is arbitrarily defined as the unit, and the question whether it really represents this unit has lost its meaning.*
>
> — (Reichenbach [1927] pp. 28-29)

Notice that the possibility of measuring the stick in Paris with Kripke's ruler is a *technical possibility*, but what Reichenbach and Wittgenstein are saying is that determining whether or not the stick in Paris *really* represents the length of a meter is *logically impossible*. What Reichenbach, and Wittgenstein, are saying casts doubt on the success of Kripke's argument that there is a "contingent *a priori*." For Wittgenstein and Reichenbach, the question of whether the stick is really a meter long, or really *represents* a meter, are one and the same. Kripke's move is based on exploiting a, seeming, ambiguity. But, the real problem for him is that introducing this stick as the "meter stick" *is* a way of giving *meaning* to 'meter'; it is not a way of singling out the length of this stick and fixing reference to that length. Kripke tells us that in the case of fixing the reference of 'meter' I am not giving the meaning, only the reference (Kripke [1980] p. 55); but if this is not giving the meaning, then what meaning, as opposed to reference, can 'meter' possess. The question is never raised.

### *i) The Singularist View and Knowledge of Actions*

We have seen that one of Kripke's arguments for the necessary *a posteriori* relies on the idea of an *epistemic situation* or *epistemic counterpart*. Elsewhere I have discussed a problematic feature of this approach, one issuing from considerations of necessary diversity. (Bayne [1988]) Despite the doubts we have raised, for now we will accept the idea of necessary *a posteriori* truths as an applicable "technology" in addressing the identity of intentional actions.

Recall that Kripke establishes the contingency of identity statements such as 'water = $H_2O$' by pointing out that we might be in the same epistemic situation in identifying a substance as water as we might be in identifying some other substance, say a substance found only on the planet Mongo (our example), even though that substance is not $H_2O$. Kripke points out that in this case we have identified a substance based on contingent properties related to the *way* the substance presents itself to us. Moreover, in the case of pain there is no, similarly, contingent property, or set of properties, by which we can identify pain but which is not *essential* to pain. What we shall argue is that what we have been calling "basic actions" are like pains in the following sense: I cannot identify my basic actions, *qua* intentional, on the basis of contingent properties, just as I cannot identify *my* pain (*qua* mental) on the basis of a contingent property. Nor can we "pick out" our willful actions by the contingent fact that they affect us in a certain way. Anscombe's insistence on its being the case that knowledge of my intentional actions is not by way of observation suggests this possibility, inasmuch as, if we do identify such actions on the basis of observable properties then all identification of them, as intentional actions, will rely on contingent properties. The possibility is left open that I cannot identify my raising my arm with my arm's going up because I cannot explain the appearance of the contingency of this identity by *imagining* an epistemic counterpart to *my* raising my arm which is not an instance of my arm going up. Just as any "counterpart" of pain is going to be a pain and, so, not an actual "counterpart," so too, there is no "counterpart" of the experience of my raising my arm which is not, itself, the experience of my raising my arm.

The difficulties are increased by the fact that intentionality is not a property of the action, itself, as Anscombe notes. If intentionality, however, is not a property, then we are hard put to say that we identify the basic action in terms of an essential *property*. But neither, then, can it be a contingent property by which it is identified. I may be in the same situation I am in when I identify water but what I identify in fact is not water; however I cannot be in the same epistemic situation I am in when I identify a bodily motion as a basic action where the action is not basic. Pains in this respect are like basic actions. At this point, we turn our attention to clarifying the source and content of the idea that the actions of agents relate causal sequences which are not instantiations of some law.

By most accounts, laws relate properties, although we have seen that taken together with initial conditions they can relate events. This is consistent with the covering law model of explanation. The singularist position does not exclude, *a priori*, the possibility that some properties of events in a relation of singular causation are instantiations of laws. What is, minimally, sufficient for the singularist position is that a singular cause have as an effect the possession of some property that is not "covered" by some law. The singularist need not deny that all properties are such that no singular sequence involving such properties is an instantiation of some law, only that there is some property caused to be had which is not covered by law on that particular occasion. In order to see this more clearly, let's consider a case attributed to Michael Scriven and discussed by Carl Hempel. (Hempel [1965] pp. 360-362)

Scriven gives an example of a causal relation that has no explanation in terms of scientific laws. I reach for a dictionary; in the process my knee strikes the edge of he table spilling ink onto the carpet. Scriven alleges that there is no explanation in terms of law. Hempel engages in a spirited defense of the contrary view. His reply to Scriven is not so important to us. What is important is what amounts to an admission on Hempel's part, an admission that has consequences for the singularist's position. Suppose we refer to the cause of the spilling of the ink '$p$' and the ink spill, the effect, '$q$'. What Hempel takes note of is that, as we add to our description of the effect, the more unlikely becomes an appeal to laws in providing an explanation. Indeed, if we describe the effect as an ink spot on a *particular* rug, laws do not enter the explanatory picture at all.

> *If, by contrast, the '$q$'-statement is taken to specify not only that the ink spilled out, but also that it produced a stain of specified size and shape on the rung, then, to be sure, no laws are known that would permit the inference from the '$p$' statement...*
>
> — (Hempel [1965] p. 361)

This is a statement of considerable conceptual and, possibly, historical significance, for here we have a singular sequence of events that is not the instantiation of a law. Its historical significance may be that it exemplifies the very thing that appears to have motivated what is "anomalous" in Donald Davidson's "anomalous monism," a view we shall, soon, discuss. For now, we are going to combine two ideas: the idea that basic actions, just like sensations of pain, are mental events and, second, the idea that singular causal sequences may not be explainable in terms of laws.

Recall that in our extended discussion of shoe-tying, we took note of a "special" kind of causation, viz. entrainment. What interests us is that the entrained motion of the shoe laces was the result of basic action associated with the moving fingers. One feature important for our purposes is that the entraining cause, the finger movement, and the entrained effect, the movement of the laces, take place concurrently. This is important because it rules out the possibility of "preemptive causes." For our purposes a preemptive cause is one which is such that, while it may not be the actual cause of some event, would be the actual cause should some other event fail to be the cause. (*vide* Lewis [1973] p.171) Such preemptive causes had been discussed by others, e.g. J. L. Mackie, before Lewis. (Mackie [1965] p. 25) Mackie cites earlier remarks by Scriven and Patrick Gardiner, but it was David Lewis who first called attention to their significance in constructing a viable counterfactualist account of causation. Without pursuing Lewis's views further, at this point, we can say this much: The more closely two events occur in time the less likely are such preemptive causes to become actual causes. In addition, as this possibility diminishes the more "fragile" the effect becomes. Fragility will be understood, here, as the property which an event has if it could not have taken place differently or at a different time. (Lewis [1986] p. 196) Singularity theorists of the radical sort will insist that *all* events are fragile. The more fragile an event the more essential become its properties. In discussing Heathcote and Armstrong we argued that their use of Kripke's argument is inapplicable to basic actions, since there is no epistemic counterpart grounded in a, merely, contingent feature of any such actions. This now becomes a consequence, at least in part, of the fact that the events in a singular causal sequence are of extreme fragility. (Lewis [1986] p. 197) Suppose the lid of a jar in my grasp is turned by the continuous basic action of moving my hand counterclockwise.

The entrainment, itself, may be characterized as subject to the physical principles associated with the analysis of vectors. Laws, therefore, relate some properties of the events involved. Our singularism allows for this, since it is only required that not all properties are "covered" by laws. One such property in this example is the time at which the event occurs. Again, it is an important feature that in the case of entrainment causation, such as this, that the cause and the effect are concurrent; the cause does not precede the effect. Where the cause is regarded as mental, as we have been taking a basic action to be, there is no point in "tracing back," a notion that we shall discover Anscombe felt to be of limited value in the treatment of intentional action. We conclude this aspect of our discussion of singular causation by bringing it back to Anscombe.

As we examine her reply to Chisholm, as well as her comments specifically directed to causation, we must keep in mind that her rejection of causal determination is a consequence of her rejection of the view promoted by Hempel and, to a lesser extent Davidson, that events in a singular causal relation are determined by law. Since there is no law that will "cover" the events, there can be no *determination* of effect by cause. We have applied these ideas in examining basic actions in particular, actions which according to Anscombe (with Davidson following her lead) are the only real actions we can attribute to the agent. In particular, we have promoted an example of singular causation related to the one earlier discussed of tying one's shoe laces, which we discovered to involve an interesting type of causation, entrainment. We, then, speculated that this type of causation is crucially related to the mental, insofar as basic actions are intentional, and it is basic actions which entrain the movement of objects in the "external world." That movement is not mental; basic action is mental. Our view is that this is the crucial nexus between the mental and the physical in action theory. It is inspired by Anscombe and, essentially, incorporates her commitment to singularism.

## *j) Feynman, Bohm, and the "Magic" Box*

Anscombe is, exactly, correct: causation is, typically, *assumed* in providing some basis for the necessitation commonly associated with the use of 'law'. (Anscombe [1971] p. 133) Although Hume is a good example of one who makes this assumption, or something very much like it, he was more circumspect than others with regard to the idea of "necessary causal relations," saying only that when there is invariance "we always conclude that there is a secret *cause*." (Hume [1888] p. 75) One philosopher/scientist Anscombe drew from has echoed Hume's sentiments: "When we find such regularities...we assume...necessary causal relations." (D. Bohm [1957] p. 4) Here, as in Hume, one finds the assumption of a connection between necessity and regularity, although Bohm's theory is more complex because he distinguishes chance from the statistical regularity we associate with causation. Causal relations are in fact, frequently, thought to explain the necessity of scientific generalizations, rather than the other way around. How this figures in identifying generalizations *as* lawlike, insofar as they support counterfactuals, will depend on how we are to properly view the relation of counterfactuals to causation. Some, e.g. D. Lewis, have argued that causation should be analyzed in terms of counterfactuals, such as when we assert 'If *A* had not occurred, then *B* would not have occurred' in the analysis of '*A* caused *B*'. (Lewis [1973]) Anscombe challenges the idea that necessity and cause are related as Hume, Bohm, and, of course, many others, have suggested.

Anscombe's objection to associating prediction with causality depends on a crucial asymmetry: we find it much easier to "trace back" a cause than to make a prediction. Prediction, here, is closely related to "explanation," where explanation is understood as subsuming events under scientific laws. Thus, Anscombe is challenging the typical association of cause and explanation, such as when explanation takes the form of a "deductive nomological" or "inductive statistical" model of the sort suggested by Hempel and Oppenheim. (Hempel and Oppenheim [1948]). Let's consider an analogy that may clarify what may be one's intuitions at this point with respect to the relation of necessary and sufficient conditions in the context of explanation.

Imagine a tree, for simplicity without leaves. This is a growing tree and growth takes place from the end point of the branches, apical meristems. We are unable to predict the precise direction and rate of growth. This is owing to a number of factors, including randomness in nature which is, currently, part of the physical world view of science. In other words we cannot assume a set of conditions that will be necessary and sufficient for predicting the position and length of the limbs at some future time. However, if we take any point from the tip of the branches and "trace back" preceding states of the limbs, moving our finger, say, towards the root of the tree, to some preexisting point on the branch we can ("*post factum*") assume that there are necessary and sufficient conditions which are identifiable in principle. This is one way of intuitively grasping the difference between "tracing back" and prediction.

Indeed, it was in the context of disputing the association of explanation and prediction that the sort of example Anscombe sets forth first appears. Her example is this: Imagine that I have had, merely, a single contact with an individual with an infectious disease. The frequency of transmission makes it impossible to *predict* whether I will contract the disease. Accuracy of prediction, therefore, is ruled out and with it the idea that my contracting the disease is a necessary consequence of exposure. However, if I do contract the disease, it is easy enough to *trace back* the cause to my being exposed to the infected individual. We have, therefore, an asymmetry that, ostensibly, excludes identifying predictability (based on laws etc.) and causation. Anscombe's approach is, almost, precisely the approach offered by Scriven years earlier in challenging the identification of causation and explanation that depends on laws.

Scriven had proposed an example where it is supposed that the only cause of paresis is syphilis and where I have been exposed to syphilis. However, exposure leads to paresis only rarely, and so, while if I were to contract paresis the etiology of my infection would be perfectly clear, nevertheless there would have been no way that a physician could have predicted my contracting the disease with any accuracy. (Scriven [1959]) Scriven concludes from this that we cannot identify explanation with prediction. The case is, almost, identical to Anscombe's.

Our ability to trace back to the point of our exposure to the disease is easy enough owing to the infrequency of paresis, unless there is exposure to syphilis, but there is some question as to whether the asymmetry mentioned is sufficient to exclude the identification of causation and predictability. Might it be the case that even though the event was not predictable that *some* lawlike connection must obtain making explanation, at least, possible? In the case of such examples as those supplied by Scriven and Anscombe, Hempel has a compelling reply: lawlike necessity (to be distinguished, of course, from logical necessity) is no guarantee that a prediction is possible. If the situation were otherwise, says Hempel, my winning the lottery could be predicted from my having bought a ticket, since we can regard buying the ticket as necessary to winning the lottery. (Hempel [1965] p. 369) In other words, there is no reason to believe that just because the doctor could not have predicted my contracting the disease that it follows that lawlike necessity cannot be associated with causation in this instance; or that predictability and causation are distinct.

The asymmetry of predictability and causation recapitulates an important difference between necessity and universality, on the one hand, and causation, on the other. (Anscombe [1971] p. 135-136)

We can know the cause without being able to predict the effect, basing our prediction on universal laws. This is what the above example and the problem Scriven presented is being used to point out. Another way of looking at matters is to see the asymmetry as resting on the fact that predictions involve a margin of error, whereas the causal case, as she describes it, exemplifies no margin of error worthy of discussion; the contrast is clear. What is not considered is that as we narrow the margin of error, experimentally, we introduce new *causal* properties relevant to our prediction, relevant in the sense that only by depending on them can the right laws for prediction be identified. As we approach the "ideal" prediction, where no margin of error exists, what we describe and how we describe it, become increasingly interrelated. Predictions depend on descriptions; a causal relation between events does not.

Hempel, and many others, including Davidson, have maintained that explanations concern only *sentential facts*. Moreover, Hempel insists that when we attend to the causal facts, i.e. when we attend to "concrete events," what gets singled out depends on the "context of inquiry." (Hempel [1965] 422) But if the context of inquiry is the context of explanation and explanation is linguistic, then linguistic considerations determine our choice of relevant properties in providing an explanation. However, if the context is one of attempting to narrow the "gap" between our understanding what the causal dependency is and the explanation of that dependency (one that would serve to support prediction), then we must reach outside the context of our inquiry towards causal properties, independently of linguistic expediece, and outside *this* context. (*cf.* Bohm [1957] p. 17). If this is accepted then Hempel's skepticism regarding Scriven's example loses force, and Anscombe's employment of a similar example in support of maintaining a distinction between universality and prediction, and causality, has a chance of withstanding criticism. Anscombe's holds that to be caused and to be determined are different things, inasmuch as a determined result is a result for which there was no other antecedent possibility. Setting aside the possibility of preemptive causes—which include causes preventing other causes from having the same effect—it must be noted that it is, precisely, because in the example cited paresis has no other "possible" antecedent that we can trace back the cause to syphilis so easily. Moreover, in the absence of any appeal to lawlikeness it is difficult to argue that any other outcome was possible, for one may ask: "Is it not the case that what is possible in the relevant sense of 'possible' is what is nomically possible? Doesn't the singularist of an indeterminist disposition have difficulty accounting for what is possible and what is not? Answering such questions is made no less difficult by the fact that Anscombe accepts both necessitating and non-necessitating causes. (Anscombe [1971] p. 144) Necessitating causes relate events *qua* kinds, indicated by the general terms used in formulating the scientific law, from which the effect is in principle derivable. In this instance, it is not possible for the cause to take place without the effect taking place, just in case there is nothing to prevent the effect from occurring. A non-necessitating cause, for Anscombe, is a cause which may "fail" to result in "its" effect, even when nothing is present that might prevent it. However, we can only speak of a cause that might have *failed* if some event in the past has "successfully" caused a certain effect or it can be predicted on the basis of a lawlike connection of events. We can say that an elephant's crossing the road *failed* to cause a snow storm only if there is some reason to believe that such crossings have been known to cause snow storms or will at some time in the future. Similarly, we say that we *tried* only on occasions where we have failed. Thus "failure" depends on some reference to prediction and, implicitly, law; and law is, precisely, what Anscombe wishes to dismiss in characterizing instances of non-necessitating singular causation. An inconsistency in Anscombe might be alleged if we can say that the very idea of non-necessitating causation presupposes regularity in its formulation.

Anscombe's notion of a non-necessitating cause, as she describes it, requires the transitivity of causation. To see this consider the example she attributes to Feynman. A Geiger counter is set next to a radioactive source. If it registers a certain reading, it detonates a bomb. She has told us that by a "non-necessitating cause" she means a cause that can fail to have "its" effect, although nothing prevents the effect from occurring. (Anscombe [1971] p. 144) We know that, if the bomb goes off, the reading will be the cause, but we cannot predict that the bomb will go off because we cannot predict the reading. The reading, which would be the cause, is considered to be (when the bomb goes off) the non-necessitating cause of this event. By "non-necessitating" we do not mean that the bomb could go off even without the reading; we mean that the reading might have obtained without the effect of detonating the bomb.

If the reading is the cause of the detonation, then *ab initio* it should be no more non-necessitating than any necessitating event in the following sense. The causal connection between the reading and the detonation is one thing; the causal connection between the emission of a certain number of particles and a certain reading is another. At first it appears that the non-necessitating character of the cause in the Feynman case belongs to this latter event, i.e. to the causal relation between the emission of a certain number of particles and the resulting reading. Since all causes are to be regarded as non-necessitating this is, certainly, the case. In fact, however, the root of uncertainty is to be found in whatever causes a *certain number* of particles to be emitted from the radioactive source. There are two events, here, at issue: the *cause* of the emission of a *certain number* of particles and the emission of *that* number of particles. We cannot "trace back" from the emission of a certain number of particles to the cause of this emission, as we "trace back" to the reading on the Geiger counter from the detonation, or as "traced back" to syphilis from paresis.

The causal relation between the cause of the emission of a certain number of particles and the emission itself is, substantially, removed from the relation of the reading to the detonation. If causation is not transitive then there is nothing "non-necessitating" about the cause of the detonation owing to the random emission of particles from the radioactive source, otherwise there would be no point in Anscombe introducing the special case relying on quantum indeterminacies. This can be attributed to the fact that the, relevant, non-necessitation of the cause of the explosion depends on the uncertainty we associate with the cause of the emission of a *certain number* of particles that, ultimately, led to the reading on the Geiger counter. Suppose Anscombe simply were to shift the example by talking of the second causal relation, that between the emission of a certain number of particles and the Geiger counter reading, as the locus of non-necessitation.

In this case the proposal would be that the non-necessitating cause was the emission of a certain number of particles and the effect was the reading, where the reading, then, results in the explosion. Now if this is a non-necessitating cause, i.e. the emission of a certain number of particles, then this is to say that it might have occurred without the effect taking place, even though nothing prevented it. But this, merely, duplicates the problem, since between the emission of a *certain number* and the reading on the Geiger counter there is no basis for asserting non-necessitation; *randomness* in this case is not an issue because we assume the number of particles is, already, given. Keep in mind that the Feynman example is part of an argument for non-necessitating causes; non-necessitating causes cannot be assumed in stating it.

What, really, need to be considered is the relation between what causes the emission of a *certain number* of particles and the reading on the Geiger counter. But now we no longer have a case where, like inferring the reading from the detonation, we can infer the cause of the emission of a *certain number* of particles from the reading. It would appear, therefore, that Anscombe is committed to the transitivity of causation. She cannot have it that the cause of the explosion was non-necessitating based on the randomness of the emission of particles without introducing a third, intervening, event, viz. the instrument coming to have a certain reading.

Accepting the transitivity of causation is a matter of contemporary interest, particularly in dealing with issues of "mental causation." There is also some question as to whether there *is* anything we might describe as the cause of the emission of a *certain number* of particles. Alternatively, Anscombe might give up non-necessitating causes, something, however, that most likely would amount to abandoning her singularist position.

It should be noted that Anscombe is, perfectly, aware that the source of non-necessitation in the bomb example is not the emission of a *certain number* of particles but, rather, what causes the emission. As far as this is concerned, she remarks that the effect is owing, merely, to the fact that there is radioactive material present. (Anscombe [1971] p. 145). But this will not suffice to locate the cause of the emission of a *certain number* of particles; that is, the number required to set off the bomb. Being in the presence of a radioactive source is consistent with any one of a number of particles being emitted. Whether these considerations are destructive to Anscombe's account can only be resolved after distinguishing two ideas, viz. determinacy and necessitation.

The non-necessity of a cause is a matter of a cause's not necessarily yielding its effect; indeterminacy amounts to being the claim that not all effects are necessitated by their causes. Thus, it might be said that in a particular case there is indeterminacy only if the cause is non-necessitating. But *does* a non-necessitating cause imply an indeterminate cause? If so, then are indeterminacy and non-necessitation equivalent? Reformulated the question becomes: Is it ever true that a non-necessitating cause is determinate? The answer appears to be "No," as long as we regard an indeterminate cause as one that might have had any one of a number of effects. It is, surely, possible that a cause which might have taken place without "its" effect might have been the cause of any one of a number of effects, effects which are such that in any case the question of non-necessitation can be raised. Notice one other thing: the idea that a cause may not have had "its" effects is not the same thing as that the same cause might have had different effects, depending on the point in space-time in which it occurs. This view is attributed to Moritz Schlick by Reichenbach. (Reichenbach [1920] p. 84) Schlick's view, much like Anscombe's, conjures up the image of an event which contains "its" effects. Needless to say, this raises a series of questions about the nature of singular causation.

If we restrict ourselves to singular causation, then it may be the case that causation is determinate but non-necessitating. This would be evident should it turn out that a cause might have any one of a number of effects without an alteration of the context in which the cause has its effect. Indeterminacy, where it involves, simply enough, statistical margins of error, is of no concern to the singularist. Statistical uncertainties are matters for regularity theorists who depend on the reality of lawlikeness. If, however, the one-many relation of cause to effects reaches into the nature of things, beyond laws and our ability to measure, then it may turn out that indeterminacy and non-necessitation are equivalent, since even singular causation would be subject to this universal fact. The bomb example, under transitivity of causation, may render this an unattainable equivalence. But, if so, then saying that the cause of the emission of a *certain number* of particles "merely happened" (Anscombe [1971] p. 145) and that the cause of the explosion is non-necessitating, may raise the problem distinguishing explosions that merely happen from those which do not "merely happen."

One wonders what in cases of singular causation allows us to speak of a *cause* when the event is non-necessitating. What does "cause" in the sense of the singularist add to, or subtract from, the conditions laid down by Hume? Unfortunately, we must leave these issues unresolved. For now, let's examine whether the Will can be a non-necessitating cause without contradicting physical law. First, let's clarify, exactly, what question is at issue.

Anscombe considers an objection directed against those who claim that indeterminacy in physics introduces the possibility of free-will. (Anscombe [1971] pp. 145-146) The objection is that those free-will proponents who latch on to indeterminacy in support of their view could be understood as claiming that, at the level of the indeterminate, an act of will can affect events in such a way as to conflict with the course of events required by natural law. Thus, the objection goes, the free-will advocate's proposal has it that the will can overrule natural law, and this is not possible. Anscombe points out that this need not be the case; she notes that this objection to the free-will advocate would only succeed if it were assumed that there is regularity between acts of will, at the level of the indeterminate, and the events captured by the statistical regularities expressed by scientific laws. Her language is cryptic, and there may be more than one way of interpreting it; however the example she constructs to illustrate her point is both ingenious and illuminating.

Imagine, then, that we have a transparent box filled with thousands of tiny beads of many different colors. Suppose, further, that we constantly shake the box. However, this box is remarkable for the following reason: no matter how we shake it we can discern the word 'Coca Cola' viewed from one side of the box, or another. No matter how we shake the box, we are always able to see this word. Each occasion of shaking the box results in the appearance of the same expression, although it occurs with many different color arrangements of the tiny pieces of glass. Anscombe's claim is that there is no reason, contrary to what the free-will critic is suggesting, to believe that statistical laws or the laws of chance are violated by the recurrence of this expression, and that, because this is true, there is no reason to believe that free will exercised at the level of quantum indeterminacy contradicts the laws of nature. Of course, exercising our free-will under these conditions does not require that the causes of action be subatomic, only that the act of Will have consequences, perhaps, at this level; nor need we assume that quantum indeterminacies operate only at the subatomic level—something about which there appears to be some controversy. What are we to make of Anscombe's example and what it is she seeks to establish? It is unlikely to be a coincidence that Karl Bohm in a remarkably lucid and original discussion of causation uses an example that approaches the one she employs. Much later in a different context she will make mention of Bohm's discussion and comment on it, but it is a reasonably safe conjecture that Bohm's work was relevant to Anscombe's 1971 discussion. (Anscombe [1983] p. 104)

If the expression "Coca Cola" appears in the mixture and we attribute this to events undetermined by physical law, would we be committed to saying that the events are, therefore, not determined? The appearance of the word is the result of some constraint placed on randomness. This constraint as an act of Will, if we were to suppose it to be such, could hardly be considered random, otherwise acts of Will would be random and the expression would, probably, not have appeared. If it is not a random event then the question arises as to whether it was determined. It, clearly, does not follow from the laws of chance. Our only alternative is statistical law of the sort we associate with scientific law, law which it is alleged is being contradicted by the repeated appearance of "Coca Cola." But how do statistical laws come into being in the first place? They come about as a consequence of perceived regularities. Theories designed to *explain* such regularities may include postulating particles having certain properties, but the laws, themselves, are not constrained by theory, as such. If the box had been shaken only once, then we would be faced with what would appear to be cancellation of some sort of the laws of chance; in this case statistical laws need not enter, directly, into the dispute. But if we were to get the same result, repeatedly, then we might arrive at a statistical generalization, one requiring explanation. If we are mixing concrete and sand we don't rely on the "effects" of statistical law in order to expect uniform consistency. (Bohm [1957] p. 23) What we rely on is chance; indeed, we expect its effects within limits. But if we wish to produce the word "Coca Cola," and if we are content to consider the laws of chance, alone, or indeterminate acts of will, then there is no explaining how we can "depend" on shaking the box to get this effect, "Coca Cola." The objector to whom Anscombe is addressing has a fall-back position.

The objector may say that the agent must have intentionally caused "Coca Cola," something that cannot be attributed to quantum indeterminacies, such would be the case, if a Geiger counter might spell out "Coca Cola" in a code formulated in terms of the emissions of particles from a radioactive source. Moreover, there is nothing that would prevent on Anscombe's assumptions the sort of situation described in H. H. Price's case of the talking leaves, or Putnam's bug, from surfacing in the case of the box. Suppose "Coca Cola" comes up, after about the third shake, and I say "No thanks, not now"; I shake the box, again, and the words "That's Ok for now, but what about this afternoon?" In such a case we might look for something in the system under examination, the box and its contents, or the way we shake it, for an explanation; alternatively, we might consider that there is an outside influence we have yet to detect. We are faced with a challenge resembling the problem of "other minds." We would not conclude that the appearance of the words contradicted modern physics. Keep in mind that Anscombe is arguing against those who claim that free-action would "falsify" natural law. Indeed, the "cancellation" of the laws of chance is familiar and required for the existence of any world which can hope to be an object of scientific inquiry. The point is that Anscombe's box example shows what the free-will advocate wants—that is the free-will advocate who latches on to physical indeterminacy—only if free-action as an event is sufficiently like the "cause" of the emission of a *certain number* of particles from a radioactive source; but it is, also, consistent with the terms of her example that the cancellation of chance occurrence is no less consistent with natural law than the cancellation of the chance occurrence of automobile accidents by the installation of traffic lights. She describes the box as "remarkable," presumably because of the appearance of "Coca Cola" among the many colored glass beads. It may be that there would be a mind directing the course of events in such a case, but what makes the situation remarkable cannot be traced, or attributed with any rational justification, to free actions resembling the random occurrences of particle emission in subatomic contexts.

## k) *Anscombe, Bohm and Mechanistic Determinism*

We have seen how it was that Russell sought to purge philosophy of the word 'cause', arguing that it could be replaced by talk about laws. This we noted was central to the claims made by the regularity theorists. But shortly after Russell wrote, there came a new challenge to the idea of causation, one that arose from developments having to do with the role of probability in quantum theory, developments that suggested an inherent indeterminacy as to what the facts of the matter are with respect to physical states such as position and momentum. The indeterminacy suggested by regarding probabilities as facts of nature led to similar calls for the abandonment of causality and the determinism of the sort Russell had defended in the form of Laplacean determinism. Thus at the same time Russell was rejecting causation for reasons having to do, largely, with logical expedience, his own position, determinism, was being undermined by physical theory. Some physicists, e.g. Julian Schwinger, sought a middle ground where determinism is preserved within the framework of indeterminacy in physics, but the trend was set and determinism was thought to be incompatible with a new view of nature and its laws as statistical in nature. This led some, e.g. Carl Hempel, to introduce in addition to deductive nomological explanation yet another: inductive statistical explanation. The notion of laws and lawlikeness were decisive considerations in many discussions of determinism, but the relation between determinism and mechanism is not a relation of identity. Determinism was entailed by the "mechanization of the world picture" (the expression is from Dijksterhuis). But mechanism and determinism were (and are) different ideas, and we must see them as such, if we are to, properly, grasp the issues of singularity vs. regularity and the philosophy of mechanism. Anscombe's views on mechanism were influenced by David Bohm. He held that the introduction of statistical methods did not motivate flight from the mechanistic picture but, rather, became part of it. A brief look at the philosophy of mechanism will afford us a clearer insight into the Bohm/Anscombe connection.

One of the clearest expositions of mechanism was set forth by C. D. Broad in his great work in philosophy of mind *The Mind and It's Place in Nature*. (Broad [1925] p. 44) Broad sketches a theory he calls "pure mechanism." His conception of the "ideal of pure mechanism" is this: first, there is only one sort of "stuff" out of which things are made; second, aside from spatial and temporal properties, there is only one essential quality, besides this stuff's causal properties: inertial mass or, perhaps, electrical properties; third, there is only one fundamental sort of change; and, fourth, there is one fundamental *law* determining how one particle affects another. It is worth noting that on this account mechanism presupposes what is a *de facto* regularity theory approach to causation. But we must ask: What is the relation of determinism to mechanism? Can a mechanistic theory not be deterministic? Although Broad's description is, clearly, idealized, e.g. requiring what is close to Davidsonian type "monism" and only one fundamental law, although subsequent accounts do not depart from it substantially.

Bohm's view of mechanism is close to Broad's idealization. Mechanism Bohm says is not a scientific but is, rather, a philosophical position, one characterized essentially by its claim that "all of our experience...can all be reduced completely and perfectly to nothing more than consequences of the operation of an absolute and final set of purely quantitative laws determining the behaviour of a few kinds of basic entities or variables." (Bohm [1957] p. 37) It is easy enough to see the similarities between Broad and Bohm: both conceive mechanism as deterministic and committed to laws as fundamental to the theory.

In rejecting the mechanistic picture of the world, Bohm likewise rejects determinism; and, while we reach new, and more revealing, laws of nature with each level we uncover, further levels seem to come, inevitably, into purview. Even though with larger and larger statistical aggregates we arrive at more and more specific approximations of the determinist ideal, the ideal is never satisfied. (Bohm [1957] p. 56). To be sure, chance exists objectively within one context, but does not exist in another, although there may be other objective chance fluctuations introduced at the level of this larger context of inquiry. The mechanistic view, as we have seen, on most formulations includes a thesis about fundamental entities constitutive of the physical world. If on the mechanistic view chance probabilities are to give way to predictability, this will depend on taking contexts closer and closer to these fundamental entities as converging to the limit of inquiry. But for Bohm there are no such limits and laws may be stacked on top of laws in a relation of reciprocity rather than "descending" contexts, without reaching a fundamental fact of the physical world. This in effect is what we take to be the essence of Bohm's repudiation of determinism and the mechanism entailing it. Moreover, the possibility of reciprocal causal relations between levels rules out confidence in even a seemingly successful form of mechanistic determinism. We now offer one item of a speculative nature on the possibility of mechanism

It may turn out that mechanism is possible only where reciprocity is ruled out, that is where there is interaction between a containing system and a contained system. This may have implications for the theory of human action. It would represent a striking turn of events should it turn out that only a self-predicting mechanism can in principle predict with absolute determination, since only in the case of such a mechanism could intervening elements of influence be ruled out. A successful self-predicting mechanism it might be argued rules out any context over and above the one doing the predicting. Only by assuming mechanism can determinism be defended in this radical form, a form where the possibility of predicting all events is possible from the perspective of one context of inquiry. However, according to Bohm, mechanism is consistent with the standard view in physics that there is an inherent "absolute chance" associated with events in nature. This presence compels a new view, one which does not reject mechanism but one which is indeterministic, whence "indeterministic mechanism." (Bohm[1957] p. 63). This form of mechanism introduces what Bohm describes as "lawlessness." But lawlessness is not exactly clear when considered in relation to Anscombe's rejection of determinative causation.

Anscombe's rejection of determinative causation is based on the idea that a set of conditions otherwise constituting a cause may fail to yield an effect. That is, while all the right conditions are present, the event simply does not have the effect law would dictate. Again, no laws are contravened; no laws are disconfirmed. But this is not the same sort of indetermination that accompanies recognition of "absolute chance" in nature. Consider the following thought experiment. Suppose that the initial conditions of all causal laws relevant to the state of the universe at some time are fulfilled, as the indeterministic mechanist must suppose. Imagine, however, that on this occasion *no* effect follows. Are we, then, to we describe the universe as lawless? At first it would appear that under these circumstances no law is contradicted and all that occurs, i.e. nothing, accords with law. Things may not be so simple.

If I suppose that no law at a certain time was instantiated; that is, no event followed from another, then it would appear that no law applied since a law relates an antecedent and a consequence and the consequence did not in fact occur. It may that Anscombe is merely asserting that this is possible, not that any such occurrence of one event without the occurrence of a lawlike related other event takes place. But if we can say of one event pair that this is possible, then why not say this of all pairs? In this case, the world would, indeed, be lawless. That *no* laws would be contradicted in a world where our thought experiment was reality is not clear, however. Would we have to suppose that no event required by any law will take place at some future time without supposing that the principle of conservation of energy is violated; but what about the law of inertia which says that a thing persists in its state of motion unless acted upon by another force? If the possibility that no event followed by another, to which it was related as the consequence of a lawlike relation to that event, were realized, then there would be no *persistence* of a uniform state of motion and, so, the law of inertia would appear to be violated.

This consideration applies in the much more limited case, the case where two events, rather than two states of the universe, as Russell understood them, are being related. The prospects for a defense of determinism based on considerations having to do with the law of inertia, while plausible, cannot be examined further, but we would otherwise be tempted to consider that inertia is not a cause and, so, the conditions associated with its instantiation do not include a cause. A disposition may serve as a cause but most dispositions are, themselves, caused or, otherwise, explained. However, inertia is neither caused nor explained, or so it would appear. Moreover, inertia raises questions about the sense of 'possible' Anscombe intends when she says a cause may not have its effect although all antecedent conditions are satisfied.

If one accepts Russell's version of determinism, then, when the conditions ("determinants") of an event fixed by law are satisfied, not only does the event which we call the "effect" occur but the *time* of that event's occurrence is predictable as well. (Russell [1912-1913] pp. 144-145) But if this were the case then should the events not occur, as they do not in our thought experiment, then determinism would fail. However, I know of no scientific law that prescribes the exact time of an effect given some causal antecedent. This could not in principle be ascertained inasmuch as there are too many variables acting in the system, ruling this out as a requirement of lawlikeness. If we are right about this, then it would appear that temporal relations between causes and their effects, if determined at the level of singular causation, elude capture by the "nomological net." If Anscombe is right, however, then it is entirely possible—unlikely but possible—that no event occurs even when what Russssell calls the "determinants" are present. But this would conflict not only with Laplacean determinism along Russellian lines, it would also conflict with "indeterministic mechanism" as Bohm describes it, while leaving untouched the view that the introduction of "absolute chance" is consistent with lawlikeness when those laws are statistical. Others, e.g. Von Mises have maintained that lawlessness prevails wherever chance rules, a view not shared by Bohm. What is most important is that Anscombe's claim that an event may not follow when all the conditions of the relevant causal laws are satisfied is not *ipso facto* a rejection of the regularity theory, a theory she, nonetheless, rejects. We conclude with a statement of Bohm's position in general terms and Anscombe reaction to his view of mechanistic determinism.

"Indeterministic" mechanism incorporates, within the main body of doctrine associated with mechanism, the idea that "absolute chance" is included in the natural state of things. It assumes finitism with respect to the number of properties in nature and a fixed number of laws. Taking a cue from Einstein, Bohm proposes that the element of chance introduced by the standard view of quantum theory is illusory and that there is a "sub-quantum mechanical level containing hidden variables." (Bohm [1957] p. 101). These variables occur in contexts of investigation that go beyond our present knowledge and are, perhaps, infinite in number. Besides the fact that this raises questions about whether a complete science is possible, it also raises the question whether nature can be understood within human means. According to Bohm, the "essential point," as far as concerns mechanism, is that the quantum indeterminacies introduced by Heisenberg and others arise from "qualitatively new kinds of factors existing in a new domain." (Bohm [1957] p. 126-127).

According to Bohm what a thing is, scientifically speaking, cannot be determined by any finite set of properties. (Bohm [1957] p. 154) Also, while mechanistic views will exclude either the laws of chance or causal laws, depending on the form they take, because nature, for Bohm, is conceived as qualitatively infinite, either exclusion must be avoided. Both concepts of mechanism may be "shadows." (p. 143). Given that nature is infinitely rich in properties, mechanism, according to Bohm, is doomed to fail. Thus when Anscombe remarks that one's being an indeterminist at one level does not rule out mechanism at a higher level she may be either expressing disagreement with Bohm or introducing a possible misunderstanding. (Anscombe [1983] p. 105)

One can be a determinist, or indeterminist, without being a mechanist, although mechanism includes a commitment to either determinism or indeterminism. Even though Bohm may be right that an infinite number of qualities rules out mechanism (recall our earlier definition from Broad and others) this would not allow us to rule on the issue of determinism vs. indeterminism. Since the contexts of investigation are infinite no resolution of the issue is possible. Immediately after remarking on the consistency of mechanism and indeterminacy, at different levels, Anscombe continues to assimilate mechanism and determinism, saying that with respect to the behavior of one kind of particle one may be a determinist, but with respect to another a "mechanist." Again, according to Bohm, a mechanist may be an indeterminist. What Anscombe's point in fact amounts to is this: for a mechanist it may be possible to be a determinist at one level and an indeterminist with respect to another; or, a determinist with respect to one sort of particle and an indeterminist with respect to another. For Bohm, however, levels are introduced by indeterminacies present at a level calling for the need to introduce a higher level which in turn will contain its own indeterminacies. For Bohm mechanism is rejected for reasons, largely, but not entirely, having to do the finitude of the mechanist's world.

Bohm's "levels" contain variables that once understood explain events that are indeterminate at a lower level. Should one reach a higher level where there are no indeterminacies, then no further levels would be required; nature would be finite and mechanistic determinism would be confirmed. But if there is a higher level where determinism prevails and a lower level where it does not, this would render the motivating cause for introducing higher levels in Bohm's case otiose. There is, then, a fundamental disconnection between Anscombe and Bohm, one which is difficult to detect in Anscombe's stated views on mechanistic philosophy. How all this relates to "explanation by intention" is uncertain. When the issue is that of whether mechanistic determinism applies to human action she remarks, saying "The question is left entirely open." (Anscombe [1983] p. 106)

## *I) Reconciling Singularity and Regularity Theories*

We have spoken of two approaches to causation: the regularity theory and the singularist theory. It has been a long held view that these positions are incompatible. We want to challenge this by maintaining that there are two senses of 'cause' at issue, and that while they are different they are related within a single framework that makes more sense than regarding them as being in competition. In order to do this we are going to make use of the idea that the two concepts of cause are related, logically, in much the same way as 'ancestor' is related to 'parent'. In order to see how they are so related let's, first, consider a formal definition of 'ancestor'.

In particular, let's begin by examining one carefully constructed definition of '$b$ is an ancestor of $c$' offered by Goodman and Quine. (Goodman and Quine [1947] p. 108). Where 'mem' means class membership, their definition can be stated as follows.

$\sim(b = c)$ & $(x)\{ c$ mem $x$ & $((y)(z)((z$ mem $x$ & Parent $yz) \rightarrow y$ mem $x) \rightarrow b$ mem $x\}$ ("mem" means 'member of' - srb)

There are a number of ways to read this. Let's settle on one: "$b$ and $c$ are not identical and for any class, $x$, if $c$ is a member of $x$ and all parents, $y$, of members, $z$, of $x$ are also in $x$, then $b$ is a member of $x$." Being an ancestor is a hereditary property. A simpler, but more schematic, way of presenting the essential idea behind being a hereditary property is suggested by Carnap, one where we drop mention of classes (Carnap [1958] p.147); here we dispense with overt reference to quantifiers as well:

F$c$ & (F$x$ & (H$yx$ → F$y$). → F$b$.

We can read this as "If $c$ is F and if it is the case that both $x$ is F *and* that if H$xy$ *then* $y$ is F, then it follows that $b$ is F. On one interpretation of 'F' and 'H' we might say that this means that if $c$ has the property F and if anything with F is such that its parent has F, as well, then b has F. In this case we would say that $b$ is an ancestor of c. One reason for switching, momentarily, to the predicate notation is that it is easier to see that the relation 'ancestor of' is transitive, and is provably so.

Where 'R' is the relation ancestor, it can be proven that if 'R$c,b$' and 'R$b,d$' is true, then 'R$c,d$' is true. This is what it means to be transitive. The following argument is valid, although we shall not include the details of the proof itself.

Fc & (Fx & (Hyx → Fy) → Fb    (cRb)

Fb & (Fx & (Hyx → Fy) → Fd    (bRd)

Therefore,

Fc & (Fx & (Hyx → Fy) → Fd    (cRd)

Having established the transitivity of 'ancestor of', we are left with two logical facts of significance: first, that transitivity has been established for 'ancestor of' and, second, that the "proper ancestral" 'parent of' is intransitive. We have it, then, that the transitive relation presupposes an intransitive relation in its definition. Returning, now, to Goodman and Quine's definition we have one other logical point to consider before applying this machinery to the problem of singularity vs. regularity in the analysis of causation.

This final logical consideration has to do with the class theoretic formulation of the definition Goodman and Quine proposed. In their formulation the only constraint on the class, $x$, is that it contain the parents of all of its members. So anything else can be included as long as this is not disturbed. With respect to '$x$' as Quine puts it, much else may be included: "ancestors, and neckties; for, neckties being parentless, their inclusion does not disturb the fact that all parents of members are member." (Quine [1972] p. 238) It has been argued that this is a disadvantage of the definition. (e.g. Lucey [1979]) What we wish to maintain, contrary to such criticisms, is that this lack of specificity in the class, $x$, cannot be purged without sacrificing the transitivity of the relation to be defined, viz. 'ancestor of'.

Lucey formulates the ancestral in terms of "generational removal." We are skeptical, at the onset, insofar as the approach requires a distinction between "direct generational removal" ("DG") and "indirect generational removal" ("NDG"). We will set this aside. In a nutshell the main proposal is to use in the definition a triadic, rather than a dyadic, relation like 'parent of': "(E$n$) DG($n, w, z$)" meaning "there is a number $n$ such that $w$ has a generational removal of order n from $z$." (Lucey [1979] p. 284) Suppose, then, that we want to formulate "w is the great grandfather of z." In this case we would have

DG (3, $w, z$).

So far so good, but introducing a triadic relation like this raises questions about how we would, then, understand the concept of an ancestor. The problem is that transitivity is affected. Consider that from

$$G(1, x, y)$$

and

$$G(1, y, z)$$

we can't infer

$$G(1, x, z).$$

Even if we introduce a defined relation as 'Rxy' = $df$ '(Ew)R(w, x, y)' transitivity would not be provable, at best it might be introduced as a "meaning postulate." So here is our claim:

If we "squeeze" out the dross introduced by a class approach to the ancestral (Quine's neckties for example), then we lose transitivity. Now this may be a reason to jettison the analysis. We offer no final judgment, but instead proceed to apply these logical findings to the problem of reconciling singularist and regularity theories of causation. In treating causation counterfactually D. Lewis introduced the concept of "fragility." Fragility will is understood, here, as the property which an event has if it could not have taken place differently or at a different time. (*cf.* Lewis [1986] p. 196). Elsewhere I have defended the view that the more closely two, causally related, events occur in time the more fragile they become, but for now I want to make a different point.

Singularity theorists trade in a concept of causation such that the events in a causal relation are fragile at the limit. We would prefer saying that for the singularist events are completely "inelastic." On the view we accept, singular causation is indicated by the relation which is analogous to the proper ancestral of 'ancestor', viz. 'parent'. Notice that this is a dyadic relation and intransitive. What we propose to do is reconcile the singularist and regularity approaches by taking causation in the singularist sense as the proper ancestral of 'cause' in the regularity sense. At this point the "dross" fits in nicely with the idea of infragility, and the usual class theoretic approach to 'ancestor of' can be preserved.

Without the "dross" the events held in the causal relation will be inelastic. The class view accommodates the elasticity of causally related events and relates, deductively, the transitivity of the causal relation to elasticity. One possible consequence is this: we've heard a lot about how probability is part of nature and that causation so conceived as probabilistic is consistent with "mechanism." (D. Bohm 1957). But we would make the following point (which coheres well with Bohm's project): only in the sense that causation is transitive does probability or chance or randomness enter into a description of causation. It is only the transitive sense of 'cause' that fits the regularity theory, and this relates to the elasticity of the events in the causal relation. Using the ancestral relation to illustrate the differences between singular and regularity theories helps demonstrate the mutual consistency of these two approaches.

# PART 7:
# Causation and Agency

If we view the world as made up of events, then understanding it will not be possible without understanding how events are, or can be, related. Some events may be thought of as, mere, *happenings*. Other events, some would say more significant events, are called *doings*. (Melden [1961]) Our interest is in *doings* and *happenings*, but only insofar as *happenings* may, also, be things *done*. Doings are human actions, and understanding how they come about, and what their existence entails, is the problem of *agency*. Happenings are events. When they are causally related, pairwise, this is sometimes called "event-event" causation; when an agent acts, the relation, if causal, relates person and event (a *doing*). We will call this "agent causation." Anscombe, never, explicitly, accepts agent causation, and she argues, vigorously, against one particular theory of agent causation proposed by Roderick Chisholm. Shortly, we shall examine her reply to Chisholm in some detail.

We have been discussing causation as a relation between events. At certain places in the ensuing discussion this should be understood as contrasting with "agent causation" or the causation of an event by a property, such as when we refer to the fact that the jar broke because it was brittle. As we have seen, Anscombe accepts the idea of causation as event-event causation determined by law in some instances but not in all. The regularity theorist *requires* that an effect follow a, certain, cause; otherwise the "law" would not be a *law* (for now we set aside the idea of statistical regularities).

## *a) The Causes of Action*

Whatever may be the nature of causation, our task is to understand and, perhaps, criticize Anscombe on the role it plays in giving an account of human action. The difference between reasons and causes, as we have seen, is central to her entire philosophy. In an essay that sheds considerable illumination on her theory of action, "The Causation of Action," (Anscombe [1983]) she entertains a commonplace example of human behavior, shutting a door, and engages the question "What made that door shut?" She considers the question under different circumstances and conditions, and in so doing isolates what is compelling about a theory of action, one where causation and reason account for different aspects of a given human action.

A door may come to be closed in any one of a number of ways. There may be a door closing mechanism such that whenever the door is open the mechanism comes into play closing it, e.g. springs attached to the bottom of the door near the hinges. It is reasonable to ask how such a mechanism might work, and how other devices and door closing processes, might accomplish the same thing. The obvious example is where someone walks over and shuts it. Questions about how this "mechanism" works are the questions Anscombe seeks to answer.

At some point this will involve identifying chains of causally related events. (Anscombe [1983] p. 92) For example, one answer might go something like this: the door snapped shut because of the movement of a spring; there was a movement of the spring because of an earlier compression of the spring; this because, previously, the door had moved in the opposite direction; and this because the agent had pushed it with his hand. Further, the agent's hand moved the way it did because of the contraction of his muscles; the contraction occurring because of a signal sent from the brain. But now why was the signal sent from the brain? Here, Anscombe alleges a break in the explanation, one that makes this explanation different from explaining the event in terms of manufactured devices such as mechanical door closing mechanisms. At this point we might say the agent did what he did because he was caused to want to do so owing, perhaps, to something he may have seen, say a wild bear headed for the door at a full run. The message from the brain to the muscles took place along the efferent nerves; the agent's cognitive awareness of the bear began as a signal along afferent nerves which were stimulated by the light from the bear to the agent's eyes. But there is a gap, a gap between the afferent and efferent nerve impulses; that is, the sort of gap that did not exist between the signal from the brain and movement of the muscles. This is not to say, however, that there is no "gap" between the efferent signal and the movement of the muscles.

The gap between the efferent signal and the muscle movement might be filled by similar physical connections; the efferent signal may have initiated chemical messaging that eventuated in movement. Should the question arise as to how this takes place, a correct answer would enable us to fill a gap between, already, established links. Up to this point, we have been talking about picking out a chain of causally related events by tracing further, and further, back the chain that might be said to answer a how-question. But in the case of relating nerves and muscles, causally, we are connecting gaps *between* links; we are not tracing back links in a chain of cause and effect relations. Thus, according to Anscombe, we are pursuing two different approaches, or directions of inquiry. The contrast is between "in and in" rather than "back and back." We continue the former until we reach links that are no longer, themselves, chains. (Anscombe [1983] p. 93) We now face a problem associated with a gap in "tracing back." In particular, we have seen that such a gap exists between the signals from the environment and the efferent signals from the brain to the muscles. Here we rely on certain "clues" in order to tell us, as we trace back, what signals to the sensory receptors are relevant to what is being sent by the efferent nerves to the muscles.

Suppose we have traced the cause of our closing the door all the way back to the incoming physical signals; but there are so many we don't know which way to go next. Compare this to having to step back in order to see a larger part of a picture for the purpose of seeing what it is a picture of. In the case of the door closing, the agent might see an angry bear running towards the door, or hear someone ordering him to close the door. We now have a "clue" as to how to proceed backwards to the cause; we trace the cause to the appearance of the bear, or the bear's running, taken together with what we already know of the state of the brain. Keep in mind that we are, still, trying to answer a question similar to the one we asked about how the door was shut; we are not asking for reasons for shutting the door, only what caused the door to get shut. With this is mind we have to come to an understanding, if our "tracing" is to be successful, as to how recognizing the danger of the oncoming bear, or hearing the command, figures in the "how" of shutting the door. Anscombe vigorously argues against the idea that once we take advantage of this "clue" we will be able to fill in the gap and arrive at a description of how the man closes the door in the way we explain, merely, mechanical door-closing mechanisms.

The view Anscombe opposes is that which says that we take this "clue," consisting as it does in beliefs and desires, and from it get a fix on which brain states intervene between the afferent and the efferent nerve impulses. On such a view our procedure would be to discover the brain states corresponding to such things as my visual experience that there is a bear running towards the door, or my aural experience of hearing the command, and once having discovered this correspondence being able to resolve the connection between the brain states of belief and desire, on the one hand, and those related to visual or aural experience, on the other, in just such a way as to explain the agent's door closing behavior mechanically, as we might explain any other mechanical door closing device. The "clue" in other words is a clue to how to go about creating descriptions that make these two enterprises, methodologically, one. In this way, explanation by way of intentions would be reduced to accounting for causal relations between brain states. Anscombe rejects this approach.

If there had been a state corresponding to the "clue," some brain state corresponding to the intention to close the door, then the causal account might go through as suggested. But, says Anscombe, it is mistaken to believe that intentions, or volitions, are isolatable events corresponding or identical to some brain states. Her example is illuminating in ways she did not consider. Suppose, to take her example, someone is attempting to make a phone call and the dial is jammed or, to update the example, the buttons on the phone are stuck. The person dialing the number applies force to the dial (or button) in order to overcome the resistance. Now the interesting part: although the agent acts intentionally, no intention is *formed*. Moreover, if he is asked why he applied more force, the agent may, simply enough, reply that he wanted to overcome the resistance. But this answer is formulated after the fact. While he was, actually, performing the action there was no thought of a desire to overcome the resistance. This is reported later. Most likely, Anscombe is right about this, but it is worth pointing out a couple of facts she does not mention.

In the first place, the example she chose is an example of what we have called a "willful act," not an "act of will"; that is, we are dealing with the sort of action that some, e.g. James, would not regard as being, even, a voluntary action. Another side of the issue is this: there are actions which are voluntary but not intentional. One example is smiling under certain circumstances. I may smile without intending to do so, although it may have been done willfully. I will not pursue this further, although there would be some irony in the fact, if it were a fact, that voluntary action ("free action") is possible only when it involves an event identifiable with a brain state. Second, this idea of a reported intention being reportable only retrospectively is not limited to such examples as these. Indeed, it belongs to an entire class of such events. Another example is reporting that we tried to do something. Suppose I am bringing my green books to the roof and I see that I've overlooked one. I reach down to pick it up and, suddenly, realize that I can't pick it up because it is nailed to the floor. At the time I was reaching down but had not, as yet, begun to lift the book, had I been asked what I was doing I would *not* have replied "I am trying to pick up this book." However, if I am asked afterwards, following my failure to lift the book, what I had been doing I might reply "I was *trying* to pick up the book." This suggests, as in the case discussed by Anscombe, that there was not some further event, a trying, that accompanied the action in question. Compare this in some respects to the pleasure of walking insofar as there is no additional experience of pleasure accompanying a pleasant walk, as Ryle noted. Had I known that the book was nailed to the floor, and had formed an intention to pick it up, then had I been asked, at the time, what I was doing, I might very well have replied "I am going to try to pick up this book." Anscombe's larger point is that purposeful action cannot be given an account, solely, in terms of efficient causation; hence an important difference obtains between explaining how a door closing mechanism works and providing an account of the agent's action in closing the door.

Those who oppose her position will, she says, take a sharply different view.

The opponents, let's call them the "Causalists," argue that in denying a role to introspectable events such as intentions in, e.g., the act of forcing the button or dial on the phone, she is not doing anything they would not allow. Indeed, the Causalists are likely to argue that there is no place for such things. Anscombe maintains, however, that *in order* to fill the gap on the Causalist approach intentions must enter the picture. But, if this is so, the Causalist approach is sullied by what from its point of view are undesirable elements. The Causalist might claim that relying on intentions was a heuristic for filtering out "noise," and that, once this was done, brain states would, then, fill the explanatory gap in tracing events related to producing the action. However, Anscombe would have a reply. She might point out that postulating intentions was *necessary* in order to fill the gap! If, indeed, intentions are required, then replacing them with brain states would be, to borrow a turn of phrase from Wittgenstein, an "unnecessary shuffle." Of particular interest in this regard is Anscombe's view that, just as intentions were not considered as constituting a natural class by Davidson, brain states alleged to correspond to intentions do not constitute a natural class either.

The argument that they do not form such a class involves the following claim: whatever brain states might correspond to a belief (or intention), say, do not, as such, amount to being sufficient for the belief. They may be necessary, but they are not sufficient. Why? Because there may be no connection between those brain states and what the belief is about. Take one example close to the one Anscombe supplies. I might have a belief that my bank is closed on Sunday. I might not have that belief, however, and yet be in the same brain state I would be in if I did have the belief. This brain state might have been induced without my ever having any awareness of banks, or my bank in particular. The methodology here is related, somewhat, to Putnam's "brain in a vat" puzzle. The point, however, is that *because* I've never, actually, had any knowledge or awareness of the bank, I cannot have a belief about it, even if the brain states are as they would in fact be had I had such a belief. Anscombe's argument has wider applications than those directed against the Causalist.

Let's ask the following question: It is, logically, possible that I might be able to cause you to "have" a certain thought by slapping my knee a certain way, but is it possible that that thought would, really, be *yours*? What would make it your thought? I had the thought, slapped my knee, and the thought occurred to you in some form. If it is not your thought, at least in the sense of your having come by it "honestly," then in what sense of 'have' is it a thought you "have"? It would appear that I cannot induce a thought that is *yours* unless I induce a belief or some propositional attitude towards its content. If what I am proposing is correct, then I cannot slap my knee and cause a belief unless I cause, by my slapping, *your having* that belief. In the case of intentions a problem arises: If I slap my knee in a certain way in order to get you to have the intention to push a ball, I need not make it your intention that *you* push the ball, only that you would have it that, somehow, the ball be pushed, or move, or some such thing. Prichard's example of a golfer is useful, although it goes back to earlier discussions of a, somewhat, different character. I may intend that the ball be sunk should I want, merely, that the ball go in the hole; but if, *qua* golfer, I try to sink the ball, as a component of the intention, then I want it to be the case that it is I who sink the ball, not merely that the ball be sunk. But in the case of belief, if I should slap my knee and get you to have the belief, I need not get you to believe that you believe what it is I want you to believe by doing this. If I did have to do this, then I could not get you to believe *p*, without getting you to believe *I believe p*. This goes to the heart of part of what Kant was driving at in his discussion of the Unity of Apperception, ideas Anscombe would, almost, certainly reject since she denied that the word 'I' even *has* a referent. There is, then, no filling the gap between afferent and efferent nerve activity by way of intentions or states of persons such as wants (for the same reasons) as the Causalist would have it. But this is not to deny that intentions don't figure in causal chain, only, perhaps, that it is causation of a sort that differs from what we encounter in chains of physiological causes and effects. (Anscombe [1983] p. 100) How, then, are we to view the difference between the causation we encounter in physiology and the causation we encounter in such cases as slamming the door because we see a wild animal charging towards us?

Anscombe's insistence that these are two different sorts of causation can be understood as a rejection of Davidson's claim that wants and beliefs enter as efficient causes of action. Davidson does not allow for this distinction of "sorts" of causation. Anscombe makes a very interesting and powerful move, one which she does not exploit to the degree she might have. She suggests that in such cases as her *Time* magazine example, where she is "made" to refuse an interview as a matter of principle, what we are dealing with is a causal sequence that amounts to being "shadows on shadow." Shadows lack causal efficacy and, yet, they are physical in the sense of being explainable as the effects of physical causes. Our intentions, etc. may be likened to shadows; they are not physical, but their existence does not conflict with physical accounts of the world. Anscombe doesn't make use of the fact that shadows are not physical, instead she focuses on the idea of shadows as subjects for "supervenient description" of what are, underlying, physical processes.

On the assumption that shadows lack causal efficacy and that the events upon which they depend are determined, it follows that the events described by supervenient descriptions are determined. (Anscombe [1983] p. 104) Supposing that supervenient descriptions are "higher level" descriptions, while descriptions of physical events, as such, are "basic level," she asserts that should determinism obtain at any level, then determinism prevails at all levels. But, should it turn out that indeterminism enters at any level then one may or may not be a "mechanist" at any level, where mechanism is uncommitted to either determinism or indeterminism. Anscombe owes her conception of mechanism, not indeterminacy etc, to Bohm. What is, particularly, interesting on Bohm's account is that mechanism is compatible with either determinism or indeterminism. In order to understand Anscombe's appreciation of Bohm, we must, at least, consider a salient historical fact associated with this sense of "mechanism."

Anscombe is impressed by the historical shift in the debate over determinism, and related matters. She observes with interest that, whereas in the early days of the discussion, the consensus was that at the basic level, the micro-level, determinism prevailed with higher level phenomena being undetermined, or so it appeared. Later, the ground shifted and the argument was made that at the micro-level (quantum level), while indeterminacy ruled, higher levels were determined as a consequence of "constancy" of statistical laws. But, even if statistical laws are constant, if in fact indeterminism obtains at the micro-level, we can assume mechanism without assuming that higher level events are determined. Indeed, she suggests, there may enter causes of a psychological sort that have the effect of these higher level events. One must keep in mind that, for Anscombe, this doesn't mean that such events are determined, since her position, which we have, already, discussed is that causation doesn't entail determinism.

There are similarities between Bohm on "mechanism" and Anscombe on "causation." Both are consistent with either determinism or indeterminism. But there is another consideration in dealing with Anscombe's introduction of causes of a "psychological sort." Recall that she has denied the causal efficacy of shadows. At first, this seems plausible, but there is room for continuing the discussion and, perhaps, for some skepticism. Suppose I am standing at the window. Further, suppose it is evening and I see a bear-like shadow. I've heard that bears are in the area. I, quickly, shut the door. In this case, it seems, perfectly, reasonable to say that the shadow caused me to shut the door. If so, then contrary to what she has said shadows *do* have causal efficacy. Consider in connection with this that 'bear-like' is not a description we would attribute to the causes of the shadow, even the bear is not "bear-like." We might say the bear caused the shadow but there is nothing in the language of physics that translates 'bear'. Further, aside from the causes of the shadow there is the shadow, itself; and, here, we might think of it as a cause of my action which is, to use Anscombe's expression, of a "psychological sort." Usually, philosophers and scientists regard shadows as "pseudo-processes," processes lacking causal efficacy inasmuch as they are incapable of carrying a signal, in the way a moving wagon may carry a passenger. Much has been made of this by philosophers discussing causation, philosophers such as Wesley Salmon, who attributes the idea to Reichenbach. (Salrmon [1984] pp. 141-147) However, it would appear that the notion of a "pseudo-process" goes back, at least, as far as Arthur Eddington (Eddington [1927] pp. 56-57) The example cited by Salmon appears to be, almost, exactly the one Eddington employs. The point to be made is that while a pseudo-process, such as a shadow, may not "carry a signal" it may *be* a signal when the events under examination are taken under the description of processes of a "psychological sort." A shadow, one may be tempted to say, may be a message but is never a "messenger." A causal process, however, is never a message but may be a "messenger." I have, elsewhere, discussed this at great length and will leave the matter as is, but the proposal is, entirely, consistent with Anscombe's views on causation where intentions are involved. Anscombe insists that nothing she has said resolves the matter of whether human actions, those involving intentions, etc. are determined: that is, whether they are, as we have noted, is "left entirely open." (Anscombe [1983] p. 106) We have been discussing general topics related to causes and actions. No commitment by Anscombe has been made on whether it is we who cause our action, or whether our actions are caused by events outside the somatic context. She directs considerable energy to the views of Rodrick Chisholm, who later appears to have abandoned many of his views in favor of what appears to be a Davidsonian position.

### b) Anscombe's and Chisholm

Roderick Chisholm contributed, significantly, to the discussion of agency. His position evolved, over the years. Although late in his career he appears to have abandoned many of his earlier views, they remain influential and worth continued attention. Anscombe's, brief, critical remarks on Chisholm shed, considerable, light on her views regarding developments subsequent to the publication of *Intention*. We proceed by, first, describing Chisholm's earlier position and, then, go on to examine, briefly, his later position which is contained, mainly, in Chapter II of his book *Person and Object*. However, his most influential single work on action theory was, most likely, his 1966 paper "Reason and Action." (Chisholm [1966]) This is the primary target of Anscombe's criticism. We will examine Chisholm's 1966 work and, then, continue with a discussion of Anscombe's reaction.

### c) Chisholm's 1966 Position on Agent Causation

Recall that Anscombe attempted to trace back events in the causal chain that led from the door closing to the brain of the agent who closed the door. There was a gap between afferent and efferent nerve activity which she attempted to fill by stepping back to get a wider perspective, a perspective which introduced sensory stimulation from an external object. Although she distinguished "sorts" of causation, she was less than explicit as to the nature of causation where it relates human action to events external to the agent.

Tracing back events to the agent was familiar to Aristotle who, while not tracing events beyond the agent, suggested that there is a "sort" of causation belonging to human agency alone: "Thus a staff moves a stone, and is moved by a hand, which is moved by a man (Aristotle [*Physics*] 256a6-8)." With Aristotle in mind, Chisholm distinguishes two sorts of causation. First there is the sort where one event causes another event; and, second, there is causation between the cause, which is the agent, and the effect which is an event or action. Agent causation he calls "immanent" causation; event-event causation he calls "transeunt" causation. (Chisholm (1966) p. 17)

When an agent performs an action, such as closing the door, he causes an event in the brain. This occurs by immanent causation, whereas the brain event causes the muscles to move by transeunt causation. (Chisholm [1966] p. 20) It is essential to transeunt causation, or what is sometimes called "agent causation," that there is no preceding event causing the agent to cause the change in the brain resulting in muscle movement. On the Russell/Ducasse/Davidson position, as we have seen, an agent's beliefs and desires, jointly, cause the action of the agent. One difficulty, commonly associated with this approach is the problem of "deviant causal chains." Chisholm has something to say on this. He addresses the problem by first examining an example. A fellow desires to inherit his uncle's fortune. He believes that if he kills his uncle he will get it. This belief and this desire evoke nervousness on his part, causing him, while driving, to accidentally kill a person who, unknown to him at the time, is in fact his uncle. This case, and others like it, illustrates the fact that a belief-plus-desire analysis fails to capture the *endeavor* associated with the action. The belief and desire, jointly, caused the action, but the action that took place is nothing that the agent, at the time, was *endeavoring* to perform. Let's consider the example of endeavoring that he introduces and which Anscombe discusses in her criticism.

Chisholm constructs the example of a man in Providence N.J. who wishes to cause a switching circuit to switch in Denver. He *undertakes* to do so by dialing a number in Los Angeles, knowing, as he does, that for that phone to ring in LA the switching must occur in Denver. Note that because the switching in Denver will take place before the ringing in LA that he is not undertaking to have the LA ringing *cause* the switching in Denver since he knows that a cause does not follow its effect. In this example, the agent is undertaking to cause a circuit to switch in Denver by attempting to complete a call to LA. In other words he is endeavoring that his undertaking to cause the phone to ring in LA cause the switching in Denver. This situation is analogous to causing the brain states that cause my muscles to move by *undertaking* to move my arm, just as I may cause the switching in Denver by undertaking to ring LA. So far, we have been discussing Chisholm's view, circa 1966, but he, later, shifted his strategy. He would, later, take as fundamental the notion of 'undertaking' rather than 'making happen'. This will prove fundamental in assessing the effectiveness of Anscombe's criticisms. What is clever about Chisholm analogy is that it supplies a solution to a problem described by A. I. Melden. Before returning to Chisholm and Anscombe, let's examine Melden's views, briefly.

### *d) Melden's Problem(s) with Volition*

"Abe" Melden, as he was called, was an affable teacher who, almost, single handedly created the graduate department at UC (Irvine). It is said that in an effort to build the department at Irvine he called Gilbert Ryle, inquiring into the possibility of obtaining someone special for the department. The upshot to this, according to Prof. Ron Barnette, was that Daniel Dennett was hired without an interview. Melden, who drove a Mercedes roadster, was an expert on wine and had a passion for opera. He would sometimes speak of Anscombe but was reserved and measured in his comments. Melden's book on action theory would become a classic in the field.

In *Free Action,* Melden discloses some important objections to the theory of volition, objections which figured in the evolution of views as diverse as those of Davidson and Chisholm. Let's take a look at a few sides to his argument since they reveal both what is problematic with past accounts of volition as well as common misunderstandings of the traditional account. It should be made clear that there has never been a theory recognized as *the* theory of volition. Much criticism, emanating from people like Anthony Kenny and Gilbert Ryle bear little resemblance to many, if not most, theories of volition advocated by those who in fact buy into the idea. Many criticisms, including some by Melden, himself, depend on straw man arguments, rather than well documented accounts of the theory under attack. Nevertheless, Melden's criticisms, as well as those of Ryle, e.g., have been useful in encouraging new theories more powerful in some cases than many of the more traditional theories, such as those to be found in, say, James or Bradley.

Melden supposes that a volition is just another act, only it is to be understood as internal, one which causes an event, such as moving a particular set of muscles. This results in another event, such as raising one's arm, perhaps, in undertaking to signal a turn while driving (to take his favorite case). This is, however, something of a mischaracterization insofar as many advocates of volition do *not* regard it as an act which is, more or less, like others, except for being internal. Most volitionists reject this option since it encourages the belief that the theory entails a regress, one requiring a further action in order to produce the volition, just as the volition is required to produce other effects, such as muscle movement. Setting this aside, however, Melden, further, suggests that each sort of muscle movement requires a different sort of volition. (Melden [1961] p. 49). This criticism is not unlike, nor unrelated, to James's criticism of Wundt's theory of "feelings of innervation." This theory violated James's "principle of parsimony" by requiring a feeling for every type of muscle movement of which an agent is capable. James dismisses the idea that a feeling is required based on violation of parsimony in much the same way that Melden objects to a theory of volition requiring a volition for each muscle movement. (James [1890] pp. 497-498) Indeed, one finds a propensity among anti-volitionists to borrow from James, an ironic development, given James's commitment to volition as a mental process.

On a Jamesian account, an act is volitional if it is caused by an idea of action clearly, and uniquely, attended to. In the case of muscle movement, the "idea" is, essentially, a brain trace associated with a past experience. These experiences provide the ideas of movement required for action. They are acquired involuntarily and in such a manner as to remind us of Skinner's notion of "operant" behavior. (James [1890] p. 488) For James the closest thing to a volition in Melden's sense is an idea, not a performance. We hold these ideas in memory and, only after acquiring them involuntarily, exercise them in taking some initiative as agents. It is this recollection that affords us knowledge of the position of our limbs without observation, a fact subject to extended discussion by Anscombe as we have, already, seen. In any case, according to James, I need not acquire an idea of a volition and an idea of movement attached to it and, finally, a causal relation between them. All that is required is an idea of the movement. Thus there is no need to learn the connections between volitions and muscle movement. Adhering to James, if possible, helps side-step another problem. The problem at issue is central to Melden's approach to action, more generally.

Melden believes the volitionist is caught in a dilemma. On the one hand, the volitionist maintains that in order to produce a volition, $v_i$, leading to a certain muscle movement, $m_i$, I must be aware of the effect of $v_i$. What this entails is that, for the idea of $v_i$ to be intelligible, the idea of $m_i$ must be contained in the idea of $v_i$. But if it is so contained, then the relation of $v_i$ and $m_i$ cannot be a causal relation, inasmuch as the concept of a cause must be independent, on Humean grounds, of the concept of the effect. On the other hand, if we begin by thinking that $v_i$ is the cause of $m_i$ then it must be the case that when I first performed $v_i$ I had no idea what was to ensue. This he takes as problematic. Let's consider the second horn of the dilemma first.

We have, already, seen that for the most "notoriously" volitional view of action, viz. James's, there is no need for surprise on performing an action for the first time. The idea which serves as the volitional component of action is acquired as the result of what later will be called by James's behaviorist opposition 'operant behavior'. In this case, I acquire the idea without surprise and, perhaps, by "accident" in some sense of the term as I learn how to control my limbs. As for the first horn of the dilemma a number of things might be said, but, instead of examining Melden's theory in detail, a challenge to his general conception of volition may suffice. Even if we think of volitions as causes, we need not assent to the belief that there is a pairing of volitions and bodily movements of the sort Melden prescribes. Instead we might think of the theory (on one construal) this way: an intention, or object, of action might be thought of as analogous to the direction we point a pistol. The volition involved in implementing the intention might be thought of as pulling the trigger. Now it is not necessary that for each direction we point the gun we require a different sort of trigger-pulling. Each idea of action is actualized with the pulling of the "trigger" but this may be nothing more than a "release" of some constraint. It need not have its own character, logically, tied to the idea of the intention. This view is not as simple as it appears; it addresses some core concerns unrelated to the immediate task of understanding and evaluating Anscombe's philosophical psychology, but it is pertinent to the matter of agency in Anscombe and elsewhere.

Melden alleges that my discovery of the connection between a volition and the ensuing muscle movement must have caused me to be "surprised or astonished." (Melden [1961] p. 49) But this is no more necessary than that an infant should be astonished that he can put his foot in his mouth, although some parents (as well as politicians) may experience some surprise at the ease with which it is accomplished. At this point, let us return to the specifics of Anscombe's critique of Chisholm. Although Melden is no longer at the forefront of current discussions of volition, his work was, highly, influential and the positions he held remain worthy of serious consideration. Anscombe never cites Melden in her published work but there is evidence of its presence, usually in her comments on others.

### e) Anscombe's Critique of Chisholm

Chisholm's example of phone dialing, where we intend to cause a switching in Denver by dialing LA, is pretty much the same as Anscombe's example in Section 23 of *Intention* of the man who by contracting his muscles, deliberately, undertakes to produce certain substances involved in the production of those muscle movements. Anscombe claims that the way most people think of Chisholm's analogy isn't, really, the analogy as Chisholm presents it.

Most people in setting the analogy beside what is believed to happen in, deliberately, raising one's arm will align the undertaking with the dialing, i.e., dialing the LA number in the endeavor to cause the switching in Denver. However, what I undertake in my endeavor to raise my arm is the physiological change required for this to happen, just as it is required in order to ring LA that a switching take place in Denver. Agent causation enters only insofar as my endeavor to raise my arm has these physiological results. The correct view is not the common view. The common view takes the dialing as the undertaking; but what is, actually, the correct reading of Chisholm's analogy is that the events associated with the undertaking are more akin to the switching in Denver than the dialing of the LA number.

In reply to Wittgenstein's question "What is left over if we subtract the fact that my arm goes up from the fact that I raise my arm?" Chisholm answers that what is left over is what I make happen in my endeavor to raise my arm. But there is a, further, question that Anscombe wants to raise if, as Chisholm maintains, what the agent causes is the physiological changes associated with the endeavor to raise one's arm, and that question is this: What is left over if we subtract from the fact that *these* changes occur from the fact that I make them occur? Anscombe maintains that Chisholm's belief that a cause necessitates its effect, along with his belief that freedom and determinism are incompatible, compels him to introduce some other mode of causation besides event-event causation (Anscombe [1979] p. 81). In other words, in order to be a free action, the causation involved must not be of the event-event sort. We have seen, however, that Anscombe, herself, recognizes different sorts of causal histories (Anscombe [1983] pp. 100-101) even though she rejects what compelled Chisholm to affirm two sorts of causation, viz. immanent and transeunt causation. It is important for understanding Anscombe that the two sorts of causal histories she acknowledges are not in competition. The reason they are not in competition has a great deal to do with how she stands with respect to the place of scientific laws in providing an account of human action. Roughly, her position with respect to these two sorts of causal history is comparable to Davidson's position with regard to the compatibility of causation by reasons and causation by events. We, next, consider a question much like Wittgenstein's, original, question but applied not to the raising of the arm but, rather, the events we make happen in undertaking to raise our arm: "What is left over if we subtract the fact that events such as the neurological events associated with muscle movement happen from the fact that we make them happen?" There is a flaw in Chisholm position, says Anscombe.

If in endeavoring to make my arm go up I undertake to do something, then, if I know that I am, indeed, endeavoring to raise my arm, then I must know what I am undertaking to do with this end in mind. But in this case, since what I undertake is making brain states come about which are preliminary to this movement, I should be aware of them; however, this is not the case. On Anscombe's understanding of Chisholm's position, the only answer to Wittgenstein's question is 'Nothing'. (Anscombe [1979] p. 84) She doesn't reject the possibility of Chisholm finding a way around this problem, but if there is a way, she cannot fathom what it might be.

It seems clear that if there is no difference, that is, if the answer is 'Nothing', then there may be difficulty distinguishing what I do in undertaking an action and what I do in performing the action. Suppose, however, that what is undertaken in the endeavor is distinct from the action I endeavor to perform. Since I am unaware of what I am undertaking, I may no more be undertaking, intentionally, than I would be undertaking, intentionally, to wrinkle the rug in endeavoring to reach the other side of the room. From the standpoint of identifying what is, and what is not intentional, my wrinkling the rug is no less an undertaking than achieving the neurological preliminaries to action. The main difference, one might claim, is that wrinkling the rug is not a "preliminary" in reaching the other side of the room. We might, then, pose a different question: What is the difference between my undertaking to create the preliminary neurological circumstances and my wrinkling the rug in endeavoring to reach the other side of the room? In some sense, one is an accident and the other is not. But any account of this difference will be as uncertain as the difference one might propose between lawlikeness and accidental generalization. Suppose this wrinkling is something I fail to notice. In this case if Anscombe is right, and there is no epistemologically significant difference between what transpires in *my* creating the neurological preliminaries to action and the occurrence of those preliminaries, then there is no difference, it would appear, between *my* wrinkling the rug and the wrinkling of the rug, except that wrinkling the rug is not preliminary to reaching the other side of the room by walking. Anscombe's critique of Chisholm reveals a significant development in her views since *Intention*. We shall, at this point, discuss how her views dove-tail in some respects with those of Davidson as well as a couple of instances where she took exception to his proposals.

## *f) Davidson and Anscombe on Agent Causation*

Anscombe does not accept Chisholm's view that there is a form of causation, immanent causation, attributable to the agent in free action. She defends the position that causes do not determine. This allows her to resist the path Chisholm took in adopting the view that there are two sorts of causation. She has maintained, as we have already noted, that there are two sorts of causal histories. But how can there be two sorts of causal histories without there being two sorts of causes? A similar question crops up in connection with Davidson's belief that reasons can be causes, even though they do not introduce causation of a sort that differs from event-event causation. The connection between Davidson and Anscombe on this matter is one of considerable subtlety, and no clear resolution of how they are related is possible, given the, presently, available documents. However, given the enormous influence Anscombe had on Davidson, it is not inappropriate to consider the possibility of some reciprocity, particularly in regard to how Anscombe viewed the causes of human action.

Recall that when Anscombe discussed tracing back events related to closing the door, she reached a point where there was a "gap" or break. At this point, she introduced "clues," and these came down to psychological states of belief and desire. It was here that causal history separate from the series of physiological occurrence became relevant. However, this non-physiological, i.e. psychological, history did not necessitate introducing anything like agent causation; this prospect was averted by recognizing that causes do not necessitate. But, if this is so, what, then, is her position on the causal role of beliefs and desires? Davidson's suggestion of reasons as causes was not intended to introduce a peculiar causal nexus between reasons and action. In addition, Davidson attempted to travel a middle course between the singularity view and the regularity view of causation.

According to Davidson, Ducasse was right in maintaining that singular statements of causation, such as 'Running over the nail caused the flat tire', entail no identifiable law, but Hume might be right, too, in his insistence that there is some law to the effect that all events similar to the first event (running over a nail under such and such conditions) are followed by events similar to the second (the tire going flat). (Davidson [1967] p. 160) Davidson's position denies that there are laws connecting the mental and the physical; however, he avers that all events are physical; he is a "monist." What is interesting and, at the time, original in his proposals is that there is an "anomalous" character to mental predicates that rules out psychophysical laws.

If Davidson is right in his "anomalous monism," then there are no physical predicates with an extension identical to some mental predicate as a matter of law. The relation of cause and effect is, for Davidson, independent of description, but laws are, very, different in this regard. Laws are linguistic in the sense that they cover events only if those events are described in a certain way. His view is much like Hempel's in this respect. The situation relates to the position he takes on intentionality, where he alleges that there is no natural class of intentional actions, only actions that are intentional relative to certain descriptions. The same holds for causes. An event is captured in the "nomological net" (Feigl's expression) only if it is described in one way rather than another. At the core of his views on mind is his rejection of Cartesian notions of privacy etc. as definitive of the mental and his acceptance *in one form* of Brentano's notion of intentionality.

Brentano's criterion of the mental requires intentionality. Davidson's emendation of Brentano's thesis makes intentionality description-relative. The distinction between mental and physical is, therefore, relative to language, whereas the causal nexus between events is not. This has implications for the concept of agency.

## *g) James, Volition, and Anomalous Monism*

Let's examine and speculate, briefly, on some of the essential elements of Davidson's theory. Recall that for James attending to an idea of action, at the exclusion of competing ideas, leads to a particular action. Although he never uses the word 'cause' in this connection, this makes him a causal theorist of a sort. The fact that attention is central to James idea of agency is made important for this discussion by the fact that if it were possible to deal with the mental, solely, in terms of a single mental notion, that of attention, then we would be in possession of a theory of the mental that differs from Davidson's in not relativizing the mental to linguistic descriptions. In addition, the claim that the mental is distinguished by the intensionality of mental reports would receive a significant challenge, insofar as 'to attend' is not an intensional verb. There is a sense of 'attention' that is not an intentional notion, assuming that if it were intensionality would be entailed. Let's explain this a bit further.

To be sure, there is one sense of 'attends to' which might be intentional. Jack may be said to be attending to Orcutt, say; but, Orcutt is a spy, and if I say "Jack is attending to a spy," there may be the imputation that Jack knows Ortcutt is a spy. But if I say "Ortcutt has Jack's attention," substituting 'a spy' for 'Ortcutt' need not impute knowledge, or belief, to Jack of Ortcutt's being a spy. The point is that there is a sense of 'attention' just as in the case of 'see' where intensionality is not a feature of the verb. If all mental acts required attention in order to *be* mental, a case could be made that the mental does not entail intentionality, where intentionality is characterized in terms of intensionality—that is, the failure of substitution of co-referential terms in the context which is, then, said to be intensional. On a Jamesian view, under this interpretation, agency would not entail intentionality. The point, here, is not to defend this view but to emphasize how it is that "anomalousness" enters into Davidson's theory only if intensionality is the criterion of the mental. For Davidson, since there are only physical events (his "monism") an event is mental only under a particular description, but what is "anomalous" is *not* that no physical predicate is coextensive with a mental predicate. What is anomalous, actually, is that all events are physical *and*, while there are events receiving mentalistic descriptions, there are no laws relating these mental events to physical events.

If it were possible to collect a class of beliefs under a single description we might be able to construct laws relating such events (and others) by way of descriptions; but in the case of mental predicates no such descriptions are possible. Since laws relate descriptions, no laws relate mental events to physical events. Such laws would be "heteronomic," relating events through descriptions that belong to different vocabularies. The key to understanding anomalousness can be expressed, as Davidson suggests, as a difference in translatability. I will depart from Davidson's account, minimally, for clarity of exposition. If we attempt to translate predicates of what we shall call the "mental language" to the physical language we encounter a problem we do not encounter in translating from one physical language to another physical language. In the latter case, it might be alleged (by Quine, e.g.) that there is some "fact of the matter" based on evidence; and, if the evidence is insufficient, this is not to say there is no fact of the matter, only an underdetermination of the theory of translation by the evidence. But in the former case, not only is there underdetermination of theory (of translation) by the evidence, there is, also, the problem that there is no fact of the matter giving a special privilege to one translation over another. Further, in this case, rationality, the concepts of belief, desire etc. enter the picture and with respect to these there is no fact of the matter to be discerned. Nature in this case will not govern our choice. What this means for the issue at hand is that mentalistic descriptions correspond to no natural class of things in the world and, thus, a lawlike relation cannot be codified relating them to physicalistic descriptions. Keep in mind that, while there is no natural class corresponding to these mentalistic expressions, this is not to say that mental attributes are not, at bottom, physical attributions. According to Davidson they are. But what is important is where the theory leaves the concept of agency and whether Anscombe does or does not invoke agency.

Anscombe does not invoke agency; but she does say (Anscombe [1983] p. 100) that a causal history of an action is of a different sort than the causal history of an event which is not an action. She does not reject the possibility of providing a, purely, physicalistic account of *how* an action comes about, but this will not explain *why* an action was performed and, so, even though she is not committed to agency in, say, the sense of Chisholm, she does not accept a physicalist account as providing an explanation of what an agent does. She does, however, lend support to what is, essentially, the Davidsonian position that correlating brain state kinds with beliefs of a sort is futile. (Anscombe [1983] p. 98). This would suggest some sympathy for the idea of the "anomalousness" of the mental, but the picture remains unclear as to, exactly, what her position is. She is, however, closer to Chisholm than some "anti-causal" theorists, like Melden, in an important respect.

For Melden, the causal theorist has difficulty making intelligible the idea of how it is that we raise our arm by moving our muscles. (Melden [1961] p. 53) The idea, here, seems to be that "we intentionally move our muscles in order to raise our arms." But before humans knew about muscles they were able to move their arms at will. Chisholm was able to avoid this problem, although he raised a few of his own. What Chisholm did was insist that instead of thinking that we move our muscles with the intention of moving our arm, we move our muscles by undertaking to move our arm, instead. Anscombe by holding tight to the distinction of reasons and causes, and by promoting the idea that there are two kinds of causal histories, not to mention two "knowledges," was able to retain what is phenomenologically compelling about the concept of agency without introducing "spooky" events. We conclude by remarking, briefly on how Catholicism influenced here philosophical world view.

It is well known that Anscombe was a devout Catholic. Her thoughts on theology would require a book to analyze and evaluate. Her Catholicism was part of her philosophical as well as her personal identity. There are no certain borders separating her theology and her philosophy. We have made no effort to indicate where they might lie. She was exquisite in her treatment of both subjects. In view of her philosophical Catholicism, her attacks on Cartesian philosophy may come as no surprise; nor, her acceptance of much of Aquinas; nor her embrace of Aristotle and criticism of Hume; nor, perhaps, her indifference to Kant and neglect of some philosophers who, like Kant, have very little significance to "Aristotelian Thomism." But to regard Anscombe as a Catholic philosopher, *per se*, would be a mistake. Her devotion to philosophy is evidenced by her intensity and, careful, attention to detail. Notwithstanding the confidence she projected, when she thought she was wrong, she said so, and sometimes did so in print. She pushed herself to the limits of her understanding and skill. Occasionally, she would hedge her philosophical "bets," but usually all her cards were on the table and there was no effort to reconstruct a problem in order to fit a desired solution. Anscombe by being an interesting person made philosophy more interesting to those who heard her speak or read her works. She was a philosopher rather than a philosopher "of" in the sense that she operated within the field, itself, rather than approaching it from some other field, such as the philosophy "of" science; or "of" mathematics, etc. To borrow a turn of phrase from her adversary May Brodbeck: "It was philosophy straight up; no chaser."

# Bibliography

Alexander, S. *Moral Order and Progress*, (1889) Thoemmes 2000.

Armstrong, D. *A World of States of Affairs*, Cambridge, 1997.

Anscombe, G. E. M. *Intention*, (1957), Harvard University Press, Cambridge, 1963.

Anscombe, G. E. M. "Modern Moral Philosophy," (1958) in *Collected Philosophical Papers*, Vol. III, Blackwell, Oxford, 1981, pp. 26-41.

Anscombe, G. E. M and Geach, P. *Three Philosophers*, Basil Blackwell, Oxford, 1961.

Anscombe, G. E. M. "On Sensations of Position," (1962) in *Collected Philosophical Papers*, Vol. II, Blackwell, Oxford, 1981, pp. 72-74.

Anscombe, G. E. M. "Thought and Action in Aristotle," (1965a) in *Collected Philosophical Papers*, Vol. I, Blackwell, Oxford, 1981

Anscombe, G. E. M. "The Intentionality of Sensation," (1965b) *Collected Papers* Vol. 2, Blackwell, Oxford, 1981, pp. 3-20)

Anscombe, G. E. M. "Causality and Determination," (1971) in *Collected Philosophical Papers*, Vol. II, Blackwell, Oxford, 1981, pp. 133-148.

Anscombe, G. E. M. "Times, Beginnings, and Causes," (1974a) in *Collected Philosophical Papers*, Vol. II, Blackwell, Oxford, 1981, pp. 148-163.

Anscombe, G. E. M. "Practical Inference," (1974b) in *Human Life, Action and Ethics: Essays by G.E.M. Anscombe*, edited by Mary Geach and Luke Gormally, Imprint Academic, 2005.

Anscombe, G. E. M. "Whatever has a Beginning of Existence must have a Cause," (1974c) in in *Collected Philosophical Papers*, Vol. I, Blackwell, Oxford, 1981, pp. 93-99.

Anscombe, G. E. M. "The First Person," in in *Collected Philosophical Papers*, Vol. II, Blackwell, Oxford, 1981, pp. 20-36.

Anscombe, G. E. M. "Under a Description," (1979) in *Collected Philosophical Papers*, Vol. II, Blackwell, Oxford, 1981, pp. 208-220)

Anscombe, G. E. M "Action, Intention, and 'Double Effect'," (1982) in *Human Life, Action and Ethics: Essays by G.E.M. Anscombe*, edited by Mary Geach and Luke Gormally, Imprint Academic, 2005.

Anscombe, G. E. M. "The Causation of Action," (1983) in *Human Life, Action and Ethics: Essays by G.E.M. Anscombe*, edited by Mary Geach and Luke Gormally, Imprint Academic, 2005.

Anscombe, G. E. M. "Chisholm on Action," (1979) in *Human Life, Action and Ethics: Essays by G.E.M. Anscombe*, edited by Mary Geach and Luke Gormally, Imprint Academic, 2005.

Aquinas, T *Summa Theologica* in *Introduction to Thomas Aquinas*. Translated by A. C. Pegis, Modern Library, 1948.

Aristotle, *De Anima*, in *The Basic Works of Aristotle*, edited by Richard McKeon, Random House, 1941.

Aristotle, *Nicomachean Ethics,* in *The Basic Works of Aristotle*, edited by Richard McKeon, Random House, 1941.

Aristotle, *Metaphysics, The Basic Works of Aristotle*, edited by Richard McKeon, Random House, 1941.

Aristotle, *Eudemian Ethics*, in *Aristotle: The Athenian Constitution; The Eudemian Ethics; on Virtues and Vices*, translated by H. Rackham, Harvard University Press, 1935.

Aune, B. *An Empiricist Theory of Knowledge*, Bowler Books, Montague, MA.

Austin, J. L. *How to Do Things with Words*, Harvard, 1962.

Ayer, A. J. *The Foundations of Empirical Knowledge*, Macmillan, 1963.

Bayne, S. R. "Kripke's Cartesian Argument," *Philosophia*, Vol. 18, 1988, pp. 265-269.

Beaney, M. *A Frege Reader*, Blackwell, 1997.

Bergmann, G. "Duration and the Specious Present," in *Logic and Reality*, University of Wisconsin Press, 1964.

Bergmann, G. *Philosophy of Science* (1957) University of Wisconsin, 1966.

Black, M. "Making Something Happen," in *Determinism and Freedom in the Age of Modern Science*, Collier, 1961.

Bohm, D. *Causality and Chance in Modern Physics*, University of Pennsylvania, 1957.

Bradley, F. H. "The Definition of Will (1), (1902) *Mind*, N.S. xi, No. 44, reprinted in *Collected Essays*, Vol. II. Oxford, 1935, pp. 476-514.

Bradley, F. H. "The Definition of Will (1I), (1903) *Mind*, N.S. xii, No. 46 reprinted in *Collected Essays*, Vol. II. Oxford, 1935, pp. 515-551.

Broad, C. D. *Scientific Thought*, Routledge & Kegan Paul, 1923.

Broad, C. D. *The Mind and Its Place in Nature*, Routledge & Kegan Paul, 1925.

Carnap, R. "Testability and Meaning" (1936-1937) in *Readings in the Philosophy of Science* edited by Herbert Feigl and May Brodbeck. Appleton-Century-Crofts, Inc. 1953, pp. 93-103.

Carnap, R. *Introduction to Symbolic Logic*, Dover, 1958.

Cartwright, N. "An Empiricist Defence of Singular Causes," in *Logic, Cause, and Action: Essays in Honor of Elizabeth Anscombe*, edited by Roger Teichmann, Cambridge University Press, 2000, pp. 47-58.

Chisholm, R. *Person and Object,* Open Court, 1976.

Chisholm, R. "Freedom and Action" in *Freedom and Determinism,* edited by Keith Lehrer, Random House, 1966.

Chomsky, N. *Syntactic Structures*, (1957) Mouton. 1985

Chomsky, N. *Aspects of the Theory of Syntax,* MIT, 1965.

Chomsky, N. *Cartesian Linguistics*, Harper and Row, 1966

Curme, G. O. *Syntax*. Heath and Company. 1931.

Danto, A. "Basic Actions," (1965) in *The Nature of Human Action*, ed. Myles Brand, Scott, Forseman, and Company, 1970.

Davidson, D. "Actions, Reasons, and Causes," (1963), in *Essays on Actions and Events*, Clarendon Press, Oxford 1980, pp. 3-19.

Davidson, D. "Causal Relations," (1967) in *Essays on Actions and Events*, Clarendon Press, Oxford 1980.

Davidson, D. "Agency," (1971) in *Essays on Actions and Events*, Clarendon Press, Oxford 1980.

Davidson, D. "Intending," (1978) in *Essays on Actions and Events*, Clarendon Press, Oxford 1980.

Davidson, D. "Paradoxes of Irrationality," in *Philosophical Essays on Freud*, edited by R. Wollheim and J. Hopkins, Cambridge University Press, 1982.

Donagan, A. "St. Thomas Aquinas on the Analysis of Human Action," in *Reflections on Religion and Philosophy*, Oxford, 1999, pp. 68-80.

Donnellan, K. "Knowing What I am Doing," (1963) *Journal of Philosophy*, pp. 401-409.

Dowty, D. *Word Meaning and Montague Grammar*, Kluwer 1979.

Ducasse, C. J. *Causation and the Types of Necessity* (1924), Dover Press, 1969.

Ducasse, C. J. "Explanation, Mechanism, and Teleology," (1926) in *Readings in Philosophical Analysis,* Appleton-Century-Crofts, Inc. 1949, pp. 540547.

Dummett, M. *Frege*, Duckworth, 1973

Dummett, M. "Language and Communication" in *Reflections on Chomsky* edited by Alexander George. Blackwell 1989. pp. 192-212.

Eddington, A. *The Nature of the Physical World*, 1968 [1927], Ann Arbor.

Geach, P. *Mental Acts: Their Content and Their Object*, Routledge, 1957.

Geach, P. "Imperative and Deontic Logic" (1957) in *Logic Matters,* University of California Press. 1980.

Goodman, N. *Fact, Fiction and Forecast*, (1954), Harvard, 1983.

Goodman, N. and Quine, W. "Steps Towards a Constructive Nominalism," *Journal of Symbolic Logic*, Vol. 12, No. 4, 1947

Grice, H. P. "Meanng," (1957) in *Studies in the Way of Words,* Harvard, 1989, pp. 212-223.

Grice, H. P. "The Causal Theory of Perception" (1961) in *Studies in the Way of Words,* Harvard, 1989, pp. 224-248.

Grice, H. P. "Utterer's Meaning and Intentions" (1969) in *Studies in the Way of Words,* Harvard, 1989, pp. 8-118)

Hare, R. M. *The Language of Morals*, Oxford, 1952.

Heathcote, A and Armstrong, D. "Causes and Laws," (1991) *Nous*, 25, pp. 63-73.

Helmholtz, L. *Ueber die Erhaltung der Kraft* (1888) cited in *Identity and Reality* by Emile Meyerson, Dover, 1930.

Hempel, C. "A Purely Syntactical Definition of Confirmation," in the *Journal of Symbolic Logic*, Vol. 8, 1943, pp. 122-143.

Hempel, C. and P. Oppenheim "The Logic of Explanation," (1948) in *Readings in the Philosophy of Science*, edited by Herbert Feigl and May Brodbeck, Appleton-Century Crofts, Inc. 1953. pp. 319-353.

Hempel, C. *Aspects of Scientific Explanation*, Free Press, 1965.

Holton, G. "Mach, Einstein and the Search for Reality," *Thematic Origins of Modern Science*, Harvard, 1975, pp. 219-259.

Hume, D *A Treatise on Human Nature*, Selby-Bigge, Oxford, [1739] 1888.

James, W., *The Principles of Psychology*, Vol. II, Dover, 1890.

Kant I. *Critique of Pure Reason*, (1787) translated by Norman Kemp-Smith, MacMillan, 1963.

Kant I. The Moral Law: Kant's *Groundwork for the Metaphysics of Morals*, translated by H. J. Paton, Barnes & Noble, 1967.

Kant, I. *Critique of Practical Reason*, Bobbs-Merrill, 1956.

Kenny, A. "Happiness" (1965–1966) *Proceedings of the Aristotelian Society*, pp. 66 87–102.

Kenny A. *Aristotle's Theory of the Will*, Duckworth, 1979.

Kenny A. *Action, Emotion, and Will*, Routledge, 1963.

Kenny, A. *Aristotle's Theory of the Will*, Duckworth, 1979.

Kneale, W. "Natural Laws and Contrary-to-Fact Conditionals" (1950) in *Philosophical Problems of Causation*, edited by Tom L. Beauchamp, Dickenson Press, 1974, pp. 46-49.

Kripke, S. "Identity and Necessity," (1971) in *Naming, Necessity, and Natural Kinds*, edited by Stephen Schwartz, Cornell University Press, 1977, pp. 66-102.

Kripke, S, *Naming and Necessity*, (1972), Harvard, 2003.

Ladefoged, P. *A Course in Phonetics*, Hartcourt, Brace and Javanovich, 1975.

Lewis, D. "Causation," (1973) reprinted in *Causation and Conditionals*, edited by Ernest Sosa, Oxford Readings in Philosophy, Oxford, 1975. pp. 180-191.

Lewis, D. "*Postscripts* to 'Causation'," in *Philosophical Papers*, Vol. II, Oxford, 1986, pp. 172-214.

Lucey, K. "The Ancestral Relation without Classes," *Notre Dame Journal of Formal Logic*, Vol. xx. No. 2, April 1979, pp. 281-284.

Makin, Stephen "Causality and Derivativeness," in *Logic, Cause, and Action: Essays in Honor of Elizabeth Anscombe*, edited by Roger Teichmann, Cambridge University Press, 2000, pp. 59-73.

Macmurray, J. "What is Action" in *Proceedings of the Aristotelian Society (Supplementary)*. vol. xvii. 1938.

Mackie, J. L. "Causes and Conditions," (1965) in *Causes and Conditionals*, edited by Ernest Sosa, Oxford, 1975, pp. 15-39.

Melden, A. I., *Free Action*, Routledge & Kegan Paul, London, 1961.
Popper, K. *The Open Society and Its Enemies*, Princeton, [1952] 1966.

Melden, A. I. *Free Action*, Routledge & Kegan Paul, 1961.

Mill, J. S. "Utilitarianism," in *Mill's Ethical Writings*. ed. J. B. Schneewind, Collier. 1965.

Moore, G. E. "Freedom" (1898) *Mind* n.s. 7, pp. 179-204.

Moore, G. E. "A Defence of Common Sense," (1925), in *Philosophical Papers*, by G. E. Moore, Collier, 1962.

Moore, G. E. *Principia Ethica*, (1903) Cambridge, 1954.

Mothersill, M. "Anscombe's Account of the Practical Syllogism," *Philosophical Review*, Vol. 71, No. 4, 1962, pp. 448-461.

Passmore, J. A, and Heath, P. L. "Intentions," *Proceedings of the Aristotelian Society*, XXIX (1955), pp. 131-146.

Plato, *Protagoras* in *The Collected Dialogues of Plato*, edited by Edith Hamilton and H. Cairns, Princeton, 1963.

Popper, K. *The Poverty of Historicism*, Harper, 1957.

Popper, K. *The Open Society and Its Enemies*, (1943) Vol. II, Princeton, 1971.

Price, H. H. "Our Evident for the Existence of Other Minds," *Philosophy*, XIII, 1938, in *Essays on Other Minds*, University of Illinois Press, Urbana, 1970, pp. 425-456.

Prichard, H. A. "Acting, Willing, and Desiring," in *Moral Obligation*, Oxford, 1949.

Putnam, H. "The Meaning of 'Meaning'" (1975), first published in K. Gunderson *Language, Mind and Knowledge,* Minnesota Studies in Philosophy of Science, vii, University of Minnesota Press; reprinted in *Philosophical Papers*, Vol. 2, Cambridge University Press, 1982, pp. 215-272).

Putnam, H. *Reason, Truth, and History*, Cambridge University Press, 1981.

Quine, W. *Methods of Logic*, Holt, Rinehart and Winston, New York, 1972.

Reichenbach, H. *The Theory of Relativity and A Priori Knowledge*, (1920) University of California Press, 1965.

Reichenbach, H. *The Philosophy of Space and Time*, (1927), Dover, 1958.

Reichenbach, H. "Logistic Empiricism in Germany and the Present State of the Problems," *Journal of Philosophy*, Vol. xxxiii, No. 6, 1936, pp. 141-160.

Reichenbach, H. *Modern Philosophy of Science*, Routledge & Kegan Paul, 1959.

Russell B. "On Meaning and Denoting," (1903-1905) in *The Collected Papers of Bertrand Russell*, Vol. 4, Edited by Alasdair Urquhart and Albert C. Lewis, Routledge, 1989.

Russell, B. "On Denoting," in *Mind*, 1905.

Russell, B. "On the Notion of a Cause," (1912-13) in *Mysticism and Logic*, Doubleday, 1957, pp. 174-202.

Russell, B. *Our Knowledge of the External World*, (1914) Routledge, 1993.

Ryle, G. "Systematically Misleading Expression," (1931-1932) in *Logic and Language*, (First Series), edited by Anthony Flew, Basil Blackwell, 1960.

Ryle, G. *The Concept of Mind*. Barnes and Noble. 1949.

Ryle, G. "Pleasure" in *Proceedings of the Aristotelian Society Supplementary*, Vol. XXVIII, 1954, reprinted in *Essays in Philosophical Psychology*, edited by Donald Gunderson, Doubleday, NY. 1965. pp. 194-205).

Salmon, W. *Scientific Explanation and the Causal Structure of the World*, Princeton, 1984.

Scriven, M. "Explanation and Prediction in Evolutionary Theory," (1959) *Science*, 130, pp. 477-482.

Shakespeare *King John*, IV, 1, 23.

Sidgwick, H. *Methods of Ethics*, (1907) Dover, 1966

Spinoza, B. *Ethics* in *The Rationalists*. Anchor. 1960.

Stout, G. F. "Voluntary Action," *Mind*, n.s. Vol. X, 1896

Von Mises, L. *Human Action: A Treatise on Economics*, (1949), Foundation for Economic Education, Inc. New York, 1996.

Von Wright, G. H. "On So-Called Practical Inference", *Acta Sociologica*, 15/1, 1972, pp. 39-53.

Walter, B. *Mahler,* Schoken. (1974) 1957.

Wiggins, *Sameness and Substance*, Harvard, 1980.

Wittgenstein, L. *Tractatus Logico-Philosophicus*, (1921) translated by D. F. Pears and B. F. McGuinness, Routledge & Kegan Paul, Humanities Press, 1961.

Wittgenstein, L *Philosophical Investigations*, Macmillan, 1953.

# INDEX

Acts (of Will), xxiv-xxv, 4, 18, 79, 89, 90, 131, 219, 220, 237
Agency, 25, 30, 33, 40, 90, 172, 177, 180, 233, 235, 237, 242, 243, 247, 251, 254
Alexander, S., xvii, xviii, 136, 137
Anomalous Monism, 189, 209, 250, 251, 252
Aquinas, T., 116, 131, 132, 254
Aristotle, xvi, 16, 19, 21, 22, 34, 54, 71, 91, 101-117, 120-123, 130, 134, 136, 137, 139, 140-144, 147, 148, 153, 160, 243, 254
Armstrong, D., 193, 194, 195, 197, 199, 210
Aune, B., xvi, 100
Austin, J. L., xviii, 3, 97
Ayer, A. J., xxii, 20, 192

Barnette, R., xv, 244
Bayne, S. R., 194, 207
Beaney, M. A., 23
Belief, 5, 6, 10, 11, 27, 32, 38, 46, 74, 79, 105, 106, 113, 120, 126, 127, 133, 154, 158, 161, 163, 165, 167, 168, 169, 173, 187-190, 236, 238, 239, 243, 250, 22, 253
Bergmann, G., x, xvi, 20, 39, 40
Black, M., 198
Bohm, D., 195, 211, 212, 214, 219, 220, 221, 222, 223, 224, 226, 227, 231, 240, 241
Bradley, F. H., xvii, xviii, xix, 143, 150, 160, 245
Brand, M., xv
Broad, C. D., xvi, xix, xxi, xxii, 24, 28, 36, 222, 223, 227

Carnap, R., xvi, xviii, xx, xxii, xxiii, xxiv, 177, 179, 228
Cartwright, N., 191
Causation, 9, 11, 15, 16, 17-19, 26, 29, 33, 35, 45, 46, 49, 50, 51, 52, 53, 54, 55, 58, 59, 73, 74, 89, 90, 93-95, 96, 101, 108, 116, 123, 138, 150; Singular causation, 172-231, 235, Of Action, 235-242, 243-244, 246, 247, 249, 250, 251, 254
Chisholm, R., 172, 211, 233, 242, 243, 244, 247, 248, 249, 253

Chomsky, N., xvi, 23, 24, 73, 74, 85
Commands, 4, 6, 7, 8, 58, 95, 96, 98
Counterfactual Conditionals, 172, 175, 177, 188, 189, 210, 212, 230
Curme, G. O., 121

Danto, A., 35
Davidson, D. 16, 17, 18, 21, 25, 30, 31, 32, 33, 35, 37-42, 43, 44, 47, 48, 49, 53, 79, 89, 92, 99. 108, 111, 112, 113, 122, 123, 127, 142, 143, 151, 152, 156, 158, 161, 162, 172, 187, 188, 209, 211, 223, 238, 239, 242, 243, 244, 248, 249-251, 252, 253
Desires, 32, 53, 120, 126, 161, 188, 189, 236, 243, 250
Donagan, A. 131
Donnellan, K. 46-50
Dowty, D., 27
Ducasse, C. J., 52, 172, 179, 187, 188, 243, 250
Dummett, M., 80, 204

Eddington, A., 241

Feynman, R., 210, 215, 216, 217
Free-will, 10, 12, 14, 34, 54, 219, 221,

Geach, P., 6, 26, 91, 126
Goodman, N., 172, 175, 176, 228, 229,
Grice, P., xv, 19, 20, 58, 59
Groban, L., xvi

Hare, R. M., xvi, xxi, 104, 105, 106, 108-111, 119, 139,
Helmholtz, L. 178
Hempel, C., 171, 175, 178, 179, 188, 209, 211, 212, 213, 214, 222, 251
Holton, G., xix
Hume, D., 52, 121, 133, 138, 145, 172, 173, 174, 175, 176, 177, 178, 179, 181, 182, 183, 184, 185, 186, 187, 188, 190, 198, 211, 212, 218, 246, 250, 254
Heathcote, A., 193, 194, 195, 197, 199, 210

Jacobson, A, xvi
James, Wm., xvi, xvii, xviii, xix, xxiv, 3, 4, 34, 51, 56, 65, 128, 142, 153, 159, 160, 162, 237, 245, 246, 251, 252
Jevons, W. S., 178, 179
Jones, R. B, xv

Kant, I., 1, 71, 113, 120, 124, 126, 142, 145, 146, 156, 178, 183, 199, 201, 202, 239, 254
Kenny, A., xxi, 15, 16, 71, 80, 81, 83, 84, 103, 118, 119, 142, 244
Kneale, W., 175
Krasner, D., xv
Kripke, S., xvi, 154, 192-211

Ladefoged, P., 154
Lawlikeness, 146, 174-177, 178, 181, 198, 214, 218, 222, 225, 226, 249
Lewis, D., 210, 212, 230
Logical Positivism, xvii-xxii
Lorenc, R., xv
Lucey, K., 229

Mackie, J. L., 210
Macmurray, J., 13, 14
Makin, S., 190
Martin, R., xv
Melden, A. I., xv, 13, 233, 244-247, 253
Mental Causes, 15, 18, 43, 51-61, 146
Meaning, xx, xxi, xxiii, xxiv, 3, 16, 20, 24, 58-59, 130, 139, 151, 157, 158, 177, 205, 207, 229, 230
Mill, J. S., 134, 135, 178

Moore, G. E., xx, 54, 104, 135, 139, 144
Morse, W., xv
Mothersill, M., 104
Motives, 53-57, 69

Observation, 8, 16, 37, 43, 47, 48, 54, 84, 86-87, 88, 92, 96, 98, 99, 125, 152, 155, 194, 202, 208, 245; nonobservational knowledge 43-46, 49, 51, 70, 85, 89, 101, 102, 151, 160; and movement, 163-165
Oppenheim, P., 178

Passmore, J., 4
Pavlick, M., xv
Plato, 121, 151
Pleasure, 109, 134, 135, 136-139, 237
Popper, K., 148, 171, 173, 175, 176, 177, 178, 197
Practical Reason, 54, 74, 100-171
Prediction, 1, 4, 5-7, 8-12, 15, 16, 50, 165-170, 212, 213-214
Price, H. H., 10, 154, 221
Pritchard, H. A., 7, 19, 239
Private Language, xxi, xxii-xxiv, 40, 63, 126, 134, 163
Propositions, 103, 108, 199
Pseudo-processes, 241
Putnam, H., 58, 154, 221, 238

Quine, W. V., xxiii, 26, 128, 204, 228, 229, 230, 252

Reichenbach, H., xvi, xxiii, xxiv, 10, 11, 201, 206, 207, 218, 241
Russell, B., xvi, xvii, xviii, xix, xx, xxi, xxii, xxiii, 23, 24, 53, 90, 124, 126, 127, 153, 171, 172, 174, 175, 176, 177, 178, 180, 181, 187, 188, 189, 196, 197, 221, 222, 225, 243

Ryle, G., xviii, xix, xx, 20, 35, 42, 55, 56, 135, 136-139, 155, 237, 244, 245

Salmon, W., 241
Scriven, M., 209, 210, 213, 214
Sensation, 2, 25, 26, 27, 29, 35, 37, 40, 41, 43, 44, 46, 47, 125, 126, 134, 136-137, 139, 193
Sense-data, xxi, xxii, xxiii, 20, 28
Shakespeare, W. 121
Shand, A., xvii
Shand J., xv
Sidgwick H., 164
Sloman, A, xv, 109,
Speranza, J. L., xv, xix
Spinoza, B., 11
Stout, G. F., xvii, xix, 34, 89, 90

Volition, xvii, 4, 20, 51, 56, 80, 90, 94, 117, 118, 120, 125, 126, 139, 141-144, 159, 160, 165, 188, 236, 244, 245, 246, 247, 251
Von Mises, R., xv, 142, 226
Von Wright, L., 71, 105, 116, 123

Walter, B., 84, 85
Wants, 5, 8, 18, 63, 71, 81, 82, 85, 102-109, 110, 113-117, 118-121, 122, 123-128, 129, 130, 131, 132-136, 138, 139, 140, 146, 149, 158, 163, 165-167, 189, 239, 248
Why-Question, 16, 20, 26, 29, 35, 42-46, 48, 49, 57, 59, 61-64, 67, 68, 69-71, 73, 75, 76, 92, 139, 147, 148, 153-155, 160, 164, 165, 167, 180
Wiggins, D., 195
Vranas, P., xvi
Wittgenstein L., xvi, xvii, xviii, xx, xxi, xxii, xxiv, 6, 7, 10, 11, 20, 35, 39, 47, 51, 63, 81, 88, 89, 90, 126, 134, 139, 148, 153, 155, 163, 202, 203, 206, 207, 238, 248

Printed in Great Britain
by Amazon.co.uk, Ltd.,
Marston Gate.